This book is wonderfully, amazii
generously shared their hard-earned wisdom with-
so many valuable truths here, and the kind you need to hear — or
read — often before you can truly own them. *Bridging Heaven* reminds
me of those *Lonely Planet* travel guides, you know the ones that make it
possible to tour Thailand and actually experience the culture? Only this
book guides you through the human experience and makes it possible
to actually own the quality of life you are choosing to live.

The common road bumps or emotions that misdirect us from the
life we imagine are brought into light and demystified in these pages,
and, most importantly, with their specific exercises and personal
stories, a mental bridge is created that can support us and carry us over
those old paths and into the life that has been waiting for us.

Deirdre Keating, Staff writer, *Moab Happenings*

Personal Strength ~ Spiritual Joy: Bridging Heaven and Earth nourishes
heart, mind, and soul and illuminates possibilities for full-out living. In
a warm, conversational style, Drs. Jan Harrell and Alan Robins invite
you to access the deep wisdom that comes with our God-given gift of
humanity and to further your quest to live with spirit and purpose.

This is a compassionate book that encourages you to fully live each
moment with faith and courage, in active, affirming partnership with
your Creator. The authors, fellow-travelers on the quest, include
heartfelt personal disclosures to illustrate their points and engaging
exercises that will prompt fresh perspectives and liberating new ways
of living. *Personal Strength ~ Spiritual Joy*, will enrich your life.

J. Fraser Pierson, PhD, Professor of Psychology

"With golden nuggets of healing wisdom and spiritual grounding, Drs.
Jan Harrell and Alan Robins help us to embrace our vulnerability as a
sacred gift that holds the key to growth into our best self and opens us
to the possibility of a deeper relationship with God."

The Reverend Michael Powell, First United Methodist Church

"Jan and Al have offered us not just a "fix" but a way to find the power
to lead a healthy and fulfilling life."

Robert W. Whitmore, Chief Executive Officer
NPOWR Digital Media Inc. & stimTVnetwork

Personal Strength ~ Spiritual Joy

Bridging Heaven and Earth

Jan Harrell, PhD
Alan Robins, PhD

Inner Peace Press
Ashland, Oregon

Inner Peace Press
Ashland, Oregon
www.innerpeacepress.com

Library of Congress Control Number: 2007926580
Harrell, Jan & Robins, Alan
Personal Strength ~ Spiritual Joy: Bridging Heaven and Earth/
Jan Harrell and Alan Robins
ISBN 978-0-9795481-1-6

Cover design by Jennifer Cohn
Cover photos by www.alisiam.com

Printed in the United States of America

~ Contents ~

~ Preface ~

Jan: My journey - From Self to God

I was born into a family of atheists. I couldn't quite feel that degree of absolute disbelief, but could also find no belief in God. It simply was not an issue that was discussed or considered in my home. By the time I went to college, I found that I was an angry agnostic. I was angry at people who used their belief in the existence of God to excuse all personal responsibility for their actions, saying that everything that happens is in accordance with God's plan.

My graduate school experience was profound for me. I felt like I had arrived home, where feelings or concepts I had only vaguely been aware of were clearly identified.   Finally, I had a way of conceptualizing the behavior of people that made sense.   I was deliriously happy. I opened my practice with great humility, often wanting to give back the money I was paid, knowing that as a beginner, I wasn't as good as I knew I could one day be. I wanted to tell people, "I'll try harder next time!" And I did try harder. Psychology felt like my calling, and I lived and breathed my knowledge and beliefs. I wanted to become the concepts I had learned. I wanted to take the knowledge I had in my mind down into every cell in my body and transform myself.

My work flourished, and I was happier than I could imagine. I was learning and growing; I even reached a point that I didn't feel embarrassed accepting my clients' money (what a relief!) As I worked, I developed clear beliefs about what it means to be a human being and about how to live so that my life had the best chance of being the way I wanted it.   I approached the Mystery of life with the determination that even though I might never understand why things happened, I could use every experience, no matter how painful, to grow and to learn - to become someone I was proud to be.

And then I started noticing something very odd. It seemed like every time I came to a moment of clarity or a new realization, I would look over and find God there, affirming the truth of my discovery. I kept finding myself walking next to God, when I had thought that I was just forging my own path, alone. Some people read the Bible and then have experiences that confirm what they have read. I had those experiences first, and then found that they corresponded to universal religious teachings. Through my work on myself in psychology, I had found God. I hadn't been trying. I hadn't even been conscious of wanting Him. But, as I went more and more deeply into my heart, there He was.

Perhaps you will be supported in your faith, through reading this book. Perhaps, as I did, you will find faith. Perhaps you will simply feel more at peace with living in the Mystery. In any case, the path of growing into our wholeness as human beings - into self-acceptance, compassion, strength and joy - is a wonderful and righteous path. It is a path you share with all people who have ever sought to reach higher than their fears and sorrows, to become more than they are. As we free ourselves from old habits and patterns that we may not even realize we have, we will come to peace with the forces that are bigger than we are, whether we call them the Mystery... Nature... the Infinite... Karma... Fate... or God.

Al: My Journey - From God to Self

When I was very young, I knew intuitively that there was a God, but I didn't know to put a name to Him. I just knew that I was getting through my life without too much help from humans. When I was a child, my parents rarely talked to each other or to me. Even though my parents were very ill and didn't have much energy to take care of me, I felt taken care of. I knew that when I was in a difficult situation, it would turn out okay. I grew up feeling very connected to God. Without Him, I feel like I wouldn't have survived. I accepted the challenges God gave me without question, and so was able to face the illnesses and early deaths of my parents. Without religious training or the influence of others, I had found peace being a child of God.

I grew up with faith that God was in control of everything and would take care of me, but I could not feel any personal strength to affect what happened to me. I had no sense of self, or any idea that I had the power to make choices to direct my life. Given faith in God in my childhood, my journey as an adult lay in finding myself.

Meeting Jan was a turning point in my life. Before her, no one had ever insisted that I pay attention to what I was feeling or that I speak up for what I wanted. It was hard for me to find those feelings and wants. I had always just done what the next thing seemed to be, and had no idea about how to make deliberate choices. I was used to living in service to people I cared about without considering my own needs. Suddenly, I had someone in my life who wasn't focused on what I could do for her, and who actually felt lonely when she didn't know what was going on inside of me. She insisted that I find and declare what I felt and needed.

My initial reaction to Jan and her mother and brother was that they were very selfish! And it seemed like they wanted me to be selfish, as well. I couldn't understand how we could get along if we were all selfish. But I slowly began to understand that they were only "selfish" in comparison to my very "self-*neglecting*" family. Her family talked about what they felt and wanted! But it was also very important to all of them to make sure that I was happy, too. They were just what I needed.

I had grown up with God but not with myself. I was completely unprepared for being a human. So I got in counseling and learned about myself. I practiced with Jan and her mom and brother. They encouraged me. It felt good! I felt strong. The stronger I got, the more I realized that I had struck gold. If I could be a person with feelings and wants, *and* do the service I felt that God expected of me, I could have it all! Ahead of me could be a great partnership with God. I could do my part and leave the rest to God!

I am still learning. I wanted to write this book with Jan in order to share what we have learned. I wanted to share my journey from God to myself. It is my hope that as you read it, you will find or strengthen your relationship with God and with yourself, as Jan and I have. I have read this book many times. I intend to read parts of it every day for the rest of my life, because now I want ME in my life in the same way I have always wanted God in my life!

Jan: Writing this book has been such a joyous experience for us. It flooded out of us in a few short weeks. I was so happy, during this time, that I had to talk firmly to myself at night: "Enough happiness! Calm down and go to sleep!" We are so grateful about how these concepts and practices are changing our lives. We hope that as you are reading, you come to share in our hope and enthusiasm about what is possible for us all and see the concepts and discoveries in this book not as rules to follow, but rather as keys to our freedom.

~ Introduction ~

All of us want to be happy, but few of us feel true peace and contentment with our lives as they are. We long for something to be different or better, so we can at last feel real happiness. We think that if we just had a better job, a better marriage, fewer problems with our children or our parents, then we could finally be happy. Our culture supports this concept in all the advertisements, movies and television programs which portray "happy" people - people who easily resolve any problem they might encounter in 30 to 90 minutes, or who pose in a photograph smiling joyously, holding the product which has caused them to be relieved of any distress. Who could doubt their happiness when beholding them: slim, fit, well-dressed, white-toothed, and often surrounded by adoring loved ones.

Of course we want that, too. So we strive to work harder, diet, exercise, shop for the right looks, cream up our skin, save up for those great cars or beautiful houses. But no matter how much we try or how great our accomplishments are, somehow they are never enough to bring the happiness we long for. And so we feel like failures. "Something must really be wrong with me if I have all of this and am not happy." Or "I can never achieve as much as other people do, because I am inadequate." or "I don't deserve any better." We turn against ourselves, rather than feel disappointed or out of control in our lives. We search for meaning in our lives, but nothing we do seems to bring lasting satisfaction or happiness.

All human beings have faced the enormity of existence and tried to make sense of it all. Some of us have a deeply embedded faith and a feeling of being closely connected with God. Some of us have belief in God but although we desperately want to, cannot feel faith, with the comfort and relief that come with it. Some of us want to believe and have faith, but do not. And some of us do not believe in God at all. Whatever we call the power that is greater than we are, it is a force which is beyond our control. It is the ultimate Mystery. It is bigger than we are. It is the infinite positive possibility that goes beyond the boundaries of human ability and power.

In our work guiding our clients toward greater psychological awareness and development, we inevitably encountered man's ultimate helplessness, and the necessity to address man's soul – the search for meaning or God. The journey toward psychological growth as humans and the journey to find meaning in life or unity with God are inseparable. Each leads inevitably to the other. If we wish to attain completeness, we must integrate the searching of our soul for God and the struggles of our emotions as we seek wholeness in this human form.

Al: Both Jan and I work with people of all different faiths and approaches to life, spirituality and religion. We try to help each of them find a way to come to peace with what they have no control over. One woman I worked with told me firmly that she doesn't believe in God. She told me "You might as well call the things that are out of control, 'luck.'" So, when we would discuss experiences where she had limited control, I started calling God "Mr. Lucky." Mr. Lucky is all that is beyond her ability to control. She has gotten into the spirit, too. She called me the other day and told me, "I had a great day, today, thanks to Mr. Lucky!"

In this book, we will be referring to God as the ultimate power and force in the Universe. For readers who relate more to Mr. Lucky, or like the term, "The Mystery" - what we cannot and most likely will never be unable to understand - we encourage the substitution. Either way, we are referring to our psychological ability to feel our humility and limitations as human beings as we face all the power and forces that are greater than we are, so we can claim the power that we *can* have. We leave it to you to choose the words that best match your spiritual and philosophical beliefs.

We will be addressing unresolved human emotions we cannot get around or jump over. They block the deep experience of peace and faith. They keep us from being fully empowered. They exist for us all, even though we do not want them to. Our approach to walking through the human experience toward God and the acceptance of our human state is based in logic and in psychology. We will show you how to integrate these two crucial aspects of life - the human and the divine, allowing you to fully experience your personal strength as well as a deeper spiritual joy.

What gets in the way of us shifting our thoughts, feelings and beliefs to live in the peace, faith and confidence we all want to attain? How can we identify and overcome the emotional blocks that are so deeply rooted in us? Despite logic and our belief in spiritual and psychological principles, why are we unable to shake off the negativity, the fear, the sadness, and the doubt that fill our hearts? The emotions which determine how we operate in the world are a matter of mystery to us, and our behaviors are often a great source of confusion and shame. In this book, we are going to explore the causes behind these mysteries through discussion, exercises and examples. We will expand our knowledge of ourselves to allow us to develop the personal strength that we long for. We offer the thoughts and tools in this book as a bridge to God for people who cannot make a leap of faith. We are going to journey with you from being stuck in your feelings to being free in your soul.

Chapter 1

~ *We Have the Right to Be Alive!* ~

All of us dream of things we would like to be different in our lives, things we would like to have or do. What interferes with being able to have a true belief that good things should and can come to us? Why do we doubt? Why do we feel undeserving or unlucky, or feel hopeless that things can change for us? Where does that negative mental programming come from, and why is it so powerful and persistent that despite all the logic that tells us otherwise, we cannot transform our thinking?

<u>Right to exist</u>

Every human being has the *right to exist*. **We were born, and like every living being, it is our turn to walk this Earth and have a life.** It is not something we have earned or need to work to deserve. It is simply a reality. Life on this planet, from the amoeba to the elephant, includes you and me. Does the amoeba ever think, "I don't deserve to be here. I have to help other amoeba or I am worthless?" If you throw a ball to a dog, does that dog ever think, "I am not worthy of having a ball. I don't deserve to chase it?" Why, then, should we have those kinds of thoughts? Are we less deserving and valuable than amoebas or dogs??? God (the Mystery) manifested our existence now. (Do you think He made a bit of a mistake, or rather that there is something interfering with our acceptance of His plan? Whether or not we will ever make sense of our existence, the irrefutable fact is: here we are!) Just as a baby has value, so do we. We are the children of God. A baby must do nothing to earn our love - our hearts just go out to embrace and claim that baby as our own. Our natural, innate, inherent value never changes, even though our bodies grow and our minds develop.

How, then, does a person come to believe that he does not have the right to exist? Why do we each look deep inside of ourselves and believe that if we were to be truly seen for who we are, we would not be wanted or loved? There are three common misconceptions that people have which lead to this belief:

1. <u>I'm not good enough.</u>

Eight year old Annie was racing around her house, getting ready for school, one morning, when she jammed her bare foot into a wall, and burst into tears. Her mother called out, "Be careful! Slow down!" - obvious words Annie didn't need to hear. Instead of comfort and acknowledgment that we all do these things, out of her upset that Annie was hurt, the mother taught Annie an unintended lesson. Instead of realizing that all of us hurt ourselves and need to learn to be careful and focused, Annie felt stupid.

We live in a judgmental world. Even if our parents are accepting and loving, we still are affected by the world we live in. There is a cultural myth that it is possible to be perfect, and so we are all judged for our imperfections. Even if no one else is aware of those imperfections, we are aware, and we live afraid that at any time, we will be exposed. Other people do not seem to have as many imperfections as we do. Something must be wrong with us. We are not good enough, and so we hide in shame. We just do not measure up. Therefore, we do not have the right to exist.

What makes life even more terrifying is that everyone else seems to be just fine. How often have you had this experience: You talk to people and think, "Wow! They seem like they are so 'together.' They seem so sure of themselves. They look like they have a great marriage, and they never talk about having problems with their children. They seem so self-confident. What's wrong with me?" We compare ourselves with others and really come out the loser. We know how much time *we* spend struggling in *our* relationships and how unsure we feel of ourselves. There is no doubt about it - we must be inferior.

Our culture also presents us, through the media, with a clear idea of what is considered "normal" - a person who is beautiful, happy, healthy, confident, assertive, wise, loving, brave, expressive, honorable, and strong. Models of these "normal" people are everywhere. We do not lack examples of this exemplary type of person. There is only one little problem - they are all make-believe people... fabricated out of our longing for perfection. We have mixed up having ideals toward which to aim, with the impossible thought that we can ever attain them.

Our role models are primarily characters in television shows and movies, actors, sports heroes or models in magazines. We watch them, listen to them, and long to achieve their excellence of character and appearance. We forget that they read from scripts other people have written, and that they represent possibility, not reality. We think that if someone possesses money, beauty or physical ability, they have a greater personal value than we do. We forget the tricks of the trade which alter the bodies of actors and models to appear flawless, and that their on-screen confidence and eloquence may be wonderfully enacted by them, but is created by writers. We forget that athletes may be agile, but all people face human struggles, just as we do. These role models convince us of our inadequacy by their very existence. But, here again is the crucial point: We have endowed these role models with impossible qualities! They are figments of our cultural imagination.

This culturally induced fear that something is wrong with us is so common. We often no more think to question our cultural belief system than we think to question the availability of air for us to breathe. It is a deep part of us that we do not even consider. And since this is not something that is questioned, it is also something that is not often discussed. It is one of those private secrets with which we suffer in agony.... all of us, side by side, suffering with our fears and our judgments of ourselves. We are afraid to let anyone know because then we will be exposed and that would be too painful to bear. Even if we escape judgment one time, there is always the next. And because each of us is intimately aware of how imperfect we are, we live in terror of being discovered, revealed to the world as the worthless beings we fear we truly are.

There is a difference between judgment and analysis. Analytical thinking makes no value judgments - it impartially and logically considers things, weighing cause, effect, price and consequence. Judgment, however, puts everything in terms of right and wrong, good and bad. Analytical thinking challenges us to grow, to expand our knowledge and abilities. Judgment teaches us that we are unworthy, unimportant, inferior and inadequate. Example: Judgment: "I made a mistake during my presentation at work. I am stupid." Analysis: "People didn't understand the point I was making. I think I need to illustrate my point with more examples." Judgment tears us down and is negative. Analysis strengthens us and is positive.

Al: I didn't learn, as a child, how to be handy. My Dad didn't putter in the garage or fix anything around the house. I never had the chance to watch someone fix things so I could learn. When Jan and I got married, I wanted to be able to fix things in our apartment. I was so self-critical about my inability and lack of knowledge that I would send her to the hardware store to ask questions about how to do our projects, for I felt ashamed and too exposed to go myself and reveal my inadequacy. When I was doing a project, I was very impatient with myself and got easily frustrated. I felt quite worthless. Of course, with this attitude, I never developed into a Mr. Fix-it. Finally, after years of this shame, I was trying to put together a television stand, and started looking analytically at the task at hand. Without my usual critical attitude, I realized, "I can do this." I was able to figure it out fairly easily, and without help. When I stopped judging myself, I could relax, and I was able to think clearly.

We all have things we would like to be able to do better. They might be tasks at work, being able to speak to our children without impatience or anger, or eating in a more healthy way. When we realize we would like to change, we often are self-critical, or feel embarrassed or bad about ourselves. We can use the same kindness to support ourselves in changing that we would in helping a child to change. Sometimes all it takes, as in the example above, is an analysis of the situation and a positive belief. No one responds well to being shamed and beaten. When we treat ourselves with compassion and understanding, we maximize our chances to grow. We are affirming that we *already* have the right to exist *just as we are.*

2.   I should be perfect.

Jan: When I was a child, I could never be satisfied with anything that I did. My poor mother was in despair at my lack of self-acceptance. Trying to overcome my self-criticism, she used to tell me that it didn't matter what grades I got, to just do the best I could and feel proud. But I was even able to turn those loving words into a standard that I could not meet. If I got an A on a school assignment, I was upset that I didn't get an A+. If I got an A+, I just knew I could have gotten an A++. Because I did not live up to the possibilities of what I imagined could be, I felt worthless.

There is a cultural belief that it is possible to be perfect, or to have no flaws. And yet, the reality is that human beings are imperfect - things do not always turn out as we hope or expect. We will never be able to become all that we can envision. If the dictionary were really accurate, we would look under "human" and see the definition: "An evolving being who journeys from ignorance toward knowledge of self and the world." (Now, notice that we did not say that we journey "to" knowledge, but rather that we journey "toward" knowledge. We are limited beings. We were designed to be that way. We are not God, and so it is impossible for us to ever attain godlike knowledge, abilities or perfection.) We fear that the only valuable being is a perfect being. Because we are not perfect, we call ourselves inferior and not valuable, and so believe we do not have the right to exist.

The fact that we are imperfect beings means that none of us has everything about ourselves or our lives in perfect order. Being imperfect makes us *vulnerable* - or **visible in our humanness.** Vulnerability is a fact of existence for all living beings. We do not have the power to choose to be perfect, so there is no way we can ever fully protect ourselves. Nor do we need to. There is nothing wrong with being imperfect. God does not mind - He made us that way.

An animal senses his vulnerability as danger. Like animals, we experience being vulnerable as a threat that we will be killed. How many times when something happened which exposed an imperfection have you said, and heard other people say, "I thought I'd just *die!*" Our logical minds know that we will not *really* die if we get a traffic ticket, get passed over for a promotion, have acne, trip and fall down.... but when these things happen, we usually feel exposed, and experience a deep sense of shame. We can tell ourselves that these kinds of things happen to everyone, but that does not make the embarrassment, shame or sense of vulnerability go away. Like an animal separated from the herd, or belly up with other animals around, we feel exposed, helpless and endangered. **Our search for perfection is really just an attempt to not feel vulnerable.**

The concept of perfection is something we have made up in our minds - (it certainly does not exist in the real world!) - as the answer to how we can keep ourselves from ever feeling vulnerable, again. But because we can never attain it, what we think will be the armor that will protect us becomes a plague to constantly make us feel more vulnerable. We are *guaranteed* to fail at being perfect, and this increases our sense of inadequacy, vulnerability and fear. Only by accepting our true state of humanness can we put "perfection" in its place. It is a thought to inspire us, not a condition we will ever become. For example, we can commit ourselves to following in the footsteps of Christ, but do any of us really think we will *become* Christ? Whatever our culture or family might tell us and expect of us, they did not design us to be the way we are. God did.

3.   I do not have the right to my own separate life.

Al: When I was a child, I loved every kind of sports and played them all year. I had been taking piano lessons since I was eight, but when I turned ten, I wanted to devote all of my time to sports. When I announced to my parents that I wanted to stop piano lessons, they reluctantly agreed, and although they did not make a big fuss about it, I knew they were very disappointed. I felt guilty and responsible for their unhappiness. What I really wanted them to say, which they simply didn't know to do, was that they were happy that I enjoyed sports so much and that they supported me in doing what was important to me. *I would have learned that it is possible for people to be different, with different goals and ideas about what is important in life. I would have learned that my parents wanted me to be* me, *not* them.

When we are conceived, we are literally *fused* with our mothers. We are one with them and connected to them. Everything that they feel makes chemicals go through our bodies. We grow until we can no longer remain inside them without the risk of death for both of us, and then we are born. At conception, we begin a lifelong journey along a continuum between *fusion*, **a feeling or sense of oneness**, and *separateness*, or *individuation* - **the growth of the individual self.** For our entire lives, we will travel back and forth along this continuum, sometimes being able to enjoy the closeness and comfort of intimate fusion, sometimes striking out on our own and having our separate needs and wants. Neither fusion nor separateness is good or bad. They are both important experiences in our lives. What happens to all of us, however, is that we can become stuck at one end of the continuum or the other, and lose our ability to move appropriately between the two experiences.

Jan: It is wonderful to be a young couple, discovering all of the similarities both share. Al and I had so many. I remember, though, walking out of a movie, one day, and having Al say how much he liked it. "What?!?" I screamed in shock. "How could you like that movie? It was awful!" He was stunned by my reaction, and, so was I! What on Earth had made me so upset so instantaneously? It was just a movie, for Heaven's sake. What difference did it make if we had differing opinions about it? I realized immediately that I had just been shocked out of my easy and peaceful fusion with my husband into a sudden awareness of my separateness. The anger was my involuntary reaction to having been ripped out of that comfortable fusion when I didn't want to or expect to be looking at the fact that we are not just like each other.

Many of us react with anger, disappointment or hurt when we suddenly experience being separate from someone who is important to us. There is a comfort in being the same. When we become aware of our separateness, we can feel shocked by the sudden sense of feeling alone, and interpret it as abandonment. We can think that something is either wrong with us or with the other person, rather than just knowing that we are different.

Fusion is an important part of an infant's life. He feels comforted and safe because of the attention his mother gives him. The mother needs to fuse with her baby in order to be able to make her needs secondary and give him the care and attention he requires to thrive. As the baby grows and starts to move along the continuum toward greater separateness, both mother and child experience freedom and relief, but also loss, as well. It is as though the reality of being two separate living people is exciting, and yet it sometimes stretches the heart to the breaking point, as we have to let go of each other. Take the kindergartner who cries on being left at school, and the mother who chokes back her tears until she arrives at her car.

It is a natural thing for all living beings to want to avoid pain, so it is common for both parents and children to get stuck at the fusion end of the continuum. The parent becomes too controlling of the child, taking everything the child does personally. The parent cannot see that the child is on his own journey of learning and that this journey is not *about* or *because* of the parent. It is the child's turn to exist as a separate person. It is the parent's gift to be able to guide his child but he needs to allow the child his own reality. If a child is afraid of leaving or being different than his parents, he or she will get stuck in being a "good" boy or girl. A child might also react to this fear by rebelling and getting stuck in being "bad." Either way, the child will feel too much loss and fear to be able to separate. Children and their parents fight their vulnerability by clinging to each other. "Good" children act the way their parents want. "Bad" children react against what their parents want. Neither are free to find their own way, feeling supported by the parents in their separating.

These children learn that their behaviors and accomplishments are not for themselves, but for others. As Al carried the burden of responsibility for his parents' unhappiness at his decision to discontinue piano lessons, children learn that their choices create pain for others. There is no separate existence where each person has his own feelings and wants, and where this separateness is accepted by everyone as right and natural. They learn that their feelings are not rightfully theirs, but rather determine their parents' well-being, and therefore the child's own security and safety.

Al: If my parents had known to tell me that they felt disappointed that I was quitting piano lessons, but that they supported me in doing what felt right to me, I would have learned that it is okay for people to feel separate. They would have been teaching me that they could feel disappointed and I could feel happy, <u>about the same event.</u> I would have been able to see that I didn't have to take care of my parents - they were strong enough to bear their disappointment and leave me free to find my way in my life.

Every child wants approval for just being himself. Parents are the foundation for the child's life. Children want to be released into the world with their parents' approval and encouragement. When parents are stuck in fusion, the children are not supported in self-awareness or in feeling that they are important. They do not receive encouragement to go out and create a life for themselves that feels right. These children become either pleasers or rebels. They cannot think about what *they* want or like. They are afraid of their parents' reactions. They have not had the support to know that it is normal to feel vulnerable when separating, and that the parents approve of their child's individuation. Pleasers and rebels do not act for their own selves. They do not make choices based on what feels right to them. They *react*. Rebels react against being held onto by their fusion object (parents, and later in life, friends and spouses.) Pleasers are scared to be different than their fusion objects. Both are afraid to let go and feel their separateness.

We are *designed* to be separate - do you see any tubes or strings or limbs attaching you to anyone else? While we have arms to hug and hold each other, to come together in love and comforting, we are designed to need to let go of each other in order to function in the other aspects of our lives. Everyone is given one body to live in and control, and to make decisions for. Your body is yours. You have the right and the responsibility to take care of the body and life you have been given by God. Only you will be accountable, at your death, for how you have used your life. Separateness is a condition we are born to that *enables* us to take on this responsibility.

Separateness eliminates the need for judgment

We once lived next door to a set of identical twins. The mother was so good humored, even though she was absolutely exhausted. She easily spoke about something that was apparent to everyone - one of her daughters was a little angel girl, while the other was tormented and often angry. She told us that when they were born, the nurses at the hospital remarked on the difference between the babies, and reassured her that they frequently saw identical twins, who from birth had absolutely different temperaments.

Although parents have an enormous influence on their children, children are born with their own distinct personalities that have nothing to do with us. When our children do something, *they* do something. Their behavior is not only based on the teachings of their parents, but also on their innate personalities. Whether their behavior receives praise or judgment from the world, it is not about us.

Most parents, as children, did not experience separateness from their parents, and so do not know how to feel anything but fused with their own children. Everything our children do is then a reflection on us. If we can separate from our children and each other, we would not feel pride *in them*. Pride in others is an experience of non-separateness. We might feel proud *of ourselves* for what we have done as a parent, or as a spouse, supporting our loved ones in accomplishing their goals. But we would feel *impressed by* them and their accomplishments, which are <u>not</u> about us.

"My child is the student of the month
at _____ Elementary School."
(Judgment: I am a <u>good</u> parent.)

"I have a meeting with the teacher about my child's behavior."
(Judgment: I am a <u>bad</u> parent.)

The concept of separateness helps to eliminate judgment. **Separateness is the idea that we have feelings and thoughts that are our own, that are not caused by anything or anyone.** We are only responsible for what we do. The actions of others are the result of their choices, not ours. Our awareness and abilities are limited. We can never do everything possible, for we do not have that kind of power. Even with our children, we can only do what we know to do. Ultimately, they are the ones who determine their lives. Each of us has our own particular way of responding to a catalyst, whether it is internal or external. Our reactions are *triggered* inside of us but are not *caused* by what is outside of us. A perfect example of this is the teaching Jesus gave on the idea of turning the other cheek. Most of us might want to hit back, or at least cry if we were struck! Because He was so highly evolved, He was able to separate from the actions of others and choose His reaction based on who *He* was, rather than being reactive.

If you were sitting next to someone who suddenly doubled over, held his stomach and moaned, you most likely would not say, "What did I do?" You would probably be concerned about him and say, "What's wrong? What happened?" It is easier for us to feel separate at the physical level, but emotional separateness is harder to attain. If someone suddenly started to cry, and you were not able to feel separate from him, you might ask, "What did I say that made you cry?" Understanding about separateness, however, allows us to know that the person who is crying is feeling sad and the tears are the expression of that sadness, not an accusation that we have done something wrong. You cannot *cause* someone to cry. Even if the tears are in reaction to something we have done or said, crying is *his* response.

While we are not responsible for the reaction of another

person, we each have the ability and the responsibility to examine our own behavior so that we act in such a way that we feel proud of ourselves. This is a wonderful power to have. There is no blame or accusation necessary when we discover more satisfying ways of acting. The idea of separateness encourages us to recognize where we have no control or responsibility, and to release the illusion that we can have control over another person's feelings. It also allows us the freedom to choose new behaviors that can give us even more pride in ourselves.

<u>How people learn and grow</u>

We all seem to be designed to learn by hindsight. This means that we will have an experience, and afterwards be able to examine it and find things we could have done or said which we would have felt better about, or which would have possibly worked better. (Again, note the word "possibly." Not being God, it is impossible for us to *know* what the outcome would have been in any situation. All we can know is that it *might* have worked out more to our liking.) If we do not understand that we are *designed* to learn through hindsight, we may become ashamed, self-critical or despairing when we look back at an experience. Unexpected outcomes, often called "mistakes," are inevitable, because our awareness of the future is limited. We fear that it is not acceptable for us to be imperfect humans. We are, after all, products of our critical world. We feel critical of ourselves because we cannot anticipate the future. This is as silly as feeling like failures because we get hungry. Both are part of the design. Instead, we can feel victorious because we have used our hindsight to learn something previously unknown.

Jan: Our first car was a 1965 Dodge Dart. It was a goodbye gift from Al's mother when she moved to the East Coast. We were both very young, and neither of us had ever had a car, before, nor a father to teach us how to take care of one. We were driving down the freeway, one day, when suddenly flames burst out from beneath the hood! We were shaken up and horrified. Luckily, we were right near an exit, so we hurriedly pulled off the road. The mechanic who examined the engine asked us when the last time was that we had added oil and water to the car. Oh.... We didn't know we needed to do that. We knew about the gas part, so it would go, but neither of us knew anything else about car maintenance. Realizing we were absolutely clueless we found ourselves a wonderful Lithuanian auto mechanic who thought we were very amusing, and took great pleasure in helping us learn how to care for our next car. (We've hardly burned up any engines since then!)

We could have judged ourselves pretty harshly for destroying a car, but the truth was, we were just innocently ignorant. Being critical of ourselves would have accomplished nothing. The task at hand was just to learn, in hindsight, what to do in order to properly care for an automobile. When we accept our humanness, it is a simple thing to take action to take care of problems and the unexpected outcomes of our acts. (Besides, how many of *you* can tell a story like that!)

All great inventions come from theory. But all inventors and scientists do experiments to test what the nature and limits of reality truly are, for theory can only indicate possibilities and a direction to try. Experiments provide inventors and scientists the opportunity to use hindsight to understand reality and improve their inventions and products. Scientists do not criticize themselves for difficulties that are revealed by their experiments. They are excited by the new possibilities and directions they are able to see *through hindsight*, and they go on to greater accomplishments. We are no different. We are the scientists, and our lives are the experiments. Like our fellow scientists, we can rejoice in the discoveries we make, rather than feel ashamed that we do not have the wisdom of God.

We are fallible beings who struggle with feelings of disappointment and limited control. But we assume having those feelings indicate that we are inadequate, rather than that they are evidence that we were born to a human life. Feeling disappointed or helpless is a natural and inevitable experience. It is rare that we will ever do *anything* perfectly. We are not born with that ability. We misinterpret the discomfort or the pain we experience when, with the assistance of our hindsight, we realize an instance of our ignorance or humanness. Pain, embarrassment, disappointment, or fear are always signals that we have the opportunity to grow. Having those feelings is not a "problem" or an accusation of our imperfection. (How can we be "accused" of being imperfect? That's like being "accused" of breathing. Both are simply part of our nature and destiny.) The feelings are simply there to get our attention - just like a fire alarm is. When we hear a fire alarm, we do not focus on how obnoxious the sound is, how blaring and assaulting it feels, and, anyway, who on Earth put it there to annoy and interrupt us! Knowing what it means, we spring to action to take steps to improve our lives - by saving them! The reaction we have when we do not like the outcome of an interaction or event is simply the alarm letting us know to pay attention: there are things we can learn that will make us smarter, more whole and, most likely, more happy and proud of ourselves. Physical pain is a call to pay attention to something in our body that needs our help in order for us to have health. Emotional pain exists to let us know that we have the opportunity to learn and grow into the people we want to be.

We are not born with the ability to know the future. Hindsight is a tool given to us so that we can increase in wisdom and knowledge through experience. Whenever we use hindsight to grow, we can feel clever for having the good sense to make use of the gift we are designed to have, the gift God gave us to help us fulfill our God-given potential.

Why are we so self-critical?

Children receive the best parents have to give, but it always is less than perfect. It is unlikely that anyone can be the parent they dream of being. It is unlikely that any parent can keep from reacting out of his own fears and needs. Each of us struggles with the fear that we do not have the right to exist, that we are inadequate, that we will be judged. We inherit the struggles of mankind when we are born, and parents can only take their children as far as they, themselves, have come. All people must struggle with being self-critical, instead of being at peace and in acceptance about being fallible, evolving beings. With no model of self-acceptance in our culture or in our families, children cannot have peace and acceptance of themselves, either.

We enter into marriage and parenthood with the highest of hopes and dreams. Yet each of us is frightened that we will be discovered as the worthless, imperfect person we truly are. ("I'm so *lucky* he's marrying me." "She wouldn't love me if she knew....") Because we are self-critical instead of self-accepting, anything our spouse or child does is a threat that our inadequacy will be revealed. And so in our fear, we actually do become critical, trying to make them perfect so we are not exposed, passing on the painful legacy of judgment.

A child has no way to understand why his culture or family is critical of him. A child simply feels the impact of this criticism. It is impossible for any child to step back and look compassionately at his family or culture and understand that criticism is the result of *their* struggles, a sign that *they* have not been able to claim their right to exist, either. So the child does the only thing he can to survive - he adopts the thinking of his family or culture and accepts his unworthiness. Even a child knows he is not perfect, and it is not a difficult thing to therefore make the leap from "I am not perfect" to "I am not worthy." No child can step back and say, "Poor Mom and Dad. They don't accept themselves." A child only knows what his parents and culture model as the way to handle that lack of perfection: criticism of others and self. This criticism can only lead to the feeling that we are unworthy, and who could conceive that God would want to give to an unworthy person?

Once we understand that we have been molded by this culture of judgment, we each have the opportunity to claim our right to exist. The proof of our claim is the very fact that we are here! Our existence is the proof that we have the same right as any other life form to have our life, and to hope to have a good life. If it wasn't our turn, we would not be here. But how do we lay claim to this right? Our logical self might clearly understand, but it seems as if there is a deeper part of us which does not. Despite what our mind tells us, we still believe that we are not worthy.

We all have a lot of growing up to do

None of us is "all grown up." Just because we leave our parents and start a life of our own does not mean that we have finished growing. The wonderful thing about this fact is that there is no end to the freedom and peace we can attain. As good as life might be now, it always can get better. We can grow in compassion and love, self-acceptance and strength, clarity and wisdom. Just because we have left our parents' home does not mean that we have come to an understanding and resolution of the many lessons and issues all people have to face.

When we look in the mirror, we see a large adult. It does not occur to us that there is a small, fearful child inside, directing the show. (Remember in *The Wizard of Oz* when Dorothy and her friends stood quaking in front of the Great and Terrible Oz? Do you remember what they saw when Toto pulled back the curtain? It was a small and humble, timid man pulling the strings.)

Our bodies may be large and fully grown, but our emotional selves may be stuck in nonlogical patterns and beliefs. It is as though inside each of us is a child who feels frightened and undeserving. When we are small children, we form a belief system about what we need to do to in order to be acceptable in the world. Young children are not very logical, however, and may easily misinterpret what is said to them, and what they see. Nonetheless, it is this part of us which reacts and *determines our behavior patterns* for the rest of our lives for when we feel frightened or threatened. And usually, although we may recognize the nonlogical or nonrational nature of our behavior, we remain puzzled and confused by it. We do not understand why it occurs or how to stop it.

Al: When I was a child, my family frequently made plans to go out to dinner or to the movies. These plans would regularly be cancelled because one of my parents would feel sick or tired. My experience of growing up was that I had a lot of disappointments. As an adult, when Jan and I would make plans for our family, if the plans were changed or cancelled, I would feel the same way I did as a child. I was so disappointed and helpless that I felt like stomping my feet like a six year old. I felt critical of myself for being so childish, so I used to withdraw in embarrassment, and wait for my feelings to pass.

The wonderful thing is that while that frightened child wasn't looking, our adult self grew up! And, while not perfect, we are intelligent, strong, kind, and fully capable of dealing with most things in the world. We may not know how to do everything, but we are fully capable of learning what is most important for our life. This strong adult has the opportunity to become the parent for our own fearful, doubting self.

Al: Since learning to reparent myself, while I still feel disappointed at times, I am able to comfort myself and remember that I am no longer that helpless child who felt totally out of control of everything that mattered to him.

I have the ability to take charge in my life and find alternatives when things don't work out the way I had hoped.

Love yourself out of the past into the present

We can take over where our parents left off, knowing that they did the very best they could do. Even if they were abusive, alcoholic, violent, or critical, they could not grow beyond their own pain to do better than they did. If they could have, they would have. But we can do more. We can begin to parent ourselves the same way we would if we took in a foster child. The adult you are today has the opportunity to bring healing to the part of yourself that is stuck, not believing that you deserve good things and that you have the right to exist. This healing will not come just from thinking about it. We need to be vigilant in watching for signs of tension in our bodies, fear, hurt, anger, or any feeling that indicates a lack of inner peace and shows that we have left our logical adult frame of mind. When we get this signal, we need to take action. (Some of us feel tension *all* the time. Well, guess what! That is the call from your vulnerable self telling you that you need *constant* attention. It won't be a problem unless you ignore that call.)

Just as we must exercise our bodies in order to maintain good health, there are reparenting exercises which we must do if we are to free ourselves from old childhood responses. These exercises will help remind us that we are no longer stuck in the past as a helpless or hurting child. The exercises will help reprogram our cellular responses. The automatic survival patterns that have developed over the years can be changed, giving us an opportunity to establish new patterns that fit our adult understanding of the world.

Exercise: (In order to get as much oxygen as possible, inhale slowly through your mouth and feel your chest fill up until it is fully expanded. Hold that breath, resting. When you are ready, slowly exhale through your mouth, and allow yourself to relax before repeating this style of breathing.) Put your hands on your heart and take deep breaths into that self who does not feel worthy. With each deep breath, take down into your body and heart the thought that it is sad that you did not learn to completely accept that you have the right to exist, but that now there is a new part of you - your adult self - who knows this and will teach you.

The healing exercises offered to you in this book will take many repetitions in order to become a real part of you. If you took a foster child into your home, *you* might love him and know that he will never again have to endure the experiences of his previous life, but chances are it will take time for *him* to come to the same awareness. You would need to have the attitude with that child that you will never get tired of reminding him that he learned very sad lessons in his old home, but that in *this* family, it is different. It would take time for him to realize that you were here to take care of him, and that he could turn to you for help. It will also take time for the nonlogical, stuck part of you to realize that in addition to that vulnerable self, you have also become a strong and capable adult. Changing our inner reality and healing pain from the past takes time. We must be patient with ourselves and be prepared to repeat these exercises our whole lives as a part of ongoing self-care.

We are often told that we can "reprogram" our minds to get rid of "hurtful memories." Our logical self believes this, but our emotional self may think, "How can I ever do that?" For example, our logical adult may absolutely agree with the idea that we can choose to be happy. That makes total sense. Why would we choose to be unhappy? But imagine that sitting right next to us is a little child who says, "I don't *feel* happy. How can I *choose* to be happy if I don't feel it? Other people seem happy. I don't. Something must be wrong with me." If that was your child, you would know exactly what to say. You'd be encouraging and positive. You'd tell that child that he is important and deserves good things, including being happy. That is what we need to tell ourselves to help us release the hurt of the past.

Exercise: Imagine your adult self telling that unhappy child: "Once your family and culture taught you that you were not worthy, that you had to be perfect. But that is not true, and it is a sad thing - no child should have to feel bad about being imperfect, for that is our nature. Your parents did not understand this, and that is very sad. But I do understand. And I will never get tired of helping you remember. I will remind you as often as you need that you were born a human being, and it is your right to learn and grow and change without ever feeling shame."

We were not born angels or saints. It is our nature to get to learn and grow.   It is our right, our *birthright*, to be fallible, growing human beings - always learning, always changing. That is a good thing, not a mistake. As a matter of fact, there is no such thing as a mistake. There are only unexpected outcomes to our actions. And how lucky we are to be able to identify when things do not go as we wish, so that we can be clever and think of other alternatives!

If it is our birthright to be evolving, changing beings, then we have the right to exist as we are right now, and we can feel deserving of having good things happen to us. Even if our parents and culture are stuck on the path of criticism, we can teach ourselves that we deserve to be a "winner." It is always an amazing paradox and puzzle that we can see the logic that we are as deserving and have as much right to exist as anyone else, but we just cannot get it down into our deepest hearts. Old teachings are deeply set. They are programmed into our cells and interwoven into every part of our lives and behaviors. We have the opportunity to reprogram ourselves with love and patience. Reparenting will be the key to our freedom. It will allow us to change patterns and thoughts that willpower simply has been unable to touch.

Exercise: Close your eyes and picture yourself as young as you can remember yourself. Look at the expression on your face. What do you see? Are you happy, eager, excited? Are you sad, scared, withdrawn? What does your adult self feel when you look at that little face? Breathe deeply into your heart and tell that child that you are here now to take care of him. He will never again be alone with those feelings.

We can find clues in our pasts about behaviors, attitudes or feelings that are mystifying. If we know how to explore the past to get clarity and understanding about where our feelings come from, it will be easier to reparent ourselves into the present, with the wisdom we have attained as adults.

Exercise: 1. Make a list of the qualities that you don't like about yourself. How do you feel when you look at that list?
2. What would a kind and loving parent say to you about each item on the list that would feel encouraging to you?
3. Without judging, use your ability to analyze to set a

> small goal of new behavior for each item on your list.
> 4.   Now list the qualities you would like to embody.
> 5.   As you look at this list, imagine a supportive parent
>   with his hand on your shoulder.

The journey from the first list to the second is called the *human journey*. It is impossible to avoid having to make it. We all start out in life ignorant and unskilled. The journey of life is about learning, growing, getting freer from fear and illusion, getting stronger, and becoming more peaceful and more compassionate. No one is born Christ, Buddha, an angel or a saint. We are born human beings, and that means that there is no way around being ignorant. It is not a fault or mistake. It is our *destiny* to grow and learn. We have the opportunity to grow from ignorance toward knowledge, just as a child has the opportunity to learn in school. If we accept this truth, instead of thinking something is wrong with us, we can feel how lucky we are that there is no limit to our becoming more whole.

Exercise: Look again at your lists. With your hands on your heart, take a deep breath and teach yourself, "It is my destiny to be a human being. If God wanted me to be a saint or an angel, He would have given me that birth - but He didn't. My journey as a human being is His plan."

Now imagine that as you are holding your heart, God is holding you. Allow yourself to breathe deeply and take into your body that you are the beloved child of God. He wanted you to exist, or you would not have been born. He is the One who designed the Human Journey, not you. As incomprehensible as it may appear to us, this is His plan. Every struggle you engage in is part of claiming your place as His child. It is <u>part</u> of the Human Journey – not a mistake. If you feel something or do something, it must be a part of God's plan and something He expects you to face. Be patient with yourself. God is patient with you. (After all, you have not been struck by a bolt of lightning yet!) When you claim your right to exist and know that you deserve things, then life can open up to you. Only then can you fully receive from God, and be God's partner in the fulfillment of the Human Journey.

We must watch ourselves as we go through our day, as we would watch a child who is too young to be able to supervise himself and stay out of danger. Rather than be surprised, shocked, upset or critical when we see old ideas and mind-sets come up, we can *expect* them to. We can expect negative feelings, fears and behaviors. We can be compassionately watchful, just as we would be with a child, to catch ourselves in the act of being afraid and feeling undeserving. If we had this attitude, then instead of feeling like a failure because we still have these feelings, we can feel successful that we are so attentive and aware of ourselves that we were able to catch ourselves in our old pattern of negativity. We can kindly reassure ourselves that we will learn. There is nothing to be discouraged about. Earlier in your life, no one knew how to reassure your fears, but that now there is a smart adult here (YOU!) who can help you remember that you have the right to exist and to thrive and be happy.

<u>Deserving</u>

Why is it so difficult to have positive expectations? What is so hard about standing forth and declaring "I deserve good things?" We may know in our smart adult minds that this is a logical statement, but there is something deep inside us which cannot accept it as the truth, which feels afraid to accept it. It is safer to think small - that is one way to protect ourselves from disappointment. It is scary to think bigger. What if we open our hearts and allow ourselves to want something, and we do not get it?

Say this to yourself: "I deserve good things." How does it feel to say those words? Everyone deserves good things in life. Our belief that we deserve good things takes nothing away from anyone else. They deserve good things, too. But in our culture, people who talk about what they want or need are often considered "selfish." We are concerned that if we say "I deserve good things" what others will hear is "I'm the *only* one who deserves good things." Who wants to hear, "What makes you think you're so special?" No one wants to be isolated and criticized for being seen as selfish, so we tend to hide our true selves and try to blend in, even if it means giving up on what we truly want or believe.

Here is an example. A couple is working around their house on the weekend. The husband says, "I'm really beat. I think I need to rest for a few hours." The wife says, "I've been waiting all week for you to help me with some projects that need two people." Is the husband selfish? Of course not. He's tired from his week. Is the wife selfish? Not at all. She just wants his help. Each one of them deserves what they want. No one is selfish. They just have to figure out what to do about having *different* needs. Rather than either of them giving up on what they need, together they can look for a way for both of them to feel important and cared about.

We are worthy

The pain we feel when we do not believe ourselves to be worthy lets us know that we can *conceive* of our worthiness. There is deep within us a rejection of the idea that we are unworthy. That pain is the true voice of a deeper wisdom. It is the acknowledgment in our soul that we deserve to have this life of goodness and that we long to claim our right to exist.

Al: I bought myself a beautiful pair of shoes on a family vacation. I usually buy very inexpensive shoes, but my family encouraged me to treat myself and get this pair, even though they cost so much more than I had ever spent before. As I opened the box to look at them, once more, on leaving the store, I started crying. I remember thinking, "I could have bought an inexpensive pair of shoes and spent the money on someone else." The truth is that I longed for those shoes but I couldn't give myself permission to spend the money to buy them. My tears came from my pain that I felt I didn't deserve to have such nice things.

Think of something you are longing for - a better relationship, job, home.... Imagine telling yourself that you cannot have it, that you do not deserve it. How do you feel? If you feel anger, sadness, disappointment or pain, *that is great news!* All of those feelings are proof that you know that you have the right to exist and only need to claim it. Our very existence is all the proof needed that we have the right to exist. Here we are! And since we're here, it is our turn. As living beings, we embody the very nature of Life – to exist and to grow. That is an undeniable imperative within us. The pain of thinking we are not deserving comes from trying to go against the force of Life within us that rebels at any denial of our right to exist. For those who call the force that organizes Life, God, this pain comes from denying the seed God planted in you that you have the right to be here. We only need to do the work of nurturing what God has planted – taking those old thoughts and replacing them with the truth of our existence: we deserve to be alive and have a good life.

Exercise: Hold your heart and imagine cradling that small child in you. Tell the child, "Once no one knew to tell you that you are a wonderful person and deserve to have success and happiness. That is a sad thing. But I am here, now, and I know you deserve all of God's blessings." Try to imagine breathing those words down into your body. Take big breaths in through your mouth and pull the love and support down into your heart.

Life and Growth are Inseparable!

The very nature of Life is growth. Given optimal conditions, all life would grow to its fullest form, as big and complete as possible. To grow into whole and satisfied beings is our **birthright!** It is nothing we have to earn or deserve. The force of Life causes all things, from people to animals to plants to push the boundaries of what already exists, in an inherent imperative towards expansion. The force of Life is so great that dandelions push their way through solid asphalt. As living beings, we are also designed to exist, to take up space. Life demands it.

Life is synonymous with growth. We have no choice. It is a biological and spiritual compulsion. Just as the most noxious of poisons are required to truly stop the growth of plants and "weeds," so we must do violence to ourselves to stop that innate natural process that we embody. As soon as life begins, has its first spark, expansion is instantaneous, urgent, insistent.

This birthright to have all that is possible for ourselves is a simple fact of nature. We need only to look around to see its truth. When we don't contain plants and animals, they grow, they spread, they multiply. They partake of the bounty of existence. Whether it is a force of nature or a gift from God, we can use the same words to describe our birthright to become big and fulfilled. In this book, use whichever concept best fits for you, but know, beyond doubt, that both support and *demand* your full existence.

Believe You Are Valuable

How is it that we have such a small view of God that we think

He would not want to give us blessings?   It must be that we have a small view of ourselves. Our world does not support the idea that each person is important. Instead, it teaches conformity. It discourages individuality and, because of the pervasiveness of criticism, makes us afraid to stand out from the crowd.

Our negative self-image limits our ability to see the truth of God. If we cannot conceive of our own right to exist, then we are saying that God, too, is small and is limited. He does not have bounty to disperse to His children. When we dare to ask with the expectation of being received and supported, then God has the opportunity to give to us. We are then living our right to exist and are not hiding in fear.

Consider this: two children are offered ice cream. One doesn't feel deserving - he will fearfully eat a little, and dare not ask for more. But imagine the other sitting with God, who says that he deserves that ice cream. That child would eat with gusto, and mostly likely expect seconds! When we feel that we have the right to exist and that we deserve good things, we can boldly expect God to want to give us His blessings.

Practice, practice, practice

Jan: I used to teach psychology at an adult school. One semester, one of my students suddenly interrupted me and said, "You're not teaching psychology. You're teaching revolution!" She was right.

The concepts that we are introducing in this chapter, as well as the rest that will follow in this book, are revolutionary. They depart from the commonly held understandings of how we should live. They are very different from what our culture and families have defined as what it means to be alive. This differentness will necessitate a deep change in how we think, if we are truly to be free. Change is not easy for anyone. Our behavior patterns are emotionally driven, not logically chosen. Response patterns get set deep in our cells, so that before we even have the chance to think, we are already reacting. Our physiological reactions are triggered long before we can identify our thoughts or feelings.

While this is not an insurmountable difficulty, to be able to make changes and heal ourselves *is* going to take a lot of attention and work. Logically understanding a concept is very different from *becoming* the concept. We can look ahead and see a mountain we want to climb, but it is a very different matter to put one foot in front of the other and keep going up the steep path until we have climbed it. Our smart left brains will be able to know the rightness of something, but our emotions and patterns of behavior are deeply embedded in us. Knowledge does not change *being*. Just as we might feel tired and discouraged climbing that mountain, so we may feel overwhelmed and despair that we might never be able to make the changes in ourselves that we long for. But we can.

We want to encourage you to have patience with yourself, to rejoice in every small step you take in having understanding and compassion for yourself. We will be helping you to remember these key concepts - these "keys" to your freedom - and how they underlie every issue we address in this book. These concepts will appear in every chapter, so that you will be supported in your work of becoming your best self.

Do you remember how long it took you to learn the multiplication tables? Do you remember endless practices with flash cards? *(Jan: and never quite getting 6x9? Well... that was my hardest one, anyway.)* Healing old wounds and freeing ourselves to be the people we want to be will also take repetition and practice. But do not worry! If you can learn 6x9, you can learn anything!!!

We encourage you to read this book with a watchful eye on yourself. As you would if you were taking care of a child, be alert so you can readily hear the pain or fear in your heart. Be ready, at a moment's notice to reparent yourself, exchanging your old reality for one that your logical adult self knows to be more true. Every time you come to a new idea in this book that feels right to you, take the time to stop. Do not let that idea stay in just your logical mind. Every time you find yourself stuck on a negative thought or feeling about yourself, take the time to stop. Do not allow that judgment to keep hold of you for one more moment! *Breathe the words and reminders deeply into your body so that they not only get down into your fingertips and toes, but into every cell of your body. Be patient. Repeat the steps we talk about until they become a part of you.* Your physiological reactions will get slowed down. You will have the chance to receive guidance from your logical adult. Your emotions will shift as you experience this love and support, and *you <u>will</u> become free.*

Chapter 2

~ *Learn to Expect a Good Life* ~

It is an appealing idea that you will get what you expect in life. Few of us, however, really believe that this will be true for us. Life feels too big and overwhelming, and we are acutely aware of our own littleness and lack of power in influencing the events and outcomes that are most important to us. It is easy to mistake our feelings of vulnerability as a signal that we should not try to achieve the goals we dream of. It is easy to be so aware of our limited power and control in the world that we give up before we even start. No one, after all, wants to be disappointed, especially if failing to meet the goals we aim for results in self-criticism or the judgment of others.

If we are not to follow the hopes and dreams which come from our hearts, what is there for us to follow? There are so many possibilities in the world. Only our hearts can direct us to the ones which are right for us. If we do not follow our hearts, we are left following fear, and fear can never help us have a full life.

The gift of vulnerability

Feeling how vulnerable we are to forces beyond our control is an unavoidable experience in life. Any animal feels vulnerable when it leaves his own territory; eyes dart back and forth watchfully, whiskers twitch, ears turn every which way listening for sounds that might signify danger. As human beings, we may experience anxiety when we venture out of our small safe zone of certainty - our home, our simple routines, the same restaurants, vacations, driving routes, television shows - into new possibilities. The world is large and overwhelming, and all of us find relief in the familiar and the predictable.

Like any animal, our adrenaline surges when we feel vulnerable or try new things. We experience this surge as either *fear* or *excitement*. This adrenaline gives us the energy to make special efforts to take care of ourselves. There is nothing wrong with that feeling, but when we call it "fear" rather than "energy" we convince ourselves without even realizing we are doing so, that we are in danger and are helpless, with no power. If we were to call it "energy" or "excitement," then it would be easier to think of the adrenaline as fuel, a positive force to help us go after what we want in the world. We can teach ourselves to harness the energy of our vulnerability, giving ourselves the power to take positive action in the world.

Exercise: Think of something you would like to have in your life that is really important to you. Let yourself feel how much you would like it. Do you feel fear when you think of it? Do you feel excitement? If you feel fear, put your hand on your heart, take a deep breath to connect with that vulnerable child part of you, and teach yourself: "I'm just feeling vulnerable. It's just adrenaline. That adrenaline is here to give me the energy to go after what I want."

Whether it is a change of job, making a move, trying a new restaurant, risking our lives on the highways, flying somewhere in one of those ridiculously small contraptions that stay aloft in incomprehensible ways... we are always stepping out into the unknown. There is no guarantee of safety, or of a positive outcome to what we try to do. It is a normal reaction to not want to feel vulnerable. It takes a lot of courage to step into the world, to get up each day and face the unknown, and many of us are able to do this by not thinking about how very vulnerable we are.

Having a negative outlook and bad expectations is one way to protect yourself from feeling too vulnerable and hopeful, and from possibly being disappointed. Not having positive expectations is one attempt to minimize the amount of fear we feel. If we open ourselves to wanting and hoping, we might get disappointed. If we hope for nothing and are pessimistic about the future, we are attempting to feel in control. (I'm holding tight to the reins of the horse. He may not be going anywhere, but at least he won't run away with me!)

We tend to think of vulnerability as being a bad thing. We do not like to cry. We do not want other people to know how deeply affected we are by tender emotions. But vulnerability is also a lovely part of being human, and we all respond to it. People sit in the dark and cry at movies when they cannot cry for themselves in their own lives. People are moved by heroism and sacrifice. We are drawn to the vulnerability of babies and young animals, wanting to embrace and care for them.

Al: Once I attended the Special Olympics. As I watched one of the running events, I noticed how moved I felt, but didn't understand why. The participants didn't have great athletic abilities, but they had something better. They raced with humility, stopping to help each other if one of them fell. They ran with strength and courage and determination, and a complete acceptance of themselves. And as each of them crossed the finish line, glowing with pride and pleasure, I thought, "What inner power!" That power can happen for each of us when we don't question or judge our humanness, but instead feel at peace with our vulnerability.

We can embrace and feel proud of our vulnerability. If we accept that being vulnerable is just part of being alive, and is, in fact, a wonderful part of being alive, then we will not need to live trying to avoid feeling it. We will be free to have big expectations and hopes for our lives. Accepting and living connected to our vulnerability gives us the greatest chance possible for God to help us fulfill our hopes and dreams.

Choice

Some people always seem to be positive and optimistic about life. Other people tend to be pessimistic, always fearing and expecting the worst. What makes the difference? Are some of us just weaker in our character and in our faith in God, and so cannot imagine that things will work out for us? Why do some people, despite any problem or difficulty they may experience in life, keep having a positive attitude?

Some people, as we spoke about in the first chapter, have a strong sense of their right to exist. They expect that good things can and will happen to them, because they deserve to be here in this life. They have a sense of possibilities and *choice*. They are aware of their power to take action. Things can be good because we can make them good. And if it does not work out one time, we will reassess the situation and come up with other alternatives that might work.

People who do not have the sense of their right to exist feel undeserving. For them, it is useless to expect more from life or God. They have no confidence in their ability to influence what happens to them in their lives. They have a distorted feeling of powerlessness, with no sense of having choice in their lives. "Things are the way they are, and I am helpless to make a difference." They might also feel that good and bad are random. People are either lucky or unlucky.

When a parent teaches a child that he is important, that his feelings and wants matter, the child learns to explore options and choices in order to find ways to influence his life and strive for the outcomes he wants. The child learns that if he tries hard, good things can happen. With a positive sense of self, the child grows to have a sense of power in the world. A child feels powerful and important when his parents respond positively to the expression of his feelings and when they seek to incorporate his needs into the family plans.

Al: This isn't an unusual experience, but I was never consulted about what I wanted for dinner. Even when my mother made something that she knew I hated, she never even acknowledged my dislike. I was never considered or allowed to have a choice. I didn't feel like my feelings mattered at all - I was just supposed to silently go along with whatever was happening in my family. And, I was told about our family's move across the country only one month before we left. No one bothered to listen to or comfort my feelings about the move. I felt just like another piece of furniture that needed to be packed up and carted away.

If a parent has not had the experience, himself, of feeling important, it is hard to pass that feeling on to his child. If the child does not feel the possibility of choice, he experiences himself as a victim. He feels the randomness of life, for no one solicits or acknowledges his feelings. He might even be punished for expressing his feelings. People raised without attention to their feelings and without being supported in their dreams have difficulty conceiving of choosing different expectations, or of choosing happiness.

Exercise: Looking for the historical roots of your sense of having choice –

1.   *Think about what was modeled in your home. Were your parents optimists or pessimists? How often did they ask about your opinions, ideas or needs?*

2.   *What were your parents' experiences when they were children? Were their parents optimists or pessimists?*

3.   *How does this carry over into your life today? Where do you feel like you have choice in your life? Where do you feel helpless about making a difference?*

4.   *Reparent yourself about the idea that you have choice. Imagine holding the child who did not get to learn that his feelings were important and that he has the right to speak up for himself and make choices. Take in the words "What you want is important to me. You have the right to your choices and your feelings."*

We will never be the victim of the ignorance of our family or culture if we take the power to reparent and heal ourselves. We can give ourselves the right to exist, and the right to use choice in our lives to reach for the good life we dream of.

What is the point of it all?

We may have had the most loving parents in the world and the best fortune and luck in our lives, but at some point we all must come face to face with a basic and important question: "What am I doing here?"

It is easy to get focused on the demands of everyday life. Bills, illness, problems in family or work are very powerful at getting and keeping our attention. And, we cannot ignore them. We *must* pay attention to them, for they are a part of what we need to do in order to survive. But at some point, it is easy to get lost in the human struggles and forget what it is we are really doing here in our time on Earth. Most of us have wondered, "Is this all there is, going from problem to crisis and back again?"

The answer we each come up with is the foundation for our very existence. Without an answer, everything we do in life is pointless, meaningless, and leaves us feeling empty, unfulfilled, and despairing. Without finding *our* answer to that question, we have no direction to follow, and are lost, floundering in meaninglessness, trying to find a way to feel satisfied and at peace. It is no accident that our culture, today, is focused on acquisition, consumption and accomplishment. Without a true sense of deep meaning and purpose, people are trying to satisfy the longing for meaning, which they might not have even identified as the drive behind their behavior. Our common cultural illusion, which is fiercely fostered by advertisers is "If I only had that beautiful house/wonderful job/lots of money/great looking wife/a better body, etc., *then* I would be happy." Yet while consumption increases to the point that obesity is a worldwide epidemic and the number of bankruptcies is higher than ever, people are no more fulfilled, and feel no more at peace within themselves.

The demands of the world *are* compelling. Worldly concerns *are* important to pay attention to. But we each need to find our answer about what we are doing here on this Earth.

When we looked at what all life forms have had in common since life began, we noticed that whether the life is an amoeba, dandelion, frog, dog or human, we all start from a small beginning, and grow, according to nurturing and opportunity, into the biggest, most developed specimen we can be. As a human being, we can not only grow physically, but can grow in our minds and spirits, as well. The world of human challenges seems to be the school for our growth as souls.

Whatever other meaning we may find in life, an underlying reality is that **we have the opportunity to learn, to grow into wholeness, and to grow to be our best selves.**

If we misunderstand this essential fact, then whenever we struggle with feelings we do not understand, or act in ways that turn out to cause ourselves pain, we will miss the opportunity to learn. We will carry pain and a feeling of failure and unworthiness. We cannot know why we face the lessons we do. We can remember, though, that we have the power to use these lessons to increase in wisdom and compassion, and to help other humans who also struggle.

Jan: When my mother, was dying, she stayed with us. We were so close, that I could hardly bear the pain of watching her fade away. I could not imagine how I would be able to continue living once Mom died. I often felt like I could hardly draw a breath, and would sometimes burst out of the house, desperate for fresh air. Many people who knew how we cared for Mom during her final weeks, complimented me on what an incredible daughter I was to my mother, that there could have been nothing more I could have done. But I knew better. I knew how fighting off feeling my grief and helplessness kept me sometimes from being there in ways that would have felt more comforting to her. No one would accept my knowledge. No one wanted to believe that I could have done more. Everyone wanted to see this as just the result of my grief.

For years, this was a secret pain in my heart. When my mother most needed me, I could not fully be available. Years later, I met Anna, who had been taken into a Satanic cult as a very young child. Along with the other children in the cult, she endured unspeakable torment and abuse, until she managed to escape at age 12. Sobbing, in my office, she told me of this, accusing herself that she did not escape sooner and take the other children with her. Her new, adoptive mother, beside herself with pain and helplessness, tried to assure her that she had done everything she could, that she had been too young to be able to do anything different than she had.

Suddenly, I knew why God sent me the agonizing lesson with my Mom. I broke into the reassurance her mother was giving her, and told her that she was right. There _had_ been more that could have been done. She _could_ have escaped with the other children. But that was not possible for _her_ at that time in her life. She had done the best she could have, given her level of development and everything she had been trying to deal with. When I said that, Anna looked at me in amazement and relief, no longer alone in her secret guilt. We looked at each other in deep understanding, and she was finally able to forgive herself.

Although I still feel sorrow for Mom not having me there as much as she needed me, I feel that I can forgive myself, too. I was only able to do the best I could, too, given my level of development at that time in _my_ life, and all that I was trying to deal with. And, best of all, now I understand the lesson and the gift in the pain.

If we remember the true purpose of life and focus our attention on it, we will be able to look at life with a different perspective. We will know that we each have the challenges God has designed for us, and it is our job to meet them, even if we do not understand them. Rather than feel unlucky when we are facing difficult times, we can look at them as opportunities to take a step towards becoming our best selves. We can have faith that the lesson will be revealed to us in time, even if we cannot know it in the present.

Expect to have homework

Whenever we face a difficult situation or feel emotions we label "negative" - sadness, fear, anger - we can train ourselves to react with a different awareness.   Negative feelings are the signal that we are receiving homework from God.   They announce the presence of a lesson.   Homework is not a punishment or sign of failure.   It is the gateway to further knowledge and strength.   When our teacher, God, lets us know through our experience of negative feelings that He has a homework assignment for us, we can react the same way a student does at school.   Sit up, pay attention, take notes.   (It's also okay to groan a little, too, and feel sorry for ourselves because the homework will interfere with our plans!)

We cannot know the *ultimate* lesson the homework is preparing us for.   And it is a waste of time to think of all the things in the past that we have done or have not known.   The point is that *right now* our Teacher has a lesson for us to work on.

Jan: Around the time I got my doctorate, I taught psychology classes at Culver City Adult School. I had talked my way into being a teacher, having had no experience before, and was very excited about what I was going to cover in my classes. But when the night came for me to actually teach, I was terrified. Al surprised me outside the building to give me a hug, for he knew how nervous I would be. And I was. I tried to breathe deeply and calm myself, and reassure myself that everything would be fine. But nothing worked. I didn't know what else to do, so I went into my classroom.

I had been told to expect 15-30 people, but more than 100 turned up. I stood quaking in front of the room, totally unable to stop my voice from ... the word "quivering" barely describes it... and said, "My name is Jan, and I'm your teacher." (It sounded more like, "My-y-y na-a-a-me is J-a-a-an and I-I-I'm yo-o-o-o-ur t-ea-ea-ea-ea-cher.") I was shaking so badly that it was as if I were in the middle of a horrific earthquake. I stood there, my tidy typed notes in hand, at a turning point.

There was no way to sophisticatedly proceed with my lesson plan, and it came to me that I needed to start the class off with the subject of vulnerability, (which I was so obviously - TO EVERYONE - feeling). We would all either have to proceed trying not to notice, or rather, pretending that we did not notice, the enormous fear shaking me at every word, or we could look at it. I decided that I would have slightly more dignity if we looked at it.

So, I talked about the facade we all put up to protect ourselves, the "How are you?" - "Great!" interactions that mask our true selves. I used myself as the living example of what really goes on: that we are vulnerable, sensitive beings. And they loved me, for I said the unsayable. I helped them to learn that nothing was wrong with them - they were just on the human journey. And I loved them, for I got to experience their love and acceptance for who I really was. (And if any of my old students are reading this book, know that I love you all, still!) Their love came pouring into me every week, healing my fears of inadequacy.

This class pulled together in a wonderful intimacy that could not have occurred if we had pretended. I knew that I was guided to reveal my humanness in order to show that this is the truth all of us live with, and it is okay. (As a matter of fact, this book may be the best thing you have ever read because you can feel, even announce with great satisfaction, Why, there's hardly anything wrong with me - just look at who Jan is... and this woman is a doctor!)

What are the steps that we should take when we become aware of the existence of a lesson?

1. Stop what you are doing. Just as a student takes out pen and paper to write down the homework, pay attention. Notice that there is something here to be attended to. You don't have to even understand what the lesson is or what you are supposed to be doing. Just stop. Note the presence of the lesson.

2. Remember God. This homework assignment is not about bad luck or your unworthiness. It is simply part of your job as God's child to be enrolled in the school of God's Plan, and to learn. It is not punishment, but an opportunity to become who God intends you to be. You are not cursed. You are receiving God's attention and the chance to receive more of His blessings.

3. Be kind to yourself. When we are suddenly presented with homework from God, chances are that we will be shocked and upset, as it tends to come rather suddenly and unexpectedly, and not always pleasantly. We live in human bodies. Human bodies receive surprises with the release of chemicals and hormones. It takes time for the body to recover, even if our minds are prepared or accepting. You may

know that an operation will hurt you, but this knowledge does not stop your body from having its reactions to the pain.

-Take deep breaths.

-Hold and support your beating heart.

-Remind yourself   of   what your logical adult mind knows – that this is just a lesson from God.

-Remind yourself that it may be hard, but that nothing is wrong.

-Focus on bringing your body and mind to a place of acceptance and calm.

4. <u>Wait for inner guidance about actions to take</u>. It will come. Do not panic and react out of the understandable and natural desire to get away from something painful. We must learn the difference between a lesson from God and a nail in our foot (although there may be much to learn from that, too!) A lesson from God is a difficult situation which has the potential to teach us to be stronger and wiser. A nail in the foot is a piece of metal that does not belong in your flesh. Take care of it as quickly as possible, and go on with your life.

Homework is a preparation for life. It helps make us stronger. It gives us tools we can use to help us create the life we want, the life we are designed to have.

<u>Living a spiritual life 24/7</u>

How do you feel when you are paying bills? You might feel nervous or scared if you do not have much money. You might feel relief if you can take care of all the bills. You might feel excited if you have extra and seem to be getting ahead. Our emotions take us on wild rides. Our hearts are whipped from one feeling to the next.

When we focus on the routine of daily life, it is easy for our spirits to sink and for us to become discouraged. When we are focused on daily challenges, we are trying our best to influence things to go the way we want them to. We are trying to be in control of our lives. If there are setbacks or failures, it is easy to feel inadequate, alone, helpless and despairing. When we stay connected to God and the purpose of life, we are remembering that we are neither alone nor in control. We can do our part, but that is all. The rest is up to forces beyond our control. God is in charge, not us.

Al: A lot of what I do with people in my office is to witness their emotional journey, and often, their physical pain.   Of course, I offer suggestions when it is appropriate, but frequently the most valuable thing I offer is company as they walk through their pain. We both wait to see what God will bring to us. In fact, one client paid me what he described as the greatest compliment he could ever pay to another person. He said "Thanks for listening to all of my words without flinching." He was grateful for the simplicity of my caring and my presence so he would not have to feel so alone. What he really wanted was company as he waited to see how God was going to act in his life. He did not want me to offer advice, try to fix him or come up with answers.

Sharing our feelings and struggles with a friend, a spouse, or members of a work, social or church community helps us remember this truth. Even when we cannot provide each other or ourselves with any answers, it is easier to find comfort and remember that this is the human journey. Without any external change occurring, there is still a lightening of spirit. We *can* help each other remember to stay connected with God. We can keep our awareness on the truth that the purpose of this life is to grow to be our best selves, and learn to be connected to God. The reality is that **there is nothing that we do or that can happen to us which we cannot use as an opportunity to become more than we were before.**

Every task, every challenge is an opportunity to become our best self, to live the way we feel proud living. We have the ability to offer up to God everything we do, every action we take.   "I offer my dishwashing up to God."   "I pay bills in the name of wholeness, fulfilling my role here on Earth as a human being."   Sound silly? Maybe, because we are not used to thinking in those terms. If you ever learned a foreign language, the words might have felt odd in your mouth as you stumbled to form them with your unskilled tongue, and remember what they truly meant. So, take a moment to consider what lies behind these words. *There is nothing we do that we cannot do in humility, in acceptance that every act can be an act of worship and of learning, a part of the human journey.* Everything that happens to us allows us to participate in the human experience. Birth is a gift, an opportunity to grow. Everything, then, is sacred, an affirmation of our right to exist as a being, as a child of God. In remembering that we are here to become as whole and complete as possible, then we can *always* succeed in life.

Regardless of the outcome of our actions in the world, we can *guarantee* that we are learning and practicing being as compassionate as we possibly can at this point in our lives. No circumstance or person can take that away from us.

Can you have patience and compassion for yourself as the child of God? If you were to see a small child struggling to do something, how would you want to react? Would you laugh at his unskilled attempts? Would you get angry and impatient at his slowness? Would you criticize and point out all the imperfections in his attempt? If you answered "no" to these questions, can you extend to yourself the same kindness and patience as you try to grow into your full potential, to become the person God intended for you to be?

Life is a very difficult school. It is not easy to face the challenges we all must face. And yet it is the design for us all. Even the most "lucky" must face the death of loved ones, and eventually his own death. Pain is unavoidable. Therefore, it must be in God's plan that we each must experience pain. If it is God's plan, then we cannot blame ourselves when we are unable to prevent painful things from happening. But like a child who is supported in learning, in analyzing outcomes and coming up with new and better alternatives, we can forgive ourselves for being inexperienced and fallible, and kindly support our own learning and growth.

None of us like to go through a painful experience. We have the illusion that life should not be painful. When we do have disappointments and difficult challenges, rather than just feel surprised, it is easy to say "Something must be wrong with *me*." This misunderstanding will keep us from thinking that we deserve good things. It will keep us from having big expectations of God. When we do mundane activities or have pain, it is important to separate from those experiences and say "That pain or activity is not *me*. It is something external to me. It is happening *to* me. It is not something I deserve. It is just part of the human journey and this is simply my turn to experience it." We can decide that we will dedicate our mundane activities and pain to our growth and to God. We will not only be able to enjoy daily life more, but we will be able to put our pain in perspective and remember that God wants great things for us. This decision allows us to face our challenges with pride in our growth, with hope and with positive expectations. Our lives will be transformed from that wild ride into a joyful experience of returning safely to our home.

Every experience holds the seeds of growth

Only when we deeply accept our right to exist can we know that we deserve the gift of life and all of the blessings that are available to us. We are no different from anyone else on this planet. Everyone is just as ordinary (we all have lessons to learn) and just as special (what a miracle we are here in our own uniqueness.) When we know that we have the right to be here, only then can we allow ourselves to feel entitled to believe that our feelings are important and that there are possibilities for our lives. When this knowledge is taken into every cell of our body and becomes a part of us, we can begin each day trusting in God and expecting His favor. It will then be possible to expect good things to happen for us if we are remembering that God is leading our lives, not us. We may not be able to understand the route we must travel, but we can keep faith that there is a purpose to that route.

Each experience has a purpose. We can choose to look at difficult times as holding the most powerful lessons for our soul's growth. Nothing that happens to us is a mistake or a problem. An event may be painful, but we can remember that life is designed so that we must each face pain. Pain actually holds more seeds for growth than happy times do. When we are sad or struggling, there are more opportunities to grow into our strength, even when we cannot understand the lesson, in the moment.

Al: When I was 19, my grandfather died unexpectedly. At the time, my mother was very ill and in the hospital. Three months after my grandfather died, my brother called me with bad news. I expected to hear that my mother had died, but instead, he told me that my father had died while visiting my mother. About a year later, my mother died. I was very shaken after these deaths, and could not understand how to feel anything but devastated by all these losses. It took time for me to realize that I had changed the way I behaved in all of my relationships. I had become a person who always told people who were close to me that I loved them. I no longer just waited for conflicts to "pass," but instead tried to resolve them. I had become someone who lived more immediately, in the moment, and with more intensity of feeling in my relationships. This was the unexpected positive lesson from all of those deaths.

The amount of freedom and sense of well-being that we can attain is unlimited. Regardless of the experiences we have had as a child, or what life has been for us as an adult, we each have the ability to strive for even greater power and peace. Our capacity for growth as a human being is unlimited. It is never too late to begin to reparent ourselves and overcome our ignorance so we can become more whole. Our intelligent and logical adult can support our emotional child in accepting that we have choice and power, and that we deserve to receive God's blessings. The negative self-talk we all engage in is simply an attempt to protect ourselves against feeling disappointment and helplessness. When we know that we have the right to exist, then we are able to tolerate those feelings and tolerate delays in attaining our goals. We can remember that we are here to learn to be whole and complete beings and that the "delays" are most likely lessons our soul needs to develop itself.

Exercise: Hold your heart. Breathe deeply into that vulnerable self. Let these words sink deeply into your heart and body: "How sad that you don't believe good things can happen to you. You didn't learn that all of us have hard times, and that nothing is wrong with you. But I am here to remind you that it is natural to feel disappointed, sometimes. When you feel helpless, when things don't turn out the way you hoped, it doesn't mean that you did something wrong. It doesn't mean that you don't deserve good things. You have the right to exist. We are just unable to know why things happen as they do. You may feel helpless, but that doesn't mean that something is wrong with you. You're not in control. God is."

Our existence has value. Even if no one else is around to tell us that, *we* can remind ourselves that we are worthy. Remember that the pain we feel when we think we are not worthy is the voice of our deeper wisdom which rejects any thought of unworthiness. Because we are worthy in ourselves, we can reject the idea that we are here on Earth to accomplish things. We are here to grow as souls. In the process of this growth, we will, of course, do and accomplish things, but that is not the point of our existence. It is extremely easy for all of us to forget that, and our logical adult "parent" is going to have to work overtime to help us remember.

Faith and hope

Many of us believe in God but cannot keep from feeling hopeless and sad. We hear words of faith and inspiration, but are unable to throw off our pessimism and heaviness of heart. We may have moments of lightness and optimism, but they do not seem to last. The idea that we can actually experience the feelings of faith and hope seems like magic, and we are unable to do it. How do you "choose happiness" or "raise your level of expectancy" or *feel* faith and hope? How can this happen? Is something wrong with us if we are discouraged? Is something wrong with our faith?

The first relationship we have in our life is our relationship with our parents. Beginning at birth, we receive lessons from them about ourselves which we understand at a very primitive level. They communicate their feelings and fears, their expectations, disapproval and love in the way they hold us, in the tones of voice they use, in the expressions on their faces. We quickly learn about our value, our right to exist, when we (mysteriously to us) seem to trigger anger, impatience, irritation, or pain in them. By the time we first hear about God, we have already learned our most important lessons about who we are and what we can expect in life.

Jan: When Michael started therapy with me, he was extremely sad and wept frequently, as though his heart was breaking. He was a deeply devout Christian, and always felt better after going to church on Sunday mornings, but often the relief and comfort he felt never even lasted until the end of the day. He left our first session knowing that he had found, in me, the mother he had never had. He "complained" at his second session that he "couldn't" even cry anymore! He knew that he had finally arrived at his true emotional "home" and that everything was going to be okay. He reported that even going to church felt different, now, since he has been learning his lessons "at my knee." To this day, although he is older than me, he only calls me "Mom." In a recent conversation, he told me "I never wanted to even admit this to myself, because I felt so bad about it, but I didn't learn the Word from Jesus. I learned it from you. I didn't want that to be true, but it is. I couldn't let God into my heart as deeply until I learned from my Mom that I deserve to be loved." Healing his human heart left Michael open to fulfill his faith and to commit to God absolutely, for he finally felt worthy of receiving God's love.

Some people have had the experience as children of having parents who were attentive to their needs. These parents may, themselves, have had childhoods where their parents were patient and loving. These parents might not have had the fears and anxieties about having children that other parents struggle with - although we all struggle with these feelings, at times.

Children who have learned from their parents that they have the right to exist and that their feelings are important, have a different experience. Their relationship with God is a wondrous continuation of the relationship with their parents. Of course God loves them. Of course He wants to give them His blessings. They do not doubt that when they want something, they deserve to get it, whether or not the parents are able to provide it. Children with parents like this can see how faith works: "I wanted a puppy for Christmas and I got one." Or, "I wanted a puppy - Dad couldn't get it for me, but he was sad."

If a child never had this experience, faith may be a difficult idea. That child will shut down hope and faith in order to protect himself from feeling disappointed and helpless when he has wants. Studies show that a baby will shut down and become listless and withdrawn if no adult comes when he cries. Parents who are responsive to the needs of their children, even if they are unable to *fulfill* those needs, teach that child that he is important. Parents can teach that God responds to needs, even if not in the form the child hopes for. A child raised in this way will be better able to keep faith and hope alive.

Everyone who struggles with sorrow or pessimism (and that is everyone, at one time or another) has the ability to develop the feelings of faith and hope. One tool that creates a bridge from our struggle to our faith is *gratitude*. Magical things happen all of the time. We simply take them for granted. And for every experience of bad "luck," there are probably many experiences of good "luck." In this moment, for example, for no apparent reason, you do not have a headache. A co-worker may have had a bad cold, and you did not catch it. Even if your family does not have a lot of money, you love each other. Your child might have died, but you got to be the one who had those precious years with him.

Exercise: How am I lucky? What do I have in my life to be grateful for? What do I see other people around me struggling with that I do not have to face in my life? What did I choose today? Where do I have power? (For example - I have an itch and can choose to scratch it. My body works. I am not helpless.)

Look for the magic in your life. Faith can come from seeing our blessings. Blessings are not just big dramatic events. They are also the "little" gifts which grace our lives that we can celebrate with gratitude. There is so much goodness in our lives that we take for granted. Remember it all! Remember that right now you are not in pain. Remember that you ate today. Remember that war does not rage outside your door. Remember that whatever challenges come to you, you deserve a good life. The presence of homework is not a sign of failure.

<u>You already live in faith</u>

You may not recognize it because you have a heavy or fearful heart, but you already operate from a place of faith. Faith is not a foreign concept that you must struggle to learn or introduce to your life. It is deeply a part of you. If you did not have faith as a foundation for your life, you would be immobilized, paralyzed by fear. We all have expectations, but, as with the blessings we spoke of in the last section, we may not focus consciously on them. We expect to take our next breath. We expect that when we wake up, we will be able to get out of bed. We expect that our clothes will be in the closet and food will be in the refrigerator. We expect our family to be alive and well. We expect the car will start. We expect that we have more time to live. These expectations are all examples of how we live in faith, not even questioning the existence of good things in our lives. The more we are conscious of how many of our expectations come true for us, the more we will feel a full and joyous faith.

The reality is that we already *do* have faith. It is not something we have to create from nothingness. We merely have to increase the amount of time and energy we spend focusing on these blessings so that we can strengthen our awareness, increase our gratitude and in doing so, deepen our faith. It is a small step to think that more good things can be coming to us, when we realize that good things are already happening to us.

If we do not realize how we already live questioning the existence of these blessings, it would seem like it would take an act of magic to "choose" to live in faith. It simply takes focusing on gratitude in order to remember the good fortune that is in our lives now. We will then be able to stay in awareness that faith is already operating in us as we face each day.

Keeping the faith in hard times

Our job as a human being is to keep a positive attitude. The future will reveal itself in time and turn out however it does. That is not ours to know or control. When we try to look into the future or take control where it is not possible to do so, we will experience worry, anxiety or depression. These are all signals that we are trying to do God's job, not our own. Whenever your heart or body feels tight, it is a sign that you are trying to edge God out of a job! Take a breath and release the control back to Him! "This is not my business. It's Yours." (If you arm wrestle God for the control over the Universe, chances are you are going to lose!)

Jan: The last day of our family vacation in Hawaii, we left our son in the rental car to guard it while we checked out of our hotel. We turned around after paying to see him walking toward us. He proudly assured us that he had locked the car to protect our belongings. He had, but he had left the keys in the ignition! We were locked out and we hadn't left any "extra" time to get to the airport.

We were frantic. People from the hotel tried their best to help us, but no one could. "Where are hoodlums when you need them," we wondered, "who routinely break into cars?" Somebody finally was able to unlock the car with a coat hanger. We had 28 minutes before the plane took off and we were 30 to 35 minutes from the airport! Al drove like a demon, with me hanging out the window, flagging cars to let us cut in. We made it in 22 minutes. Abandoning the car at the curb, Al and the kids struggled with the packs, boogie boards and umbrellas, while I ran ahead to the gate, thinking, "What am I doing?!! Al and Megan are the runners in this family!"

I kept feeling like I was going to fall, for I couldn't feel the ground beneath my feet - it felt more like I was flying. It was all I could do to banish those thoughts and just run.

When I reached the gate, I couldn't even speak. They had already loaded the last passengers onto the plane and were about to pull away. I gasped out my story, and they kindly opened the plane door, again, so we could get on. Just then, Al and the kids burst into view, laden with luggage and beach gear. I gave the keys of our car to a stranger sitting by the gate, beseeching her to return the car for us. And then, we were hustled onto the plane.

In emergencies, even nonthreatening ones like we just described, people tend to act in faith. We did not waste our time or energy getting angry or worried. We leaped into action and worked together. Without even thinking, we acted in faith that we would be able to make our plane – or at least, we had to try. This was one of those situations where it was absolutely clear that we could only do what we could do. We believed for positive possibility, against all the obvious odds.

Jan: When we got on the plane, and finally sat down, we had one more thing we needed to do. We traded our son for a box of chocolate-covered macadamia nuts! (Just kidding! But it did cross our minds.) The crew gave me a bottle of wine in recognition of my run. And, that lovely stranger did return the car to the car rental company!

It is important to be able to distinguish what is our work, and what is God's. We can take steps now to do what is in front of us, but then we must release the outcome to God. We are helpless to know or guarantee what any outcome will be, regardless of how important it may be. All we can do is be in this present moment and follow our inner guidance. It will turn out to be as we hope, or it will not. That is beyond us. We will often have outcomes that are surprises, and be able to see with hindsight what might have worked better. Remember, this is unavoidably how we learn, and we are not to be blamed for not knowing ahead of time.

When we are threatened with something bad, it is a normal human reaction to try to take control to protect ourselves. Sometimes that is absolutely the appropriate and essential thing to do. If we step on a nail, pull it out. Do not sit there and wait for God to. Perhaps you have heard this joke:

A man lay dying in a hospital. His family sent in a specialist to look at him, but he sent the doctor away, saying, "God will save me." He grew weaker and weaker. Despairing, his family sent in another specialist, who was also sent away with the words: "God will save me." Finally, when he was at the point of drawing his last breaths, one more specialist was sent in, only to be turned away by "God will save me." The man died. He went to Heaven, and marched over to God demanding "Why didn't you save me?!" Shrugging in bewilderment, God responded, "I sent you three specialists!"

When we do not like an outcome, it is sometimes easier to blame ourselves than to just feel our helplessness and disappointment. We call ourselves failures. We accuse ourselves of not being faithful enough. We judge ourselves as hopeless, or not good or deserving enough. We feel shame that others - family, friends, coworkers, God - will judge us or be disappointed in us. It is never easy to face negative outcomes, but we all must, for nothing works out perfectly for any of us.

Exercise:
1. Think of something you did that did not turn out as you hoped it would.
2. Without judging yourself or anyone else, just allow yourself to feel sad about the disappointing outcome. Just say, "I feel sad. I'm disappointed."
3. Try not to explain why it happened - just feel the sadness.
4. Allow yourself to not understand God's plan. Say, "I don't know why this happened, but I trust that God knows."
5. Try to identify if there is something you could have done in this situation that you would have liked better, without blaming yourself for not having known it beforehand. If you can identify something, congratulate yourself! You have used the lesson well. If you cannot identify something you could have done differently, allow yourself to comfort yourself that sometimes hard things just happen, and there is either nothing we could have done, or we have not yet learned enough to have known what to do .

Our power lies in living in faith. Whatever happens in our lives, we can commit ourselves to being in faith. We can dedicate ourselves to using what happens to learn and to better ourselves. We can remember that "problems" can be looked at simply as challenges, and are a natural and inevitable part of life. We can affirm that they are a part of the human journey. Every situation has something to teach us. We can be victorious by choosing to learn, rather than by being discouraged and defeated by things not happening the way we hope they will.

The message from our culture is clear: something is wrong with you if events do not turn out the way you want them to, if you are not in control. There was recently a television commercial in which the actor actually says to the television audience, "Get *what* you want *when* you want it!" We are being *brainwashed* by our culture to have a distorted idea of our relationship with God, and to think that we have the power to control what is God's to control.

Remind yourself: "I am only responsible for my attitude about the day - the rest is in God's hands. If the *outcome* of my day is not what I hoped for, it does not mean my *attitude* was not good. I did what I could."

We can separate what is our job from what is God's job. When we do our part and have a good attitude, we are victorious. If the outcome is not what we hope for, it does not mean that we did something wrong. We cannot know God's plan or control His behavior by our attitude. Every time we say "I'm going to have a good day," we are 100% successful. Our power lies in choosing to live with a positive attitude, in hope and faith, knowing that the outcome of events is in God's domain.

Freeing ourselves from negative thoughts

Negative thoughts are a reaction to feeling vulnerable or surprised. They are like thinking our car is about to crash, and bracing our body for the impact. Every time we have the experience of vulnerability, it is as though we have forgotten that we survived the last time. (Mr. Lucky pulled us through!) If we again focus on feeling gratitude for all that has gone right in our lives, and remember that these blessings occur all the time, it will be easier to feel faith that we will be fine this time, too. We will be able to have the faith that something good can come of whatever is going on.

Negative thoughts come from not remembering or focusing on being grateful for what is also true. (I may not be married, but I have such good friends, or such good health.) When something happens that we do not like, we are presented with an opportunity to grow. We are challenged to use the situation to learn something we did not know. We have the chance to expand our knowledge. This can be our attitude, as opposed to feeling like the victim of bad luck, or being critical of ourselves that we are stupid.

Jan: A client of mine, going through an agonizing divorce, decided to allow herself to feel the anger at her husband that he would not work on the marriage, but instead insisted on leaving. This was a very painful thing for her to do, for until then, she had insisted on hoping that he would recommit to their marriage. Finally realizing that this would not happen, she made a time for herself to be alone at home. She had a few drinks, to loosen up her anger, as this was not an emotion she often allowed herself to feel.

The next thing she knew, she was being revived by paramedics, who just barely arrived in time to save her life from the overdose of medication she had no memory of having taken. When I called her at the hospital, she was embarrassed, and said, "I guess you must think I'm crazy." She was stunned when I said, no, that I thought that in her ignorance and inexperience, she had simply not realized how drinking would affect her, that it would bring out feelings of despair which led to her trying to take her own life. What a horrifying experience to go through, and yet, looked at properly, it can be seen as an opportunity to learn many things. Feelings, when kept hidden, sabotage our lives. Drinking, when used as a "therapeutic tool," leads to disaster. But she was correct in believing that she had many feelings to uncover. And now, having had this "negative" experience, she is so much wiser and more prepared to commit herself to learning and growing in a way which can help her be a more fulfilled and complete human being. She also learned many lessons to pass on to her children. Where she would have turned to self-criticism and shame, I invited her to rejoice in the blessing that her life had been saved, and to be glad that she has the opportunity to grow and to help others who also might not have realized these lessons.

It is not a failure to have negative thoughts and to be as yet unable to live in faith and gratitude. We can choose to allow ourselves to be the still-growing children of God. Although we might not understand the process of growth, we can accept it, and trust ourselves and God. As we can see by watching children, it takes time to grow and to learn. We do not judge a kindergartner for not knowing algebra. If a child were to be angry that he could not do higher mathematics, our hearts would ache for him, and we would probably be bewildered at the unreasonable expectation he had for himself.

We can be the same loving, understanding adult for our own vulnerable self, knowing that we are going through a process of learning, just as children do. Our "school" has these challenging spiritual and psychological lessons. We do not have to judge ourselves. We will only "graduate" when we die. Some may despair at this thought, for it means that we will always be learning, vulnerable, fallible beings, and will never be perfect. What many long for in that desire to be "perfect," is to be free from the threat of criticism and shame. We can free ourselves from criticism and shame *now* by simply deciding to accept the nature *God gave us* as human beings. We were *born* to be fallible, and ignorant and evolving. Nothing is wrong with us. It is the very nature of our species to be this way. This is the journey. Every time we have an unexpected outcome to our actions, rather than call it a "mistake," we can proudly say that we are fulfilling our destiny! And the good news about always having more to learn is that we have *infinite* possibilities for growth, peace, and wisdom as we free ourselves from illusions and fear. If things are good now, they will only get better as we use our experiences on this Earth to become wiser and more compassionate. That is an amazing blessing.

We must teach our nonlogical "child" what we believe to be true. Just as we set boundaries for children to protect them - "No - you may **not** play in the street!" - we must be firm with ourselves. We can tell that critical voice inside us, "I will **not** feel ashamed of who I am. You may **not** make me feel bad for how I was created! You may **not** have my soul! I was **made** to be an evolving, growing being." We can also just remind ourselves when we begin to start to feel critical that we are just feeling vulnerable and out of control.

Understanding our human destiny, we can rid ourselves of the fearful and negative thought that if we are not perfect, we do not deserve to have a good life. Do we only give presents, or dessert, to children who are perfect? We are no less deserving.

Self-fulfilling prophecy

If we live in an attitude of faith and hope, when possibilities come, we will be able to recognize and grab them. Feeling that we have the right to exist and that we deserve good things, we have the opportunity to participate in life as God's active partner. Faith is realizing that something will come of the waiting that we cannot foresee. Our vision is too limited to know the lessons which lie in our experience. But they are there, even if we have no way of understanding why we are going through them.

Living in faith and hope means that we must tolerate the vulnerability of wanting and yet not being in full control. Negative thoughts try to protect us from that vulnerability, *as if it is too hard* to feel it. That is an illusion. Things may be hard, but they are not *too* hard. We are strong and enduring beings, even if we do not always feel like we are. Think of how many difficult things you have lived through, and yet you are still here. You endured and survived them all. We simply are not used to thinking about ourselves as strong. But we are.

All of us have faced disappointment, sadness and difficult challenges. While they were hard, they were not *too* hard. Go look in a mirror. Look! There you are! You survived all of those experiences. You are victorious. None of them killed you. You not only survived, but here you are reading this book, on a quest for greater knowledge and freedom *because you honor yourself enough that you know you deserve good things.* That is the truth of you, or you would not even have picked up this book. Breathe that knowledge down into your heart and body. Let it fill you with gratitude. You believe in yourself and want good things.

Good things are already happening

If we cannot envision something, we cannot move toward it. If we recognize that we already are blessed by many good things, then it is a small step to thinking that other good things can happen, as well. We are not just stuck with having to visualize out of nothing that good things can happen to us. We have the foundation for *knowing* they can happen - in our recognition and in the memory of the blessings we already have had and continue to enjoy.

We tend to take things for granted. For example, you have your eyesight and know how to read, so you can read this book. Other people are in so much pain that they cannot focus on reading, or they do not have enough money to buy a book like this. We tend not to think these thoughts of gratitude, so it is more difficult to remember that more good things like these can be in store for us in the future. When we immerse ourselves in the experience of gratitude, we are more open to recognizing and appreciating the positive forces and events in our lives.

Al: When I was eight, I learned an incredible lesson about gratitude. A boy I used to play with tried to ride his bike over some railroad tracks just before a train came. He didn't make it, and was dragged 200 feet before they were able to stop the train. He lost his leg. I went to visit him in the hospital. When I walked into his room, he got a big smile on his face and said, "Hey. I got to miss a bunch of school and I'm going to get a really cool artificial leg!"

Release the outcome to God

It is so tempting to blame ourselves when things do not turn out the way we hope. We think that we are not good enough to deserve the outcome we desire, or that we did something wrong and the lack of success is our fault. If we feel responsible for the outcome of events, we will be filled with fear and self-doubt.

People tend to wrestle with God constantly for control over themselves and the world. They seem to think that they, not *He,* have the control over what will happen. It is understandable that we all have *hopes* and *desires*, but we tend to go one step further and become *attached* to a particular outcome occurring. "It *must* happen or I will be miserable/I am a failure/I'll be so ashamed/I'll never have another chance...." on and on we go with our horror stories about how our lives will be ruined, we will never be happy again and how we are totally worthless. If we do not get our desired outcome, we take it personally. We would rather take it out on ourselves than just feel helpless and disappointed. At least if it's our fault, we can maintain the illusion that it is possible for us to be in control of our lives. "If I try hard enough," we tell ourselves, "I'll never be helpless."

A parent may say to his child, "If you are good, we will go out to dinner." What part does the child play in making this happen? The good behavior. The rest is up to factors beyond the child's control. All kinds of things can interfere with the parent keeping his promise that have nothing to do with the behavior of the child.

People do have sad things happen to them, but this does not mean that they are failures. Sad things just happen. Faith means living in gratitude and with a positive attitude, understanding that the rest is not in our control, but is up to forces beyond us, and often beyond our understanding.

Remind yourself: "Unexpected things happen. I am not responsible for them happening. I can accept them happening without thinking that it is about me or because of me."

Worry, anxiety, depression, fear are all signals that we are trying to do God's work. Our bodies are reacting in a way to try to get our attention and let us know that we are trying to do something that is not possible for us to do. *Of course* we humans hate to feel powerless and out of control. We just love it when we can be creative, influencing the world and solving problems. But the reality is that we are not ultimately in control of anything except our own awareness and how we choose to act. Everything else falls into God's area of responsibility. We can try to be the best person we can be, someone we feel proud of being, but that does not mean that we are in control of external events. God is.

If we strip ourselves of the illusion that we are in control of outcomes, then we can *really* turn over to God what is His to control. We have the power to be the person we want to be, to think and act positively and with compassion, to work hard and give our best efforts. But ultimately, we cannot guarantee an outcome, because it is not within our power to do so.

Like all parents, we wanted everything for our children. We really wanted to have children, and took our responsibility very seriously, always examining our hearts and exploring our beliefs, trying to be the best parents we could be. We agonized over their hurts and struggles and tried to support and teach them as best we could. The pain we had in the process was due to our being attached to the outcome. It is difficult to release the outcome to God when something so important is at stake, like the well-being of your children. But finally we yielded to this reality and now take comfort in the fact that we wholeheartedly did everything we knew to do. Now it is clear, as they are young adults, what has always been true - their destiny is between them and God. We can still love them, and help them where we can, but it does not lie in our power to guarantee them a safe or fulfilling life.

The act of thinking positive thoughts requires being separate from the outcome. If we feel responsible for the outcome, we will be frightened and filled with self-doubt. There is a difference between having a positive attitude, and having power. Feeling positive is not about whether or not something turns out the way we hope. It is about changing our inner experience. Every time we say to ourselves "I'm going to live in faith and have a good day" we are victorious.

God loves us unconditionally

Our culture, parents, and media have all shown us conditional acceptance. We are taught that we will only be accepted if we are successful in the world or if we do what people want us to do. We desperately fear rejection, and so we fear to reveal who we truly are. People who give conditional love are frightened, and have probably only received conditional love. They love and accept within the limitations of their humanness and experience. They do not know any other way.

Having only received conditional acceptance, we do not feel deserving of being cared for. We come to believe that we are not valuable, that only our actions are valuable. It is painful to think we are not loved for just being who we are. No wonder we try so hard to be in control and think we are at fault if something does not work. We are trying to keep from feeling that sadness. The thought that we can be loved completely and unconditionally is hard to imagine, although we all long for that kind of love.

Al: When I was a child, I learned how to be a chameleon. I learned how to anticipate what people wanted me to do or say. I was so afraid of disapproval that I became an expert at changing my behavior to please whoever was there. Although I was successful at getting conditional love, I always felt sad, because I never felt like I was loved for my true self.

Our sadness can help us remember that we have the opportunity, now, to give ourselves what our parents and culture did not know to give us. We can know that we have the right to exist and are worthy of love, as a baby is - just for our being here.

Jan: No matter what I did, I could not get to the point where I felt deserving and loveable. I could not get over feeling that I would only be wanted if I were funny or helpful. What allowed me to grow beyond this was to focus on the fact that I did not <u>like</u> to be hurt. I told myself that even if I were the meanest, ugliest, smelliest, stupidest person in the whole world, it would still hurt my feelings to be judged and treated meanly. Being the ugliest, smelliest, stupidest person in the whole world would be hard enough, with its own natural negative consequences, without my beating myself over the head, in addition! This realization led to my feeling compassion for myself.

Compassion led to feeling accepting of myself, and that led to feeling that I deserve to be accepted for who I am and treated kindly by everyone, including me!

Loving ourselves is based on the idea that there is no evaluation process. There is no right or wrong. There is no good or bad. Once we are able to accept and have compassion for ourselves, it is a natural step to know that God, who is free from all of the fear and insecurity we humans struggle with, loves us just as we are.

Staying connected with God

Why would we struggle so hard to try to be in control? Perhaps although we may believe deeply in God, we do not feel connected to Him. Not feeling that connection leaves us feeling intolerably vulnerable in this world. We feel alone and we desperately try to take care of ourselves by controlling what is happening around us.

So the question then must be - how do we stay connected with God? How do we remember that we are His children, and that we have no need for shame, for He designed us to be as we are? If we are designed to be born ignorant and spend our lifetime learning and growing, there is no reason to ever be critical of ourselves for anything. Everything we do is an opportunity to deepen our knowledge and commitment to our growth. Criticism is a waste of time. Imagine someone steps on your foot without realizing it. When you ask him to please move, instead of moving and a simple "Oh, sorry!" he stands there and berates himself for being so unaware. This is not taking any positive action that will help you or your foot! It is wasting precious time in self-criticism that you would much rather be spent in pain-lessening activity!

If we remember that we are designed to grow to our fullest potential, then everything we do is an opportunity to practice. Every act is as sacred as any other, for it is an opportunity to act in integrity and compassion. Things we struggle with just let us know where we have something to learn. That struggle is not a sign of inadequacy, lack of worth or failure. If we are able to understand and accept this with a young child, can we not accept the thought that God feels the same understanding and acceptance for us?

Our life experience is not about control, judgment or outcomes. We are on a human journey with all of its challenges. We do not have choice about that. What *is* in our power is whether or not we remember the purpose of this journey, even if we do not understand it all the time. We are here with the opportunity to learn to be our best selves. If we live in this awareness, then we can dedicate every challenge to our growth. We can feel successful and victorious that we are even aware of the areas in which we are trying to grow. Each obstacle is simply a challenge that we can accept, feeling proud of ourselves. We do not need to fight the reality of our humanness and fallibility, or feel discouraged and worthless when we are not all-knowing or in control.

God wants great things for us. But we have to expect great things from God. We can have great dreams and hopes for ourselves. God's part is to give us the blessings that He knows are right for us. We have a part, too:

* We can live fully in the present moment, focusing on the Now, not the past or future.

* We can let go of the illusion of being in control of anything except our own inner state of mind.

* We can lovingly accept that once we knew less than we know now. We can proudly congratulate ourselves for the wisdom we have gained through hindsight.

* We can accept that the future will reveal itself according to forces that are beyond our control.

* We can act, with integrity and compassion, to become the people we want to be.

* We can turn the future over to God, and know that our helplessness is not a reflection of our inadequacy.

* We can remember that misery and regret are symptoms that we are trying to hold onto the illusion of control, trying to do God's work, not our own.

* We can remember, in gratitude, the many blessings we already have.

* We can live with faith that although we will always have challenges, we deserve to expect great things, for we each have the right to exist.

We will never be in control of what happens in life. There are too many factors we can never know about, which influence outcomes. But we are absolutely in control of our inner reality. We have the power to create a good life inside of us. We can remember that as a child of God, we deserve to have a good life, and that with our gratitude and positive attitude, we can create a good inner life.

Chapter 3

~ *Doing Our Part* ~

One way to really give yourself the willies is to visualize looking at yourself through the lens of a camera. Now imagine that the camera is pulling away from you, away from the Earth, away from the Solar System, away into the vastness of the Universe. Whew! You are quite small, aren't you?

Most of us, without even doing this visualization, feel small and insignificant. We desperately try to keep this feeling away. We keep busy. Trying to hide our feelings of inadequacy, we buy things that make us feel better looking or look more successful. It is hard to allow ourselves to just be the little speck of life in the Universe that we really are, without making a judgment that we are inadequate and worthless. And it is difficult to *really* take into our hearts that as many of us as there are on this Earth and as small and humble as we may be, we each have the right to exist. We are each important to God.

There are many stories in our culture that describe the victories of the poor and humble, as they dream of and pursue happiness with the belief that they are deserving. This is true for all of us. We are here, having our life, and we deserve happiness. If good things are possible in this life, why would they not be possible for us? But if we do not believe for positive possibilities, we will never have the courage to do our part to make those good things happen.

Clinging versus a leap of faith

If we do not feel our importance, how could we possibly think that God would want good things for us? And if we feel little and adrift, not the valuable children of God, who keeps His eye on us, we will cling to whatever comfort or security we have, feeling lucky to have it, and too frightened to reach for more. Even when opportunities come our way, we may be too afraid to act on them. How can we tell when it is necessary to take a chance, or when it is important to hold on? How can we distinguish between times when we need to take a leap of faith versus cling for dear life?

It is not a simple distinction to make. If we were far out at sea on a life raft, it would be important to stay in it, not take off swimming for shore. If we were in a burning building, on the third floor, we would not want to, but it would be clear that we would need to take that leap of faith out of the window into the firemen's net. We would naturally be afraid. The logical self would need to acknowledge that although the fear is understandable, jumping is the only solution. And after the jump, we would need to do lots of deep breathing to get our hearts out of our throats back into our chests, and lots of congratulating ourselves for our strength and courage!

Jan: When our son, a very open-hearted and vulnerable child, turned four, we realized that unless we taught him big city survival skills, we would have to move out of Los Angeles. We drove through a great little town in Oregon that just felt right, and decided then and there that this was to be our new home. I had lived in Southern California since I was six, and was very attached to my "territory." When we finally made the move, I felt terrified. I kept thinking, "What am I doing here!?" I just knew that I would never learn the one-way street system (reality: there are only two of them!) Used to the tall buildings of the city, this town was just too short. Fortunately, I recognized that this was just the voice of my nonlogical child speaking. I kept telling myself to breathe, that my fears would pass, that it was the right move for us to have made, and to keep eating my cookies till I felt better!

The need to reparent ourselves will come up throughout our whole lives. We will always need the guidance and support of our logical adult self. The experience of fear or of any negative emotion is the call for help and support from the emotional self to the logical self.

Something can be logical, and yet we may hesitate to take action because of an emotional or historical conflict. We may hear words from our past that are discouraging and make us afraid to act, now. We may remember being criticized for not having known something or not succeeding. We may have been mocked for having different ideas than others had. We may also confuse our *vulnerability* with *inability* - the fact that we are vulnerable, with the fear that we are incapable. I may be scared to jump out of that building, but I am capable of doing it.

It is easy to be confused about which choices to make, especially when we are filled with fear. We can make lists of pros and cons and discuss things with our friends and family, but be no more clear about which choice to make.

The illusion that it is possible for us to be perfect appears in disguise as the thought that we can find a "correct" or "right" decision. There is no such thing. There *can* be no such thing because we do not have the power to know outcomes. Once again, we are faced with the dilemma that we must act in the present while leaving the future in God's hands. We will someday know the outcome and by hindsight be able to see what would have been best, but there is no way we can ever have this knowledge in our present moment of choice. And yet the present belongs to us, and we have no choice but to act. Not choosing is still choosing.

It is easy to become frozen by fear if we do not embrace our helplessness as just one of the conditions of being human. There is nothing wrong with either being helpless to know the right choice, or with making choices which do not turn out as we hope. Remember that we are here on Earth to learn and grow (and obviously, by the number of times we seem to repeat this fact in this book, we are not going to let you forget it!) In a sense, then, the outcome of our choices is not as important as the fact that each experience is an opportunity to take another step in becoming our best selves.

Al: My father died when I was 20. He left me a small amount of money from an insurance policy. Jan and I had no idea what to do with it (besides spending it on toys for me, which stupid-head Jan thought was not a good idea. Can you believe it?!). Jan's mom suggested we go to a financial adviser and he recommended that we buy a house. A house? We had never thought about being able to do such a thing, as we were so young. Anyway, we bought a house! We were quite scared and insecure, but we both thought it was a sound idea. More importantly, the adviser said it was the best choice to make at the time. When we thought about it from the perspective that it was the best choice at that moment in time, it felt less intimidating. It felt overwhelming and grown-up, and we reassured ourselves that if it turned out to be a mistake, we would just have to figure out what to do, next.

The first factor that makes choice possible is to remember that **within each of us lays guidance as to what *seems* to be the best thing for us *at the moment*.** If we keep ourselves open and at peace, that guidance will have a better chance of being clear and true, not fear based. We can keep from being fear-based by doing our reparenting constantly, with every breath, taking in compassion and support for our vulnerability. Rather than wait for an emergency, we can always keep a kind and watchful eye on ourselves, as we would on a child. We teach children to be aware of their environments. We teach them to pay attention to possible dangers. We teach them to watch for cars at a crosswalk. Imagine if we didn't! We would all get up to the corner and have heart attacks in shock and surprise when a car whizzed by.

The second factor which makes choice possible grows out of the fact that we are worthy and deserving. We can allow ourselves to have the right to have a dream, to pay attention to our wants and hopes. Those feelings come up in our hearts from our deepest selves, without planning or thought. They are the guidance giving us direction in our lives. There are infinite possibilities in the world - types of cars to buy, career choices to make, movies to watch, food to eat, people to befriend. If we did not have some system of choice, we would be overwhelmed by the existence of so many alternatives. Our individual dreams and wants let us know which of all of those possibilities *seem* to be the correct ones for us, *at this moment in time*. That is all we can know. When we follow our dreams, we are doing our part. We then are able to stay open for guidance and alert to possibilities.

<u>Be in active partnership with God</u>

It is our willingness to be open to guidance, help and direction from God that allows us to receive opportunities for more in life. When we do not turn to God, we are in the illusion that we are in control. This illusion leads inevitably to two possible types of behavior. We may feel our fear and the desire to stay huddled where we are, for the world seems too big, and we feel too little. Or, we may brace ourselves against our vulnerability and push our way into the world, trying to control it.

When an opportunity occurs, we may first feel excitement, but that may quickly turn to fear, for we feel our vulnerability and are aware of how powerless we are to guarantee outcomes. We can remember that we deserve to have our dreams and wants even though it is our destiny to be helpless to know the future. This will allow us to face the infinite possibilities of the world, feeling God behind us. We can be confident in our wants, for we are not alone and so can be bold. *Because we have the right to exist, we can be in an active partnership with God.*

A big part of our side of the partnership is allowing ourselves to feel worthy of receiving from God so that we can be open to receiving the dream or idea, and hearing His guidance. If we do not feel the right to exist, we will not be able to be open to reach for what is possible for us. To meet God, we must accept ourselves. Being a good parent to ourselves means being in constant awareness of what we are feeling. Just as we would not pay attention to our son or daughter for 10 minutes and then say, "See you next week," we cannot do that to ourselves. With every breath, we must strive to stay connected with our emotional self. If we do not, that nonlogical, emotional and vulnerable self *will* be the one to run the show, making decisions based on fear rather than on what is right to do. Whatever we do, all that is important is that we try our best. It is not necessary that we be perfect, for it is the spirit in our heart that matters.

We were very moved by reading Joel Osteen's book, Your Best Life Now. We suddenly became inspired to write this book. We felt that what we have to offer has a lot of worth - it certainly totally changed our lives and the lives of our clients! We knew that we had this book inside of us, and that we could trust in God to help us put it down on paper. We played with doubts like, "Lots of people write books and they don't get published." and "We won't be able to write it." But we knew that we wanted to do it. We rested in our confidence that God would help us reach inside of ourselves and the words would come. We would bring the dream, intent, knowledge and hard work. The rest would be up to God, our partner in this project.

When we face difficult situations in our lives, we often forget God. We can remember Him quite well when we are in church, but facing an immediate crisis, we often strike out on our own, driven by fear. Fear clouds our vision, and is based in the illusion that we are alone and disconnected from God. The fear says, "I won't be able to find a solution." Or, "*I* have to find a solution." Neither acknowledges God nor asks for help. Neither allows us to open to that magical sense of inner guidance.

When we stop and remember God, we are able to wonder what He has in store for us. We can remember we have just received a homework assignment. When we remember this, we can feel the relief that whatever is happening is not about us, anymore. God is in charge. Our vision is limited. We cannot see outcomes. Fear says "The tunnel is too dark. We will never find our way." Hope says "There's got to be a light in here somewhere." Partnership with God says "There is a lesson for me in this dark tunnel. My job is to have the courage to walk as far as I can, and God will show me the rest of the way."

Some people, on the other hand, become like passive children, going immediately to "God will find a way." (Remember that joke about the man dying in the hospital?) Where is their active partnership with God?

It takes courage to act when we do not know the outcome. The hard reality is that we will never have any positive outcome guaranteed to us. Negative outcomes are certainly more likely when we do not use our power to take action where we can. (If you do not jump out of the burning building, you will not like the outcome.) Whenever we lose our inner peace in either excitement or because of the tightness caused by a negative feeling, we can open ourselves to guidance as to the actions to be taken. We can open ourselves to connecting with God. We are not alone, and when we take the steps to yield to the lesson God has in store for us, we become an active and worthy partner with God. Then we will have the opportunity to become our best selves, as we live the truth that there is endless possibility open to us as children of God.

Chapter 4

~ *Laying the Past to Rest* ~

It is impossible to have human birth and not have struggles. All of us experience challenges which result in victories and tragedies of varying degrees. None of us is so blessed that we do not experience pain. We each have a personal history that is rich in experiences. We all have memories which are filled with deep emotions.

For all of us, though, there are some experiences which haunt us. We cannot come to peace with them. The trauma of such experiences impact us so deeply that the feelings get stuck in our bodies and we don't know how to release them. We are filled with intense pain, fear or regret and cannot break free of these feelings. They drive our lives in the present, with as much power as if the events which triggered them were occurring in the present. It is as if we look out at the world through glasses that are tinted by our past, and so everything feels as if it is the same as it was in the past. An upsetting or traumatic experience impairs our ability to differentiate between past and present. An accident at a particular street corner makes us always afraid at that same street corner. Or, similarly, victories and happiness of the past make everything in the present seem shallow or insignificant by comparison. Nothing can come close to measuring up to the joys or triumphs we once experienced. A high school football quarterback may never again experience the sense of importance and success he enjoyed in his teens. Life in the present is dull and he cannot find meaning or value in the man he is today. We can get stuck in the past, and not know how to free ourselves to have a richly satisfying life *now*.

Intense feelings can become frozen in time. Without even being conscious of it, we keep reliving our past, now. Fears we cannot overcome limit our ability to be fully alive, now. Comparisons which leave us always feeling inadequate make it impossible to feel the confidence to reach for new victories, today.

Nonlogical vs illogical behaviors and feelings

Our (Al and Jan's) definition of adulthood begins when our logical, capable self takes over from where our parents left off, and becomes the parent for our nonlogical self. There is a difference between *illogical* and *nonlogical*. *Illogical* means that something is incorrect. *Nonlogical* is a neutral word, describing that something is not of the world of logic. Nonlogical behavior, feelings or reactions are not wrong; they are, rather, of a different world than the world of logic. They belong to the world of emotion or of history. In order to understand nonlogical behavior and feelings, we need to explore our history so that our emotions and reactions make sense. Most of us are embarrassed by behavior which does not make sense to us. Feeling exposed when we behave nonlogically, we judge ourselves. We need to continue exploring until these feelings *do* make sense. Otherwise, we will miss the opportunity to learn something very important. We need to look for the *rightness* of our reactions, not the wrongness.

Healing the past

How do we heal the past? How do we identify where we are trapped in the past? Events which have created the stoppage of time may be remembered, but often are not. "Negative" feelings are the indicators of where we are trapped in ignorance. They illuminate opportunities where we have the possibility of more growth or internal freedom. Nonlogical reactions let us know that we are not responding to what is in front of us, but that our vision is being distorted by unresolved experiences from our past. Nonlogical actions indicate that we are attempting to control something that is not happening to us in this present moment. They are the actions of the past which we unconsciously repeat now, as if we are living in the past. It is as though we are taken over by that nonlogical and vulnerable child who does not realize that while he was not looking, while he was struggling desperately to survive, time has passed, and a strong and logical adult has grown up. Once he was alone to cope with life as best he could, but now, an adult has become a part of him and that adult is quite capable of facing the world. That adult can analyze the present and choose an appropriate logical action. That adult can take over from the unequipped child.

Our task is to heal the past and bring ourselves into life in the present. Many of us have had the experience, as children, of feeling like nothing we did was ever good enough. Our parents might have loved us, but their words reflected judgment, not acceptance and approval. Their words did not provide loving guidance - they conveyed critical disapproval and rejection. Those words still affect our self-confidence and our sense of self-worth.

Jan: When my father was a child, his mother would frequently recount the story of his birth to him, and to her friends, in front of him. She would describe the agonies she went through, how he ripped her open and how she almost died. She would end her story, each time, by putting her arm around him and saying, "But he is such a good little boy, and he is worth every bit of the suffering I went through." She even told me this story, when I was a child. I was horrified at the description, and had no idea about what to do with that information.

My father, however, deeply internalized this account of how he, in all of his innocence, had almost killed his mother. He was left with a deep shame and the belief that by the very fact of his existence he caused trouble for those he loved most. He spent his life trapped by her words, trying hard not to exist too much. He disappeared into a benign level of alcoholism which allowed him to function in the world, but helped him hide from being too big. He was loving and kind and funny, but never felt that he had the right to exist. He could not separate from his mother to see that she was struggling with feelings she didn't know how to deal with, that really had nothing to do with him.

My father is gone now, having died long before I learned what I now know about healing ourselves, which is a sadness to me. I was never able to help him understand how to overcome the lessons his mother taught him. Even his death was in keeping with his life. He was down in Louisiana, staying at a motel while he did some contracted work. He chose the most decrepit of motels, for he never felt he deserved to be treated well. One night, the broken-down gas heater sprung a leak, and he suffocated to death from the fumes.

If he were here today, I would want him to do the healing exercise which offers all of us the opportunity to come to peace with painful experiences of the past. It is possible for us to release them and forgive our parents (and others) who did the best they knew to do, even if their best was painful for us.

We can go on to live in the reality that we have the right to exist and are deserving of good things.

Exercise: Think of an upsetting thing that has happened to you in your life. Allow yourself to feel the emotions that accompany your memory. Imagine that you are holding the vulnerable and frightened child who is stuck. Breathe deeply into your heart and body. (Take your time! Feel each step deeply.)

1. Take in the words, "It is really sad that this happened to you. It's painful to go through an experience like that." Allow yourself to feel compassion for the traumatized self who had this experience. Breathe that compassion deeply into your body.

2. Now tell that self, "It's over. It was really awful, but it is over, now. You survived." Repeat these words to yourself, reassuring yourself kindly.

3. Tell yourself, "Once you were alone, and you did the best you could do to survive, but I am here, now. I am strong and smart, and I will take care of you. And if I don't know how to do something, I'll learn. You'll never be alone, again."

Now repeat these steps imagining that it is God who is telling you these words.

It is not easy to release feelings that are lodged deeply in our cells and in our hearts. It is not a matter of choice or will power. Chemicals that are released in our bodies during a traumatic experience will impact us so deeply that our feelings get stuck in our bodies. Even if we do not remember the experience, it is still there, at the cellular level. Logic, alone, cannot change physiological reality. For true healing, we must be willing to repeat the exercise above, and all of the exercises in this book, many, many times - more times than you possibly can imagine or may think necessary. Perhaps the first step will be as much as you can do for a long time before you can move on to the next step. We all have an inner timing that we must follow as to when it is right to move to another step. Healing old hurts and traumas takes time. Many of them happened during childhood, the most vulnerable time of our lives. Other hurts and events, while not occurring in childhood, affected us in the most vulnerable parts of our being, and got stuck there. But with love, compassion and reparenting, you can and will heal yourself.

When an experience is painful, it is hard to release it and allow your body to know that it is over. When our body has been shocked, it *feels* as if the experience is continuing or will repeat itself. When we relive the experience and react as if the past were occurring now, we are attempting to protect ourselves. We are trying to control the situation so that we are not hurt, again. We are fighting the feeling of vulnerability. We may live a diminished life, but we will not be surprised. When we experience or anticipate experiencing pain, we move into fear and we attempt to be in control, instead of moving into faith. Here again, we have the ability to be an active partner with God. Learn what is yours to learn, do what is yours to do, and leave the rest for God to take care of. All we can do is be in this present moment and do our best. There is no way to avoid vulnerability. It is a condition that all humans are born into. We are not born into control and power over what happens to us.

When we are adults, we can also experience upsetting events that get stuck in us. Because we are not taught how to be at peace with being vulnerable and having limited control over our lives, we get traumatized by events which make us feel especially vulnerable and helpless. We are unable to come to peace with them and let go so that we are free to live and create the life we want to have, now.

Al: Like lots of other people, I used to be afraid to fly. The whole idea of getting on an airplane, trusting that all the people who built it, the mechanics who maintain it, and the flight crew were dependable and careful and would take care of me was more than I could do. (I don't like to trust people when I'm <u>that</u> far off the ground!) Obviously, this is not about them, because those people have proven over and over that they are trustworthy. This was about my not wanting to feel vulnerable and out of control. For years, I was either in terror, or would limit how much I traveled. It was preferable for me to live a diminished life than to be so frightened. Finally, I just got tired of feeling so restricted in my life. I worked hard to find a way to face my feelings of vulnerability and helplessness and reparent myself so that I could have more freedom and possibility in my life.

Exercise: Let your logical adult self talk to your vulnerable, frightened self:

1.   Affirm the feelings: "It is hard to feel so vulnerable and have such limited control. This is natural, though, and is just what it means to be human. Everyone has these feelings. There's nothing wrong with them."

2.   Think about what you want for yourself: "I want to be able to do my life. I want to feel free to follow my dreams and have a normal life even if I'm scared."

3. Feel your strength: "I have already lived through challenges. I will continue to walk through whatever I need to so I can have a full life."

4.   Remember you are not alone: "My power in life is to choose my direction, do the best I can do in each moment, and live with hope, faith, and positive expectations. The rest is up to God."

The logical adult can look at the past with eyes of compassion. We can look for and understand the lessons we received from experiences. We can look back at our past to see what these lessons taught us - how they increased our adult knowledge and wisdom - and how they transformed us into the people we are today. We can know that all human beings are ignorant and suffer. And knowing this, we can forgive ourselves and others. None of us are born knowing how to deal with the pain we encounter in life. We all bravely try to forge on, like wounded animals, creating the best life we can, limited by our ignorance and not even realizing it.

As we grow into adulthood and have more experiences, we develop logic and strength which we can use now to liberate ourselves from old, self - defeating patterns.   Our fear lets us know where those patterns keep us stuck and unable to develop the potential we all have inside of us. Our logical adult can watch for all negative feelings our vulnerable self has, so that we can reparent ourselves into greater freedom.

Stuck in the past

Vulnerability is the awareness of being out of control. Animals instinctively protect themselves against being vulnerable. They react intensely to a situation, with either unnecessary fierceness or yielding, because they do not stop to logically analyze what is going on. For them, the experience of vulnerability feels like a threat to their survival, a matter of life and death.

All human beings struggle with the feeling of vulnerability, as well. Instinctively, we interpret that feeling as signaling danger, and instinctively, we react to protect ourselves. We are a species that has always attempted to remain in control of ourselves, of those around us, and of our environment. When we feel in control, we feel safe - at least for a while. We repeat old behaviors because they were the best we knew to do then, and they have become an automatic survival reaction. They *seem* to have worked to keep us safe.

Jan: I remember reading about studies with animals in a psychology class. In one, a rat was given random electric shocks. This particular rat happened on a behavior that looked like dancing, and he "danced" with great determination, believing that he was keeping the electric shocks away. When he did receive another shock, he danced all the harder, not able to understand that his behavior was not working to keep him safe.

We are all like that rat, doing the "old soft shoe" for all we are worth, in times of trouble. Those old behavior patterns are what we have come to believe kept us safe in the past - even if they do not seem to be working, now. Unless we really stop and think about it, we have no other alternative to try. It *seems* as though those behaviors will keep us in control of our well-being. This is a natural reaction. The difficulty is that we are *not* in control. We tend to hold on to whatever is familiar and gave us the *feeling* of being safe, even if the reality of that holding on makes us stay stuck. It seems as though we are less vulnerable when we hold onto the past. Even if it is negative, it gives us the illusion of safety, because it is familiar. We know the worst that can happen. Who knows what could happen if we make changes in our lives?

Al: The only way I could feel any power growing up as a child was to withdraw. My mother wanted me to talk to her, so when I was angry at her, I shut myself off from her. That became my method of coping with most of my other feelings, as well - hurt, disappointment, fear. It worked. When I met Jan and felt any of those feelings, I continued my survival pattern of clamming up. Jan sincerely wanted to know what I was feeling so we could talk about problems. I knew she was genuine, but I felt very frightened to expose my feelings with so much vulnerability. For the first years of our marriage, I continued this pattern, even though I could see that it caused her great pain.

We have to be willing to feel vulnerable if we are to strive for something new or better than we have had. To leave our known environment and seek something bigger and better is leaving the "territory" we are accustomed to and feel safe in, and exposing ourselves to the unknown. We are torn between our fear, which makes us cling to what we have known in the past, and our desire for a more full life in the future.

Here, again, we need to rely on our logical adult self to support our fearful self in making the changes that we know are right. We have the right to exist and we deserve better than we have had. We can support our right to have new dreams and wants. This can give us the courage to move beyond our pasts.

Getting unstuck

How do we even know what is making us stuck in the first place? How do we get unstuck? Some of us have had no role models to help us know that it is possible for us to have more in our lives. If no one supported us, or even worse, if they discouraged us, it is difficult to imagine letting go of the known to reach for more. We become stuck in fear and hopelessness, living a life of limitation. We live feeling that nothing can be better in the future, because nothing was better in the past. We have inherited an attitude of defeat that is based not only on our past, but on the past of our parents. Failure begets failure. We become stuck in pain for two reasons:

1. We do not know how to lay the past to rest. The re-parenting exercises in the section "Healing the past" are one way to address this. Things may have happened to us in our past, but now we can comfort our feelings of helplessness and grief, so that we can lay them to rest and replace those feelings with hope. We may have been victims *in* the past, but we are not the victims *of* our past. We may have been victims of ignorance at an earlier time in our lives, (even if that earlier time was only five minutes ago!) but we have the opportunity to learn and choose differently, *now*. We are empowered to change our lives, *now*. When we remember that we had no choice about being born ignorant and vulnerable, we can forgive ourselves for being fallible. When we accept that in our ignorance, we will do things that are painful and not know how to handle painful things that happen to us, we will be able to lay the past to rest and go on, now.

Al: Early in our relationship, I came in to visit Jan in the hospital after she had minor surgery. I guess I expected to see her smiling as usual, saying, "Hi! I'm so glad it's over." Instead, she looked like she had just come out of surgery. I was shocked, and the words came flying out of my mouth, "You look terrible!" As soon as I said that, I felt sick, but it was too late to take them back. I didn't know what to do, so I did nothing. At the time, I only knew to feel terrible about myself for saying such a hurtful thing, but the truth is that at that moment, I didn't have the presence of mind to handle it any differently. (Anyone out there in the hospital who needs a visitor, feel free to contact me! I always know the right thing to say.)

When we look at the painful experience in our past, we tend to interpret it as though we are inadequate, instead of just feeling sad and accepting that if we had known how to do it better, we would have done it better. We are unable to know more than we know. Instead of feeling helpless, which none of us like to feel, it seems as though it is easier to turn against ourselves and be critical. Blaming ourselves is a way of not having to feel helpless. It is an attempt to maintain the illusion that we are in control: "If I had only done this differently, these bad things would not have happened to me." But this is not necessarily true. First, we cannot know how something would have turned out if we had acted differently. Secondly, we will never be in control of forces that are operating in our life that we cannot even identify and that are larger than we are. There is power in allowing ourselves to accept an experience without interpreting it or trying to maintain the illusion of control. The truth is that we are just feeling disappointed. In doing this, we are releasing God's power back to Him, and we are able to focus on the lesson in front of us without obscuring it with self-criticism, or fighting it as though we should already know everything.

The other way to lay the past to rest is to hop to attention when we have a negative experience or feeling, and ask ourselves the question, "Where is the lesson here for me?" This is a positive attitude. It recognizes our power to learn and to change our lives. There is nothing wrong with us - we are simply being faced with an opportunity to grow. We can use the gift of hindsight to educate ourselves rather than judge ourselves. We could not have done anything differently or have known any better *until we had this experience.* The gift of hindsight enables us to increase our wisdom.

    2. <u>We must have the courage to grow beyond our parents</u>. Our parents did the best that they knew how to do. Like any other human being, they only knew what they knew. They, too, suffered with fears and feelings and did not know how to handle them any better than they did. Unfortunately, when we are small children and depend on our parents for our survival, we do not question them. Instead, we blame ourselves. No child can say, "Oh, no! Look at how ignorant my parents are." Instead, children say, "If I were a better girl/boy, *then* my Mom and Dad would love me." No child can separate emotionally from his family in order to logically analyze the struggles and suffering of his parents, and why they act the way they do. That is beyond the capacity of children.

    Al: My father had his first heart attack when I was three and he was 36, so I never knew him in good health. Occasionally, he would play ball with me outside. After a few minutes, he would hold his heart and say that the activity was making it hard for him to breathe. He would go inside, and I would feel guilty and responsible for making him sick.

    The way children cope with their family situation and keep from being overwhelmed is to blame themselves. This is a survival tool to prevent them from feeling too helpless. Adopting the family attitude of defeat and limitation is the way children keep from feeling too alone and too separate in the world. Children swallow their pain and blame themselves in order to fit in. We find our place in the world by being like our parents, for no child can bear to feel alone. Without even thinking about it, we become like our parents and live in the same pattern of hopelessness. While this is not logical, it is a natural result of being human. Some children survive by being the opposite of their parents. They fight their pain with anger and rebellion. In order to feel intact, they are so busy being not-Mom and not-Dad that they do not live as their true selves. Any child would rather have the love, acceptance and approval of his parents without having to leave them. Separating is painful and disappointing. As angry or hurt as a child may be, it is still painful to leave the parents behind.

    For us to grow beyond our parents means having the courage to separate from them and choose to be different. It means having the strength to feel vulnerable in stepping out into the unknown. While it may be restrictive, there is a comfort in "how it has always been."

It is also painful to have things our parents did not have. In doing so, we may feel the pain of their suffering, whereas if we all suffer together, it is not called into question.

When we got married, we were acutely aware that no one in either of our families had ever had as good a relationship as we had. In addition to being grateful for our happiness, we both felt pain that our parents and grandparents had never experienced the blessings of a good marriage. Each joy was also a reminder of their pain that they had never been able to live with blessings like we had. Feeling the sorrow for those family members we loved enabled us to enjoy our blessings without feeling guilt, which is the disguise sorrow often takes.

Remind yourself: "You can do it. You can let the past go. You deserve a good life, *now*. And the greatest power in the Universe is behind you." (You might want to write this down and tape it on your bathroom mirror, you refrigerator, and your calendar or appointment book, so you can remember that you deserve to create a good life for yourself.)

Be right here, right now

Our power as a human being lies in bringing our full awareness to this present moment. Whatever happens, our job is to do the best that we can, right now, without judgment. That simple goal releases our power to be the best self we can be. We cannot know the future result. All we can do is apply ourselves fully to this moment. Our job is simple: release the past, be fully in the present without judgment, remember God. His plan determines results.

Remembering God allows us to live in faith and with positive expectations. We are not alone. Faith is about God. We do not determine the future or any outcomes. Being in the present is about us. We empower our greatest strength and potential when we bring our focus and energy to what we are doing in this moment, without distracting ourselves with thoughts of the past or fears or hopes about the future.

When we release what we cannot control and apply our energy and attention to what we can do, then we are making room for God to do His part. We are in active partnership with God. We can be focused and at peace, knowing that we are doing our job. We can train ourselves to be conscious of the present moment. Like a good parent, we can set a boundary for our frightened self who wants to be in control. We can kindly and firmly remind ourselves that the outcome is not our area of concern. We can take pride in being fully present, and at peace with whatever might happen.

There is a story about a conquering army sweeping through a land, killing and pillaging as it went. A particularly cruel captain heard of a monk who refused to run away. Dismounting, the warrior drew his sword and said to the monk, "Don't you know who I am? I could run this sword right through you without blinking an eye." The monk gently replied, "And don't you know who I am? I could receive that sword right through me without blinking an eye."

In being present and releasing outcomes, the monk attained power and peace in that moment. The rest was not his - it was up to God. When he accepted his vulnerability and helplessness to determine the final outcome, he was freed to do what he could do in that moment. He did not take on the battle at the physical level with swords. His "sword" was his hope, faith, positive attitude, and willingness to have the future be whatever God determined.

What is the end of the story?

The captain, recognizing the greater power of the monk, sheathed his sword, bowed and left.

We all have the opportunity to choose to be like that monk - accepting our vulnerability, doing in each moment what we believe is the right thing to do, and releasing the outcome to God.

The future is also a trap. We can get caught in feelings of fear or excitement and yet have no ability to act, for the future is *not here*. Trying to anticipate the future is stressful and unbalancing for us. Just try to go up stairs before you arrive at them - you will lose your balance and fall. We can challenge ourselves to make each moment as full and rich as we can. We can try to be as present and alive in each moment as we can. Then we can trust that we are doing what we can to make room for the future to be good, for it will be made up of a series of moments that are good. This allows us to feel peace with what *is* and release our expectations to God.

Don't have cheap faith

Sometimes people wonder why they seem to attract negative people or events to themselves. There *are* plenty of people with negative emotions, behaviors and expectations out there, and if we are not careful, they can *attach* themselves to us. We need to set a boundary to keep them from coming into our lives. It is not that we *attract* negative things, but if we have no strong boundaries, our lives will be filled up with the negative, and there will be no space for positive wants, hopes, expectations or faith. We need to commit ourselves to demanding good things and good people for our lives. We need to listen to our inner guidance which tells us what feels *right* and *good* for us. We cannot listen to the voices from others or from inside ourselves that are negative, or that tell us, in judgment, what we *should* be doing. If we do not listen to ourselves, who are we to listen to? We are each the only one who has the ability to know our inner truth. If we trust our inner knowing and give ourselves the right to set boundaries, there will be no place for the negatives to attach to us. Negatives will be repelled by our positive energy and by our refusal to allow them in.

Marion was a woman in her late forties who had never been married, but had a history of dating men who were uncommunicative and not willing to make commitments on a weekly basis, let alone for a lifetime. She always complained, "You have to accept whatever you get from men. They never change. They act like children. If you don't accept whatever they give you, they'll go out and find another woman who will. You'd better count your blessings that at least you have a man." Marion's negative expectations created her reality. The men in her life knew that they didn't have to give their best, because she would accept whatever they gave. Her negative expectations kept her from setting a boundary which would turn away a man who was unwilling to have a committed and meaningful relationship, and leave her open to find one who would.

Not having large expectations is another way to try to be in control and not feel vulnerable. When we allow ourselves to dream big, we do not limit our possibilities. We are alive on a big planet, with the whole world before us. It is a cheap concept of faith to not recognize ourselves as children of God who deserve good things. Faith is the recognition of the relationship and partnership between us. I do my part, and God does the rest. The roles are different, but it is a relationship of two worthy beings. Both are of value and are necessary.

There is a difference between contentment and settling. Settling reflects a way of living which is restricted. Instead of going for broke after what we really want, the fearful part of us grabs onto something "good enough," and is afraid to go on and try for the best. Fear diminishes the self, which feels no right to exist. What is important is that we have the freedom and right to wonder, to dream, to question and imagine. If we have this freedom, we will each find our place of contentment. While there will always be more available, we will find that at some point, we have enough. The popularity of game shows reflects how all of us seek to find the right balance for ourselves. "You can have what you've already won, or you can go for the next, biggest prize and risk losing everything." Our culture hangs on the answers of the contestants, as we struggle with our own fears and hopes.

We have already been successful

We fear that we will not be able to change and to grow. It feels safer to stay stuck. But there is an experience we have all gone through which proves the human ability to transcend our past and our lack of ability. There is an experience we have all had of succeeding: we went to school. Once, you could not read. You could not spell. You could not add or name any of the states. Regardless of how interested you were in school – it is not everyone's calling, you know! – here you are reading this book. You succeeded. You transcended over your ignorance. You might have felt overwhelmed, embarrassed, self-conscious.... but you succeeded.

We all have the inner strength to mobilize ourselves and get through hard times. We simply do not think of that as an accomplishment. But it is. And if we can do that in *any* area of our lives, we can do it in *every* area of our lives. Because we have the ability to persevere, learn and transcend, it is just a matter of committing to do it, and putting our focus and energy to work. *(Jan: Except statistics. Nobody can learn statistics..... well, all right.... I couldn't learn it.)*

Despite our fears, we all have dreams, and the right to pursue them, whatever the outcome might be. If we also work to have an active partnership with God, we will recognize that His vision is greater than ours, and the possibility of receiving His blessings is unlimited.

The joy of NOW

Have you ever had the sun come out from behind clouds, and you just felt happy in being alive? When we immerse ourselves in the present, the past and future disappear. All that exists is this moment. All we need to do is be fully in the now. When we do this, we enable ourselves to feel the joy of being in this eternal present. It is so easy to be distracted by the demands of our lives. It is so easy to be pulled out of this present moment by experiences and feelings of the past or fears about the future. But we can train ourselves to stay focused in life, in the "now."

Exercise: Quiet yourself by finding a comfortable place without distractions where you can breathe deeply and slowly for five minutes. With every inhalation, take in the words, "All I can do is be right here, right now. And that is enough." When you exhale, imagine your breath gathering up all of your negative feelings and thoughts, and all of the expectations and judgments of others. Blow them out of your body. When the five minutes are up and you turn once again to your usual activities, try to remember to continue this conscious breathing and awareness.

We must move within the world, but we can keep another part of us watching in calm awareness. We do not have to be distracted by activity into losing our awareness and inner peace. Every moment is a gift, a chance to celebrate our connection with the eternal and with God. With every deep breath we take, we can pull ourselves into this awareness. We can free ourselves from the prison of the past and the future to feel the blessing of being fully alive now.

Chapter 5

~ *Dare to Want. Dare to Dream* ~

Our existence is a fact of reality, and living consciously means attending to *all* of reality, not just selected parts of it. Even more than having the *right* to pay attention to our feelings and wants, we have the *necessity* to do so, or we are ignoring a crucial part of the information available to us. We also have the *responsibility* to do so, for each of us is accountable for our life. Our feelings and wants are gifts to us, a reflection of our individuality. They are tools to help us find our own unique path in life. Attending as fully as we can to information allows us to be open to receiving the best guidance possible from our inner truth, and from external sources. When we are solid in our right to exist, we have a great power.

We may never really understand why we were born, but the fact is, here we are. Since we exist, we have the responsibility and the right to create a life that is right for us. No one else is responsible for us, and no one else can know what we most need and want. With this affirmation of our permission to be here, we have the right to make choices and to be different from family and those around us. We have the right to take a separate path than they have chosen. We have the right to want and expect favor in our life. All of this results in a positive self-fulfilling prophecy. Knowing that you are wanted, deserving and loved will give you confidence and make you shine. Shining will make you stand out in a crowd and increase the possibility of receiving favor.

We deserve everything

Jan: I remember buying our first couch. It was a scary thing to do. It was the first thing Al and I owned that could not be loaded up into our little car so we could drive away in freedom. Now we were "furniture owners" – which felt very settled down, to us. I remember Al sitting on that couch, one day, with me sitting on the floor in front of him, asking him what he wanted for dinner. "Anything's fine," he replied. I knew he didn't feel he had a right to ask for what he wanted, and that he had never had support to speak up for himself. (Remember his mother and his dinnertime experiences?) I wanted him to be able to have preferences and to speak up for them. "What would you eat if I weren't here?" I asked him, to which he responded, "Pizza." "That's a want!" I exclaimed excitedly. "Even if it's just a little want – not 'I'm going to die if I don't have pizza!' - it's a want! It counts! It's important"

When we are not supported in our right to exist, it is a scary thing to allow ourselves to have our wants and our preferences. We do not expect them to matter to anyone else, and we get tired of feeling disappointed and unimportant. The easiest way to handle the pain of feeling unimportant is to shut down our awareness of our feelings.

Jan: My Great-Aunt Stella used funny sayings. One of her favorites was "There's joy and there's sorrow." As a child, I couldn't understand what she was referring to. She was just a delightful old woman who always made me laugh, and who sighed odd clichés, and then laughed at herself. Now, though, I understand what she meant. When we open ourselves to receive joy, that opening is not a one way door for just joy to flow through. Any feeling that has been locked up tight behind that door will seize the opportunity to come bursting through to get release and healing. Just as our physical body has a natural process that enables it to heal, our emotional being automatically seeks to do the same by releasing emotions so we can comfort them into healing.

If we are to have a life of possibility, we must be willing to allow ourselves to want and to expect. For many of us, this will mean that feelings of sorrow will emerge for all of the times we did not let ourselves feel deserving of our dreams. Because we did not know any other way to treat ourselves, we lived diminished lives. It is common for all of us to look back on some part of our lives and wish that we had known to live more fully. The grief that may come from this lesson of hindsight can give us the fortitude to not waste one more moment in diminished living, but to allow ourselves to strive for all we can conceive of.

Jan: I used to cry a lot when I realized something I would have liked to have done differently. Then, something shifted inside me. I accepted my humanness, and the tears seemed to go away. Instead of crying, I found myself pulling the sadness, with my breath, deep into my body, down along my spine. I felt like that sadness was literally building me more backbone!

When we do not learn that we are important, feelings of wanting and preference are threatening. They threaten to reveal us in our vulnerability and expose us to the possibility of anything from disappointment to criticism. One way to protect ourselves is to stop thinking about what it is we want. And if this is difficult, self-criticism is one way to shame ourselves into silence.

Al: My brother-in-law, Bruce, was raised so differently than I was. His mother, Bette, cared very much about his needs, and they used to discuss and negotiate everything, it seemed to me. The first Christmas Jan and I were together, I asked him - he was 16 at the time, two years younger than me - what he wanted for Christmas. I was stunned to receive three pages of gift possibilities, starting with a $2000 stereo and working its way down to a pair of socks! I was horrified, and thought him the most selfish person I had ever met. But the truth was, Bruce grew up knowing that he was important, and so he allowed himself the pleasure of answering my question. Making the list, in itself, was a fun game to him, really allowing himself to think about his wants. And, as he told me years later, he would have been very happy to have received that pair of socks. I would have told myself that I was being selfish if I had allowed myself to make a list like that.

Self-criticism, while protecting us from feeling too exposed, also interferes with our being open to recognize and receive favor, for it makes us feel unworthy. When we live in compassion for our humanness and in knowledge of our right to exist, we are able to transform self-criticism into loving acceptance. We can know that it is our right to want. And, it simply *feels* better to have, as the foundation of our being, acceptance of the idea that we are entitled to a good life.

Exercise: Call up in your memory an image of yourself when you were a little child. Look at your young face. What do you see? How did that child feel about life? Now say to that child, "You don't deserve anything. You're not important." What feelings do you have when you say that? Does it feel familiar? Does it feel painful? Is it hard to say? If you find that you agree with those words, is that a good feeling, or a bad feeling? If it is a bad feeling, or if you feel sad, or find you just can't say those words to yourself, that is because that message is wrong! And deep in your heart where the truth lies, you know it is wrong.

Now say to that child, "You are supposed to be here. This is your turn to walk this Earth and have a life. You are supposed to be human - God made you human, not a tree or a fish or an angel! You're just right!"

Releasing the outcome

Of course, the truth that God wants to give us His favor does not mean that we know what God's favor is. Only He knows. It may not be linear or what we expect: "I want this so I should get it... now!" He sees the bigger picture, just as a parent does. A parent does not give his child everything the child wants because that would not allow the child to grow in strength or wisdom. We may not get exactly what we are hoping for, either. We are also not going to manipulate God to get what we want by having a positive attitude. He is in control, not us. Our job is to accept our place in the Universe and try to deeply internalize that we deserve to exist. We must remain separate from the outcomes.

Al: A friend of mine always prays for what he wants. Recently he has become discouraged because he doesn't feel like God has been listening to his prayers. Actually, when we talked about it, it turns out that God is just not giving him what he wants. God is not doing His job according to my friend's job description! Even my friend can laugh at himself, but he still keeps praying, with great determination. Recognizing that we are not in control is acknowledging that God will answer prayers based on His terms.

We are all children of God

Everyone is a child of God, and everyone has the same right to exist. When we remember this, we can approach other people with love. We are all family. There need be no competition, for we are all on the same team. If we honor each person we encounter with this attitude, they will feel seen and loved.

Often, situations arise in which people seem to have conflicting or different needs. If we remember that we are all the children of God, it will be easier to try to find solutions which consider everyone's needs, leaving everyone feeling like a winner. Our attitude can be that *of course* we want to help each other and find a solution that makes everyone feel honored and important.

Jan: When we were a young couple, Al always wanted to watch the Sunday game during football season. I wanted to get out and do things together. Al used to feel like I was trying to control him and tell him how he should spend his Sunday. He felt resentful and thought I was criticizing him about how he wanted to spend his time. I felt hurt and resentful that he didn't want to spend time with me. It finally occurred to us that we just had very separate, or different, needs. We loved each other. Neither of us wanted to hurt the other - we were just different. He wasn't watching the game to avoid or to hurt me. I wasn't trying to control his time or criticize him for enjoying lying around and watching the game. When we each could step back and simply <u>see</u> the other person's needs without taking it personally, it became simple to find a solution we could both feel good about.

It is easy to get in a power struggle with other people. It is easy to get feelings of hurt, righteousness and defensiveness triggered in us, and to get reactive. Separating from the other person helps us focus on being the person *we* want to be. We can each simply reveal our own truth, our own thoughts and good ideas. We do not have to become reactive to the other person's tone of voice, facial expression or words. We can remember that other people, also, have their suffering, and are struggling souls. They, too, are ignorant and have their lessons to learn. We cannot expect them to be a perfect adult in their response, just as we are not perfect adults, either. With each comment, question or challenge the other person might make, we can keep the focus on ourselves, and try to illuminate more and more clearly our thoughts on what we want and how it can work. We can acknowledge their concerns, and yet stay focused on a positive direction which would allow everyone to feel content.

It is natural to want what we want, and to hope for certain outcomes. Separating from the outcome and releasing it to God allows us to focus on doing our part. This mobilizes a great power within us. If we are involved in a situation which involves other people, feeling separate from the situation can make us feel free and powerful. When we are attached to the outcome, we automatically create tension inside of us, and between us and the other person. If, however, we separate from the outcome, there is no fight. There is no interpersonal conflict, no threat or challenge, no right or wrong. There is nothing to argue about.

Al: Recently I was in a minor car accident. When the cars collided, I checked myself to see if I were physically hurt, which I wasn't. I noticed the other man getting out of his car, so I knew he wasn't hurt, either. My body was shaking, just from feeling so vulnerable. I rolled down my window and asked him if he was okay. He held his fists up, challenging me to a fight. I asked him, again, if he was okay. He kept his fighting pose, and I looked at his eyes and saw that he was also shaken, but couldn't admit it. His way of dealing with his vulnerability was to want to fight. I looked at his vintage car and could imagine that the car was probably really important to him, and that he probably couldn't respond in any other way than to get mad at me. I felt bad for him that he was so upset, but it was a relief to not feel responsible for his upset, or that I had to get angry, too. It was just an unfortunate situation that no one wanted to have happen.

It is a challenge to stay separate, rather than become reactive to whatever the other person does or says. If they are angry, our adrenaline surges, and we heat up, as well. If they attack, like assaulted animals, we counterattack or join them in criticizing ourselves. If they make an accusation, whether or not it is true, we defend ourselves and often accuse them right back, or, in the case of an established relationship, dredge up old hurts and resentments. It does not take long for a discussion to escalate out of control and what might have started as a simple matter is now a full scale war. The power of being separate eliminates all of this.

Here is a common type of exchange married couples have:

<u>Wife</u>: You were supposed to be home an hour ago. Where were you?
<u>Husband</u>: I had to stay till I got my work done.

<u>Wife</u>: Why can't you at least call me when you're going to be late?
<u>Husband</u>: Right - I'm there having a great time staying late because I enjoy getting hungry and tired.

Here is how the exchange could go if both of them could speak from a position of "separateness," remembering that they are on the same team, not adversaries out to cause each other misery:

<u>Wife</u>: I'm sorry you had to stay late, again. I know you don't want to. I get upset when I don't hear from you, though. I'm here waiting for you and wondering what is going on. Sometimes I get worried, or feel unimportant. Maybe you could give me a call when you realize you're going to be even a little late, and then we both can relax.
<u>Husband</u>: I keep trying to hurry, thinking I'll be done any minute, and I forget that you would have no idea what's going on. I'll make sure I call from now on.

It takes lots of practice to be able to relate like this. We get reactive with each other, as if we think our spouse woke up that morning thinking, "What could I do today to make him/her feel bad?" Of course, in some relationships people do treat each other that way. They intentionally hurt each other. But in most relationships, these painful events are "accidents" - with neither party wanting the other to get hurt. Most people have not learned how to express their frustrations or feelings without sounding as if the other person did something wrong. In the example, both the husband and the wife wanted the other to be sympathetic about what they were each going through.

We are not responsible for what another person feels or how they react. No act inevitably results in a given response. The way a person responds is not our fault or due to anything we have done. If we walk in front of a target where someone is practicing shooting arrows, would we yell at them, "<u>Hey</u>! Why are you shooting at me?" No. We would know that the other person was busy in his reality, and we just happened to wander by. When someone responds to us in a way that does not make sense to us, or feels out of proportion to what we have said or done, we can know that we are not connected to their reality. Something is going on that we do not know about. If the interaction is like this: "Please pass the salt." "I HATE YOU!" we can know that they are having feelings we know nothing about! Rather than take it personally, we can ask what just happened. Our startled or hurt reaction lets us know that we need to communicate more clearly with each other about the feelings we are having.

Each of us has a style we have developed, usually unconsciously, to cope with the challenges of life. When we begin to look at ourselves in the ways we are talking about in this book, we have the opportunity to consciously develop a way to work with our own emotions and reactions, as well as to work through situations with other people.

When negative feelings come up between people, we each have the opportunity to look inside ourselves and consider, now that we know the outcome, what we each could have done to have made the situation better. We can then clarify: "I was feeling defensive/angry/hurt/ (or whatever the feeling was) and I would have liked it better if I had just said ...."

Separating and inviting the other person to share his needs and consider our ideas, rather than acting as though we were adversaries, allows the person to be more open to their inner guidance and to God. He will have less fuel for any tendencies to fight. There is less chance that he will get reactive and defensive or frightened. Without these human issues getting stirred up, it is easier for God's way to be allowed to operate more easily. When we speak from our hearts to another child of God, we are able to speak with a confidence that people, if touched, will want to help us. We will be speaking in a way that lets them know that we want them to be okay, too. This is speaking from the feeling of being in God's favor. We can say what we feel and want, knowing that we are deserving. Our separateness and understanding for the needs of the other person can disarm them. There is nothing to fight against. We can, instead, create solutions together. We are all on the same side: God's.

When things go wrong

Because we are born to a human existence, we are going to have trials in our lives. The greater the trial, the more difficult it is to remember that we have the right to exist and that we are in God's favor. It is easy, during these times, to go back to feeling undeserving and in judgment of ourselves.

All challenges and struggles can be used for our growth. Every difficulty provides us with the opportunity to learn how to strengthen ourselves and be the person we want to be. We can choose to accept that we will always have lessons, and that our growth potential is unlimited. (Remember that is a good thing! We can always grow into greater happiness and peace.) We can choose to live in harmony with God's plan by remembering that as God's children we have the right to exist. We can keep a positive attitude of hope, faith and expectation. We can choose to be someone we feel proud being. We can choose to not be defeated when life is hard. We can describe this as "living in faith," "being connected with God," or living an "honorable life." It does not matter, for it is all the same.

During World War II, people of many faiths and walks of life were interred in concentration camps. In the most bleak of situations, each person still had the power to choose how to live. Some people gave up and went meekly to their deaths. Some took the place of others chosen to go to the gas chambers, so those others could live. Some cared for and tended the people weaker than they. And others collaborated with the Gestapo to try to survive or retain some sense of power and control. Circumstances do not dictate our behavior. Even in circumstances as horrific as these, we can choose to be someone we can feel proud of being. We can live Christ-like compassion.

The gift of separating

The more difficult the circumstances are, the more separating from the outcome allows us to keep conscious of being in God's favor. If we just focus on the reality of being in our bodies, it is easy to feel punished. It is easy to lose the sense that we have the right to exist. God's plan, especially during difficult times, is a mystery.

Living in faith means that we can only do what we can do, in such a way that we feel proud of ourselves. This moment is all there is, so our power lies in being as fully present in this moment as possible. We are helpless to do anything else. We are helpless to control outcomes. We will become distracted from having a full focus on what we *can* do if we are attached to the outcome. It is impossible to not hope or want a certain outcome, but we can teach ourselves to release it to God, and to focus on being fully present, in the NOW. When we do this, we are free to do our part, knowing He will do the rest according to His plan. "Convincing someone else is not my job. My part is to remember I am a child of God. With compassion for those around me, I have the right to declare myself, boldly."

Chapter 6

~ *Life Without Judgment* ~

Human beings are interesting. We are a species that does not accept its true nature. Although we are born in ignorance with some instincts, we have an enormous brain which is designed to allow us to acquire a tremendous amount of knowledge. We are resourceful and inventive so that whatever happens in our lives, we have the ability to face and form our environment. We possess extraordinary abilities to analyze and problem solve. Yet, we do not accept that this is our nature, or rejoice in all the amazing powers that we have. Instead, we dream of an impossibility - being perfect - and compare and judge ourselves by an ideal that *does not exist* as a possibility for mankind! In our imaginations - another incredible gift - we have created a *perfect being*, and then we live comparing ourselves to that being, which is *not real*! And guess what the result of *that* comparison is? Right - we feel inadequate and ashamed of who we are, and fearful that others will also judge us to be worthless because we are not perfect. With all the gifts we have, what is going on that we turn away from our true nature in self-judgment and wind up feeling insignificant?

The human condition: vulnerability and helplessness

It is a condition of being alive that we are vulnerable. We are not in ultimate control and so at a very basic animal level, we fear for our lives. We react in nonlogical vehemence to situations which do not call for such intense emotion. We are desperate to succeed and to win, so that we do not have to feel our vulnerability. We are desperate to not feel our limited control, and to not allow another person to be "better" than we are or to be in a position of power over us. At a primitive level, we experience that as the threat of death.

Al: During the years when I was (really) afraid to fly in a commercial airplane, I used to find myself doing something really funny. The pilot would turn the plane after takeoff toward its destination, or to be in the correct position to land. If he banked the plane to the right, I would automatically lean to the left, in my seat. If he banked to the left, I would lean to the right. Without knowing it, so many people owe their safe arrival to the efforts of one 175-pound man balancing the 340-ton airplane so that it wouldn't spin out of control and fall!

Because we are attached to outcomes - the basic one being living! - when we are not successful, we feel vulnerable and out of control. People often talk about those two experiences as though they were emotions. The truth is that they are *conditions*. We are born into the state of vulnerability and ultimate helplessness. While we can control many things, such as our daily behaviors - I can work hard to balance my checkbook - we cannot control the big things. Vulnerability and limited control are as natural and inevitable conditions of being alive as is the important need to eat. We are designed to be beings who need to eat and breathe, and who are vulnerable and have limited control.

Now, granted, often the experiences of our limited control and vulnerability are not pleasant ones. But that is because we have decided that something is wrong with having those experiences. They are not inherently bad. They are natural. If we were to accept that this is just the way life is, then when it is our turn to have such an experience, we would just have it without judgment. We could think: "I had my turn to be a child. Now I'm having my turn to be an adult.... get married.... be ill... die. All of these experiences are simply part of the human journey. There is nothing wrong. It is the plan."

We are aware of our vulnerability and experience it deep within our bodies when we feel our lack of control. It would be the same thing as taking off our coat in the middle of a snowstorm - we would have a chill that reached our core. Because we feel our ultimate fragility so powerfully, we often mistake this experience as a limitation. Vulnerability is a *feeling* awareness. Our *behavior* is not limited by our awareness of it. Look at how fiercely a threatened and vulnerable animal can fight. On becoming aware of danger, it does not think badly of itself, but instantly goes to survival mode: fight or flight. As human beings, we have the possibility to do the same. Knowing that we are vulnerable, we can consciously choose our behavior. Sometimes it is best to do the flight mode and separate either emotionally or physically from the situation.

Jan: I walked into a changing room at a water park with my daughter and her friend, and glanced around the room before supervising them as they washed their hands. About 20 minutes later, a woman came up to me and started yelling at me for being critical of her daughter. I stared blankly at her, feeling very taken aback and shocked, for I had no idea of what she was talking about. I said, "Pardon?" She repeated herself. I was shaken by her anger, but still didn't know why she was yelling at me. I told her, "I'm sorry, but I have no idea what you are talking about." She finally told me that I had been critical of her daughter breast-feeding her baby in the bathroom. I looked at her blankly, and told her I still had no idea of what she was talking about. At that point, she gave up and walked away. (I realized much later that I had vaguely noticed a young woman with a blanket over her sitting in the bathroom when I glanced around, but hadn't thought about it at all, and hadn't even bothered to wonder what she was doing.) Even though I felt startled and vulnerable from her attack, I knew that whatever was going on in her had nothing to do with me, so I was able to choose to separate emotionally and not get triggered into matching her reaction with anger of my own.

Frequently, mistaking our vulnerability for *inability*, we lose the opportunity to go for broke and try our best, doing our part to make life what we want it to be.

Al: For 14 years, I have sung in a barbershop quartet which has enjoyed an enormous amount of success. In the beginning, however, my legs shook so badly and my throat used to close so severely that many times I thought I would have to walk off the stage. I almost quit, after the first couple of performances, thinking that I felt too exposed and vulnerable to be able to continue. I loved singing in the group, though, so I chose to allow my legs to shake and my voice to quake. And then, at some point, they stopped. I survived what had seemed to be an insurmountable stage fright. Choosing to go for broke has resulted in 14 years of joy - touring and sharing our music and laughter.

We are all capable of so many things. It is a matter of whether or not we step up to the challenge. Life without judgment frees us to take advantage of the possibilities that come our way. Vulnerability is just a part of the experience, not a sign that something is wrong.

<u>Right to exist, again?</u>

Throughout our lives, we will always need to remember and affirm our right to exist. We will need to remind ourselves that we were born human. Accepting that truth *totally* eliminates the existence of judgment. Self-acceptance is essential. *Everything* that we struggle with is a part of the human journey. There is *nothing* wrong with us. We are only at the stage of learning that we are at, just as a first grader is not yet a second grader.   We are just the growing children of God who have the *right* to be more ignorant now than we will be later.

Positive   self-image   comes   from   deeply   accepting   our humanness and the reality of our human journey. If we deeply accepted ourselves and all it means to be human, would we fear to step out from the crowd to voice our own thoughts and find our own way? The reality of our right to exist is proven by our being alive. If the greatest power in the Universe wants us to be here, who are we to argue?   Our right to be human is absolute, not based on fleeting appearance or difficulties. It is our birthright. It is the design.

Exercise: Holding your heart, read this letter from God to your undeserving self:

Dearest Beloved Child,

You are my child. Your birth was not an accident. I chose to have you be born and have a turn walking this Earth. You have as much right to exist as any of my children. I gave you feelings and wants so that you could guide yourself, and know how to take care of yourself. When you hear this guidance, know that it is as good as hearing My voice, for it is My gift to you.

Be kind to yourself. Listen to the voice of Truth within you. It is My truth, as well. Speak it clearly and proudly. Speak it with compassion, for all of my children are as vulnerable in their hearts as you are.

I love and cherish you.
God

<u>Judgment vs. analysis</u>

People confuse *judgment* with *analysis*. Judgment involves the concepts of right and wrong. Analysis involves understanding. Analysis can help us to evaluate a situation and increase our knowledge. Judgment is about the self: "Am I worthy?" Analysis is about the lesson: "What can I learn here that will allow me to grow?" Judgment leads to discouragement and defeat. "I can't do anything, because I am worthless." Judgment leads to hopelessness. Analysis works with the concept that we are evolving beings. Our ability to learn and grow will always be unlimited. Self-acceptance makes analysis and learning fulfilling and exciting.

Judgment	Analysis
"I am fat."	"I'd feel more comfortable and healthier if I lost some weight."
"It was dumb to buy that car."	"Next time I buy a car I'll research more than I did this time."
"I'm not smart enough to get a good job."	"I want to work on my job skills so I can become more marketable and get a better job."
"My mother is selfish."	"I think I'm not making my needs clear enough to my mother."
"I'm a weak person."	"I need to figure out why I don't stand up for myself."
"I'm a slob."	"I don't like to come home to my house looking like this. I think I'll put more energy into cleaning it up."
"My husband's ugly."	"I wonder if Brad Pitt's still single?" (Just kidding!)

Judgment serves no good purpose in our lives. Rather than helping to make our lives better and assisting us to become more than we are, it detracts from life and makes everything harder and worse. It distracts us from the matter at hand and brings our attention back to ourselves. It is a desperate attempt to avoid feeling vulnerable and out of control. It tells us a lie: "If only I were perfect, bad things would not happen to me." We try to control ourselves, with the illusion that if we do, we will be in control of life, as well.

The gift of self-acceptance

Hindsight is how we are designed to learn. We do not just have experiences - we look back at our experiences. We evaluate them. When we accept ourselves without judgment, we are able to make the most of our learning opportunities. Judgment looks at us with the eyes of others, making us mere objects to be evaluated for our worth. It takes us away from ourselves. We are no longer the center of our experience, the one who knows. We become the frightened child who is scared of rejection and who does not remember that he has the right to exist. When we judge, we are watching from the outside in, rather than living from the inside out.

An example of this is the focus many of us have on our weight. When we read our weight on a scale and say that we are fat or (whew!) not, are we in touch with the truth of our self? No. We are making a judgment based on an external thing. We are looking at ourselves, not living as ourselves. If, on the other hand, we feel comfortable in our body, we would not even need a scale. We would live connected to what is going on in our bodies and how we feel. If we felt uncomfortable, we would make adjustments to our eating patterns based on wanting to feel better. Scales are sometimes a measure not of our weight, but of how out of touch we are with ourselves and how frightened we are of the judgment of others. (It is also easy to judge ourselves for judging! Whenever we notice a behavior that is not loving and compassionate, we have a choice. We can judge ourselves, or embrace our vulnerability, and love and support ourselves into behaviors we value more.)

The mind which interprets and evaluates good and bad takes us away from centered living. The mind cannot be allowed to turn its only ability, that of analyzing, on itself. We are not subject matter, a situation or an interaction to be judged. Our value and worth are already set and cannot be changed, regardless of what happens or what we do. We have been given this life and deserve to have our human journey without judgment. We do not have to earn acceptance or justify ourselves. Our right to exist is a gift.

How can I see myself as God does?

"God, please help me to be the person my dog thinks I am." Those of us who have dogs in our lives know the experience of unconditional love. We can come home, having left our dog for hours all alone, and receive a welcome that is exuberantly joyous and loving. We can be in a bad mood, exhausted, cranky, dirty, and still face no judgment - only love.   Our dogs live the example of absolute acceptance. They are able to just "be" in each moment without having the burden of a brain which interprets everything it experiences. They do not judge us, or themselves, either. They provide a role model for how we could love ourselves.

We all fear the judgment of others. We all fear that we will be rejected as unworthy. But if we follow the example of our dogs, we will not need to go to judgment when things happen. We will be able to see an experience as just an event of the moment - a snapshot of a moment in time, not a pronouncement about our value as a human being or a prediction about the future.

Al: I was at a party talking with a man I hadn't met, before. In the middle of one of my sentences, he looked at me with a strange expression on his face, turned and walked away, without saying a word. I felt flushed with surprise and self-consciousness, then thought, "Well, I've felt that way, before, too!" And then I started to laugh. I could see the event for what it was and didn't have to judge myself or him. Not everyone is going to be interested in me, and I'm not going to be interesting all the time.   Then I laughed even harder as I had a flash of that interaction being a scene in a movie.

Our right to exist is a given. There is no debating it, for we are here, just as all life is. We are all having our turn. We are at least as worthy as the other life forms put on this planet. We have as much right to be here as a dandelion does! Do you think a dandelion stresses over what other dandelions think? Does it get embarrassed when its seeds blow away? Or does it just live its life, stretching out to meet the sun, rejoicing in the rain?

Instead of judging, we can allow ourselves to simply have the feelings which accompany an experience. We can have compassion for ourselves. We can remember that we are having a human experience (we are human and we just had an experience) - therefore it is natural, and we can have compassion for how it feels to go through that experience. We are designed to be incomplete and learning, so we will always be surprised by outcomes that are different than we expect. But the fact that we are surprised does not mean that something is wrong.

It is our destiny and birthright to be evolving and growing beings. We can accept ourselves and declare against judgment. We do not even have to be at the point where we feel deserving and valuable to do this. We can take a hint from the amoeba, which automatically and immediately pulls away from sharp things. "Judgment hurts. I do not like to be hurt. Life has enough naturally painful consequences without my beating myself up in addition."

Remember, judgment is an attempt to not feel out of control. It is an unconscious attempt to protect us from a feeling that *seems* as if it would be more painful than judgment is. It is easier to be critical and get mad at ourselves than to feel our helplessness when something happens that is upsetting.

Jan: When I moved to Oregon, one of the first things I did was attempt to get my Oregon clinical psychology license. I sent proof of my licensure in California, but was asked for proof of my course of study in graduate school. I was very excited to be in Oregon, and eagerly and promptly sent off all that was asked of me. Each time I heard from the licensing board, they wanted more and more, and were never satisfied, although I went to a nationally renowned and accredited university. They kept questioning the validity of my schooling and experience. After a while, I started to feel hopeless. I did not know how to convince them of the wonderful schooling and training I had received. I began to feel like I had no value, that I was unworthy of a license. That's when I realized that instead of feeling the sadness about <u>failing</u> to get through the hoops the licensing board puts up for new residents, I was seeing <u>myself</u> as a failure. This clarity did not resolve my feelings, but it put me back on track. For three weeks, I felt as though I did nothing but stagger around my house, my hands clutching the claws of the enemy, which were imbedded in my chest. I felt like I was fighting for the possession of my soul. For long three weeks I fought that enemy, judgment, denying him myself: "You may <u>not</u> have me!" And then, it was over. And while I may feel deep pain about things that happen to me, or that I have caused through my ignorance, I have never again felt critical of myself. Over <u>anything</u>. I won. And if <u>I</u> can win, you can too!

When we turn away from judgment, we can see ourselves as growing children, for we will never lose the ability and necessity to grow and expand ourselves. We can simply allow ourselves to feel the emotions that come up inside of us as we go through our life experience. These emotions let us know about our inner truth. Who are we going to be if we are not ourselves? We can yield to our fate, and choose to accept who we are designed to be.

When we jump to judgment, we short circuit a natural learning process. We are attempting to be in control. Because this is not possible, our attitude and actions distort reality and are therefore self-defeating. It is harder to find our true way in life when we limit our growth and our awareness, just like turning off the lights makes it harder to move around a darkened room freely and with confidence. The path may be hard, but we are equipped with all we need to make this journey.

From self-acceptance to feeling God's acceptance

Acknowledging our right to exist provides us with the foundation for having a positive self-image. There are four steps that can take us to God without having to just *hope* we get there by magic, grace or some other mysterious process. The process is not complete without all of the steps being included. The Steps to Inner Peace are the foundation for self-acceptance and for a positive self-image.

1.   Without judgment, acknowledge your feelings and the actions you have taken.

Jan: After working a busy 1 ½ hours, one Thanksgiving morning, I popped the last of my two pies, two cakes and a pudding into the oven. I was in the middle of happily congratulating myself on what an efficient and excellent job I had done, when I turned around and saw two cubes of butter lying on the counter, each of which should have gone into a cake! What perfect, humbling timing! How easy it would have been to get angry that I had forgotten to add them to the ingredients. How easy to take my surprise and such clear evidence of my lack of perfection, and beat myself for being stupid.

When we feel emotions, we immediately have the experience of feeling vulnerable. Our instinctive reaction is to fight against feeling that vulnerability. (Remember, it is an animal reaction to associate vulnerability with the threat of death.) Judgment is the strongest tool we use to beat that vulnerability down. We get angry with ourselves for things we have done, calling ourselves stupid or weak, rather than just allowing ourselves to be in the reality of feeling vulnerable and imperfect. We might also become angry at the person or thing which elicited our vulnerable response. (*Stupid butter!*) Judgment supports the illusion that if we were only perfect (or at least better than we are) or if the people in our world were better, (*Al should have reminded me!*) we would be in control and would not have to feel vulnerable.

We also judge when it is acceptable to have feelings, and when it is not. Certain events or experiences, as a tragedy or death, fall into the category of "acceptable" and we do not feel critical of ourselves for our emotional response. (As long as those emotions do not last too long.) Other events or experiences, like feeling sad at the outcome of a football game (it is easier to get angry) or touched by a movie, fall into the category of "unacceptable." This is a particularly difficult issue for men, who do not have the same cultural acceptance for their vulnerable feelings (sadness, fear, tenderness) as women do.

We have the right to acknowledge our feelings without having to justify or explain them. We can allow ourselves to simply be who we really are. "I feel sad because I feel sad." Vulnerability is one of the conditions of being human. Experiencing deep and vulnerable feelings is a part of being fully alive, and is nothing to be ashamed of.

2. <u>Feel compassion for your feelings and acceptance for your actions.</u>

Jan: I had a breathless moment where my emotions could have gone in any direction, but they settled on accepting that I do not need to be perfect. Once I would have felt shame or embarrassment, feeling exposed in my imperfection. I would have feared the judgment of others, and so would have judged myself, first, and gotten angry. But over the years, I have learned to accept myself in all of my humanness. I have spent many hours soothing my vulnerable child feelings and teaching myself what my logical adult knows to be the truth: we are destined to be imperfect. So, on that Thanksgiving morning, I was able to allow a surprise to just be a surprise. My acceptance let me see the humor of the situation and be able to laugh, especially at the contradiction of my feeling so self-satisfied with my efficiency, and the reality of being so inefficient!

Reparenting is a crucial part of this step. You may say positive things to yourself and your logical adult may hear and believe them, but unless you connect with your vulnerable child, those positive things *cannot get in.* Many people do the right things, and say the right things to themselves, but see no changes in their feelings or behaviors. That is because they are only operating at the logical adult level. This leads them to feel even more judgmental of themselves and eventually, to feel hopeless.

Vulnerability opens us to receive the messages which can heal us. When you are a compassionate parent to your growing self, a magical thing happens. It may only be *your* hand which is holding your heart as you breathe kindly into your body and say supportive things. But guess what! Your vulnerable self does not know that. All he feels is love and compassion coming toward him, and it does not matter *whose* hand it is. This feeling experience of being cared about can deepen the ultimate re-parenting experience - being parented by God. *He* loves me, and I know what love feels like because I have been able to give it to myself on this human plane.

3. <u>Choose a course of action and keep a positive attitude.</u>

Jan: I was not sure what to do - was it too late to save our desserts? Despite the moans and worries of the family, I pulled the cakes out of the oven, melted the butter, and stirred it in, right in the pans. I had no idea if I would wind up with "Swirled Grease Cakes" or something close to the cakes I had intended to make. But I felt adventurous and clever to have come up with a solution, and I trusted that it would all turn out just fine.

While *ultimately* we have limited control, we are not (thank goodness!) completely powerless. We always have the choice of our attitude. Why not have a positive attitude about what you have chosen to do! But we have more than that. Even though we cannot control the outcome, we *can* analyze situations to see if there is anything that we can do. The purpose of the mind is to organize and assist our survival by problem solving and finding ways to take control where we can. The mind is not a useful tool until we are at the stage of an experience where we need to do analysis. It is not the job of the mind to judge us for being in a predicament. Its purpose is to help us consider alternatives and make choices. Having the right to exist allows us to consider what we want and to consider how to get it. If we do not feel the right to exist, we will not even look for choices. We will be more likely to feel like a victim of the situation. We will most likely get stuck in step 1 or 2, feeling frozen in our feelings without having any place to go. In addition, if we do not have permission to feel separate, our choices are limited to what we think other people want us to do, or what we think will be better for other people.

Jan: Because I feel the right to exist, I was able to consider choices to see how I wanted to handle this situation. Because I was able to feel separate, I was able to make my decision about a course of action that felt right to me, despite the fears of my family. I did not have to feel that I had ruined everything for everyone (remember their moans and worries?) or that I should choose to throw away my baking and buy dessert at the supermarket just to make sure no one was upset.

4. Release control.

Jan: Except for having Pumpkin Chocolate Swirl cake, instead of Pumpkin Chocolate Chip cake, both cakes turned out just fine. But what really pleased me was that I could laugh and let it be okay from the beginning, regardless of the outcome. That was something to be thankful for! (Al: I'm glad she felt so self-accepting, but in one of my bites of cake, I had 1/3 of a cube of butter!)

Once we have taken the first three steps, we must recognize our limited control and know that the outcome is ultimately not ours to determine. "All I can do is do the best I can, given the level of my development at this moment." Now it is time to allow God to do His part. Forces greater than us are always at work, and we cannot know about them. But knowing that we have the right to exist, we can live allowing ourselves to have our feelings. We can live with hope and with positive expectations, knowing that whatever happens, it is not about us - we are separate from the outcome. We cannot know the purpose of what occurs in our lives. We can only continue to live in faith. *(Jan: And sometimes that great Cook in the Sky comes right through for us!) (Al: Well, for some of us.)*

Forgetting the butter in cakes is a minor but clear reminder of our humanness. Most of us have done things that haunt us with deep pain and regret, although we may keep them secret from all who know us. But these acts, though more painful, are truly no different than forgetting that butter. They all provide us with the necessity to forgive ourselves, and accept ourselves as children of God who, in our ignorance, could do no better. They are all opportunities to learn from pain, and to grow into more compassionate and accepting people.

Using the Steps to Inner Peace

All of us would like to feel happy, fulfilled and successful. These feelings *can* be ours. The four step process is based on logic, and it works! This process results in feeling proud of and at peace with ourselves. It allows us to connect with God, feeling our right to exist, and that we are loved and deserving. How could we not feel happy with this result?

We are aware, at a deep level, of our lack of control in the world. This makes us feel vulnerable and afraid. When things are not as we wish, we have negative thoughts. Our mind is trying to control the situation, even if the result is that we undermine our chances of success. If we do this four-step process, however, we can grow into inner peace with the knowledge that we are 100% victorious, just because we have done what we can and have been God's active partner.

If you knew who my Father was you'd never judge me!

Negative thoughts do nothing to help us have a successful and happy life. There are two ways we can eliminate them. There is a psychological way to attain this state of mind that does not even need to rely on faith. The first three steps to inner peace are based on our right to exist. Do you remember how it felt in the exercise in the last chapter to tell yourself that you are not deserving? The pain we feel at those words tells us that those negative thoughts, and *all* negative thoughts and judgments about ourselves are *wrong*. Our deepest truth tells us that we must feel our worth, or our whole body objects. The last step, releasing the outcome and accepting that we do not have ultimate control and power acknowledges the truth of what it means to be human and therefore, limited. There is no shame or blame in this - it is just the truth of being alive.

The spiritual way to free ourselves from negative thoughts is to remember that we are children of God and that God wants us to have a positive life. Our job is to do the first three steps of the process. And then, we can release the outcome, knowing that we have done all we could think to do. We can release the outcome, and allow ourselves to be at peace with our ultimate helplessness, knowing that God is here for us. We have to remind ourselves that we are here for us, too. God is ultimately in control. Hope, faith and positive expectations come from doing our part correctly, as well as releasing God's part to Him. The end result of this whole process allows us to have a deeper connection with God and a greater peace about being human.

We have the power to bring ourselves into acceptance of our true nature and of who we really are - the children of God. Only then can we live as the strong people we are designed to be, and be God's active partner.

Chapter 7

~ *You Are Already Good Enough* ~

We love a good vacation, don't we? There is something wonderful and freeing about the feeling of having all the time in the world, the feeling of being away from it all where we cannot be reached. Vacations make our souls expand. They make everything feel delightful. Every act can feel like a new adventure. Each experience is just what it is. There is nothing to compare it to. We are simply out in the world, exploring, like a child does on a warm summer day when there is nothing to do and the world holds endless potential and mystery. And we feel fresh and childlike as we encounter new places and experiences. When we are on vacation, we can leave our cares behind and just be in *this* moment. We are so filled up with just *being* that there is no need to watch ourselves or to judge.

Life on vacation has an immediacy to it. Each moment is rich and full with experience. We never know quite what to expect, because we are in unknown territory, so we are more in the present moment. We can appreciate things and events for just what they are, unless we constantly compare (as some do) "Well, this isn't how we do it at home!" or "This isn't what happened last time!"

Imagine that this was to be how we lived our "normal" lives. Each moment was just that moment. Each person was just who they are. We could just appreciate what we have. We could travel light-hearted through life and not take judgment on the trip with us. Without comparing and judging, everything and everyone would be simply what they appear, and we could value what is there.

Al: For a while, after the loss of my mother, father and grandfather, I found that every moment with someone I loved felt so sweet. Life had taught me that all I had was this moment, and that I couldn't take anything or anyone for granted. Although the deaths were very traumatic for me, the gift I received was a deeper appreciation of each moment of life. Like everyone else, I struggle to stay in that awareness, now. But that experience showed me how it is possible to live.

Immediacy - live *this* moment

If we journey through life without expectation, without judgment and without comparison, we are able to see the preciousness of life. If we have had a good experience in the past, it is very tempting to compare the present unfavorably. It can be hard to just allow the present to be what it is. But we hold ourselves hostage in the past, by comparing, and are unable to fully be in this moment: "This is not how it was before or should be, now." When we think about painful situations in the past we can get scared to do anything because we fear those bad things could happen, again. Both comparisons are subtle protests against current reality. They hold us back from full living, *now.* We become frozen in time, in a futile attempt to control what happens.

The only control that we have in the present is over our choice of actions and our attitude. Rather than split our focus between what is happening now and what *should* be, what *could* be, or what *used to be*, we can appreciate what *is*, in all of its richness and in all of its uniqueness.

Jan: I remember eating lima beans (ugh!) and Brussels sprouts (yuck!) as a child. How disgusting! They did not taste at all as delicious as chocolate cake or grilled cheese sandwiches. But as an adult, I was shocked to find that I actually enjoyed the experience of eating them. I could enjoy the unusual flavor and texture without thinking about what they were <u>not</u>. I just tasted them for what they <u>were</u>.

We can look for the perfection of the moment, valuing whatever is here, now. We do not need to have anything else, or go anywhere else, because there is enough value right here, in *this* moment. And, we can see that *we* each have value, *now*, as well. Especially since, being human, we will *never* be perfect, let's not wait! We will miss a lifetime of appreciating each other.

Jan: One day I was really annoyed at Al. I don't even remember why, but I do remember suddenly thinking, "If he died, this wouldn't matter at all. All of the little things that bother me would just be funny eccentricities of his. I would really appreciate and love him." With a shock, I realized that my annoyance was just a way to avoid feeling vulnerable and fully present with him. Suddenly all that annoyance just disappeared. I didn't want to wait to love him fully. I wanted to love him, now, and not waste one more moment of my life focused on the insignificant differences between us.

How many people wait until someone dies before they suddenly realize how much they valued that person? How many of us do not think to say kind and appreciative things? How many people suddenly realize that all of the things that were not "perfect" about that person just do not matter at all, but it is too late to tell him?

We do not need to wait for perfection in ourselves, either. We can appreciate *ourselves*, now, as well. We can remember that we are evolving beings, and look at ourselves with the same approving eyes with which we look at a toddler who is struggling to walk, but keeps falling. We can accept that we are always learning and appreciate ourselves for who we are at this point in our development. "Oh, look at me! Look at how hard I'm trying to learn. Aren't I adorable? Look what I just did. How sweet!" We are not who we once were - we have grown and changed. And we will continue to grow and change. Why not be compassionate and take pride in this fact, rather than be impatient and judge ourselves? Why not say "How clever I am to realize this!" instead of "How stupid I am not to have known this sooner."

We can refuse to allow expectation and judgment to ruin our peace and our fun! We can train ourselves to focus on what is *right*, rather than on what is *wrong*. We can look for the good in life. Why look for what is missing, rather than appreciate what is here?

Al: For my 9th birthday present, my parents agreed to drive four friends and me from our home in New Jersey to a New York Yankee game in New York. About halfway there, the car broke down, and we pulled off the road right near one of those famous New Jersey slaughterhouses. The smell was disgusting! And we were completely stranded. While we waited for a tow truck to arrive, my friends and I played tag and hide-and-go-seek in the corn fields by the road. Every once in a while, when someone was hiding, they revealed their hiding spot by screaming "I can't stand the smell!" We laughed so hard and vowed to never eat meat again. By the time the tow truck came, it was too late to go to the game, but we had all had a wonderful time. As a matter of fact, I just realized that I don't even remember my 8th or 10th birthdays!

Things do not have to be perfect to be wonderful. Our attitude makes all the difference in our experience. When we appreciate what is here, we are standing solidly in the present. When we look to what is missing or could be better, we are focusing on the past or the future. But we're not living in the past or the future... we are right here, right now! The past is over - there is nothing we can do about it. The future is not yet here – we cannot live in it. All we can do is make each present moment as rich and fulfilling as possible in the faith that all of these moments will join together to make a good life. Besides, the future is God's domain. To be mucking about there is to be interfering with His work. We are powerless in His domain, and if we try to spend our time there, we will be missing what is ours to enjoy and change, right now.

If we stand solidly in our right to exist and in acceptance of our human destiny to be growing beings, we will take joy and pride in who we are in each moment. We can only be just where we are right now. And, until we have had the experiences which wake us up and allow us to learn more than we know, at this point in our development, we are stuck where we are right now. When we stop judging and fighting this truth, we can simply enjoy the journey and compassionately support ourselves in learning. Remember, why arm wrestle God? We will not only lose, but life will not be very much fun, and will pass us by without our ever having the chance to find joy in it.

There's no such thing as a "mistake"

Our culture has the illusion that it is possible to attain perfection. There is a big difference between *attaining* perfection, and living our lives *aiming for* perfection. The first is a goal, a destination that we may wish we could actually arrive at. The second is a life path which dictates how we live. The biggest difference between the two is that success on the first is measured only when we arrive *at* the destination. Well... that is not ever going to happen, because we are not designed with perfection as a possibility. Success on the second occurs every time we take a step *toward* the destination.

Al: A few years after Jan and I were married, I had a small cut on my finger near my wedding ring. On a bike ride, my ring kept rubbing against the cut and irritating it. I took my ring off, and put it into my pocket, not even thinking there could be a problem. But when I got home, my pocket was empty. Jan and I went back and forth over the route I had taken, looking for my ring, but could find it nowhere. I felt so stupid. It was so painful that I couldn't keep from beating myself up. (Jan never should have let me go out and ride a bike all by myself!)

What we call a "mistake" is no more than an unexpected outcome. We think one thing will happen, but it does not. Some other thing happens. We may not be happy about it, but there is no way that we will be able to make flawless decisions, because we are limited beings and we do not have access to all of the information about life. There is no way to be able to know all of the possible outcomes of any action.

Sometimes we call a decision a "mistake" when we feel that we really "knew better" and just did not listen to ourselves. But there is always a reason for what course of action we take. Even though some part of ourselves "knew better," we must not have been fully convinced, and so we had to try it again, possibly in a slightly different way. Experimentation is not a bad thing. It has led to many wonderful discoveries and inventions. But when we do an experiment and are upset by the outcome, it is hard to remember that we had a reason for making the choice of action that we made. We are punishing ourselves by saying that we made a "mistake," rather than just feeling the disappointment at the outcome and our vulnerability in feeling the limitations of our ability to know. In other words, we are fighting being aware that we are ultimately out of control.

While we are on this subject, we might as well address the related concepts of "faults" and "flaws." "Mistakes," "faults," and "flaws" all assume the possibility of perfection. They overlook what we are doing here on this Earth – *learning*! And the way humans are able to learn is by using the tool of hindsight. So there is no such thing as a mistake. And what we call faults and flaws are ways we try to deal with life that we have just not yet refined as much as we will with more practice. They may bring their own problems, but they are the best ways we have found, *so far*, to handle our feelings.

When we are troubled by a "fault" or "flaw" we have another opportunity to learn something about ourselves. There are always feelings behind every behavior. If the behavior gets us in trouble, we can judge the behavior as bad, or we can look for what feelings are behind it, and try to find a more satisfying way to handle those feelings.

Either that, or we are saying that the Most High God of the whole Universe made a major flaw in how he designed his greatest creation.

Can you hand me that tool, please?

We are a work in progress. Because we are not and will never be complete, we have endless opportunities to measure that "progress" and to refine ourselves. A crucial question then becomes, what is our measurement tool? Any good workman knows that unless you have the proper tool, no matter how hard you try, you will not be able to do the job very well. If you try to dig a hole with an eggbeater, you will not be very happy. Tools are designed for specific purposes, and must be matched well with the task at hand, or you will not accomplish what you hope. If our job as human beings is to grow and develop, then what would be the proper tool to measure that development?

Human beings, not liking to feel vulnerable or out of control, made up the tool of *judgment* to measure ourselves. Judgment can only come up with measurements of good or bad, right or wrong. It is a limited, faulty and not very useful tool. Using judgment, we only get value-laden pronouncements that either make us feel horrible about ourselves, or relieve us that we do not have to feel horrible about ourselves *this* time. It keeps us in fear and dread. Judgment does not help us get the information that would really help us in our task of evolving into more conscious and compassionate beings. This is not a tool God gave us and it does not serve His purposes.

If we accept that our task is to grow, then what *would* be useful? Compassionate analysis allows us to accept ourselves, without fear, as an evolving being. We can see ourselves as a child of God. We can understand that as a child, we have far to grow, and we need not feel frightened of the experience of not knowing. Learning, itself, is then a valuable activity, and if we do our best to learn, we are successful regardless of the outcome.

John Wooden was one of the greatest basketball coaches of all time. He was a quiet and gentle man, trained as an English teacher, who did not focus on whether his team won or lost. He <u>loved</u> practices because he saw them as a classroom. That was where his players' learning took place – to grow not only in their basketball abilities, but as men of honor and character, as well. He was not that interested in the actual games, for the only measuring tool used for success was if the team won. He was interested in something far greater than worldly success. He was interested in guiding his players in becoming the best human beings that they could be.

If, knowing that we are not in control of the outcome, we make the best decisions that we can, with a positive attitude in that moment, we have done our part and can feel proud of ourselves. Then it will be easier to believe and take into our hearts that we are loveable, and good enough, already – just as we are in this moment. We do not need to be perfect to be valuable. There is nothing **we** need to do to deserve to be loved.   If we can love noisy, messy little **babies**, is God less able than we are to love His children?

Chapter 8

~ *Live in Faith* ~

We human beings *really* like to feel in control. Although many people just love being on a steep roller coaster and having the illusion of wild abandon, in our non-amusement park mode, we do not find that feeling amusing in the slightest! And we are stubborn, sneaky little guys, too. We come up with all kinds of ways to try to control what happens to us... in other words, to try and control God! We think if we beg or pray enough, if we are humble enough, if we do enough good deeds, if we make a bargain to do something or give something up, *then* perhaps God will think kindly of us and give us what we want. But it is hard to imagine that God is taken in by us any more than we would be taken in by a wheedling child. He has determined His plan for our upbringing, and that is just how it is!

Take the control you *do* have!

Control is not a bad thing, but it is often used in ways that are self-defeating. When we bemoan the passing of time and experiences, we are not accepting that the past is the past. We are fighting to have it not be over. When we get too focused on what will happen in the future, we are fighting God for control over his domain – the outcome. We do not win there, either. But the place where we *do* have the ability to exercise control is in the present. We have the power to appreciate what *is* and to make choices about our attitude and actions.

We cannot control God with our behavior or with our attitude. But our attitude has an enormous impact on *us*. When we live in fear, our spirits shut down. Our bodies are flooded with adrenaline. We have shallow breathing, and abnormal heart rates. We are like frightened, hunted animals, focusing on one thing – survival. We are attempting to be in control so that we will not die. Many people live this way. It is a negative experience, but they are always on guard, so they have the illusion that they are in control. They live as though there is no God, and everything is totally up to them.

Because the future is up to God, and since we have limited control, anyway, we might as well expect good things. We can choose to have a positive attitude. We can focus on what we can do in the present. We can allow ourselves to be open and receptive. Then, if God *does* happen to send some blessings our way, we are in the best position possible to notice and receive them. And if it is not our time for those blessings, we will not be wasting our time in misery. Life will bring enough challenges and heartache to us all without our also being miserable in anticipation of them coming!

Jan: When my brother, Bruce, was eight, he was diagnosed with an eye disease that would gradually make him blind. At 19, he realized that the time was near when he would totally lose his vision, so he quit school, and set off to Europe. For almost two years, he hitchhiked alone, making friends and having great adventures. He finally went blind on an island off Spain, found God, who guided him safely down from being lost on a mountaintop during a storm, was dubbed by a Scottish newspaper "The Bravest Hiker in the World," and felt his way through an entire crystal store in Ireland to buy me just the right water goblets. He turned tragedy into triumph, refusing to be a victim of his physical reality. And this is how he continues to live.

Deepening acceptance

It is easy to say "Choose to be positive!" but exactly how can we do that? Just because something is the logical thing to do does not make it an easy thing to do. If we do not have the positive beliefs and optimism that allow us to choose a positive attitude, are we doomed to negativity? Some people seem to effortlessly remain cheerful and positive. Why can't we?

When we fight our helplessness, we fight reality. When we anticipate negative outcomes in our lives, we are trying to protect ourselves from the sense of being ambushed or startled by life or misfortune. The problem with this approach to living is that it is based on the illusion that by being alert we can control our fate. Certainly alertness has its place! Who would want to get into a car with a drowsy or inebriated driver, or someone who couldn't stop chatting on their cell phone? But there is a difference between a restful alertness and pessimism.   Alertness does not necessitate feeling stressed or having a negative attitude. When we are alert, we are simply present in this moment with our full attention. The very act of being alert is an acceptance of our ultimate helplessness. Nothing is taken for granted. Anything can happen. But we are in acceptance of this truth, and ready for anything.   Pessimism is not present in this moment. Pessimism is busy anticipating all of the scary outcomes that could possibly occur.   Pessimism is a denial of our helplessness, for it provides the answer to the ultimate question we all have "What is going to happen?" Pessimism answers "Nothing good!" Pessimism is a signal that we are not taking care of our feelings of fear and vulnerability.

The "choice" to live in faith is based on the ability to yield to our helplessness. Yielding to our helplessness can only occur when we lovingly comfort our frightened feelings and support ourselves in finding peace with the one true power we have - to be with our own true self.

Jan: When my children were born, I found a new and unexpected part of myself. I had read about women who went to their deaths, during World War II, rather than be separated from their children in the concentration camps. Part of me was always mystified by that: "I could search for them, later. I would want to cooperate so that I wouldn't arouse the anger of the captors and risk greater punishment." But when I held my babies in my arms, I knew exactly why those women chose as they did. I would die without question just so that my children could face their own fates or deaths looking into my eyes and knowing that I loved them.

Realizing the importance of reparenting ourselves, we now have the power to be with ourselves to the death. Ultimately, we cannot ever control or determine what our fate will be, whether it is a minor occurrence, or facing death, itself.   But we can absolutely guarantee that regardless of whatever happens to us, or what we might ever face, we will be with ourselves, holding our hearts, breathing lovingly into our souls, comforting ourselves through everything. Life will definitely bring heartbreak to all of us, for in the end, we will all need to say the ultimate goodbye to those we love. But even then, we can choose to live in gratitude for all that we have had, in acceptance of the rightness of the human experience in all of its joy and sorrow, and alert for whatever adventure comes next. In this way, we can transform pessimism into peace and acceptance.

Turn helplessness into faith

When we are at peace with our helplessness, we no longer fight what we cannot control. We are able to accept that our power does not lie in knowing or controlling, but in being alert. Alertness is a neutral experience, neither negative nor positive – just present. When life gives us a challenge, we have the choice of how to handle it. We have no choice about being vulnerable and ultimately not in control, but we can choose to live in fear or in faith. (Reparenting ourselves is a necessary prerequisite to being able to choose. We can focus our energy on lovingly comforting the vulnerability we feel, knowing that ultimately all we can do is be present with ourselves. We must be an attentive parent, or our fears will rule us. We need to be vigilant in watching for and taking care of our vulnerability, or that frightened part of us will run our lives.)

By focusing on our hopes and wants, we can make that transition from helplessness to faith, without sacrificing our alertness. Embracing our helplessness as a given, we can release the future, knowing it is not ours to control. We can choose to turn our awareness to our positive desires, choosing to live in hope and faith. What do we have at stake here? Not the outcome. It was never ours to control. What we have at stake is how we feel as we go through life. We might as well choose to live in faith. Faith opens us up. Fear shuts us down. A positive attitude allows us to take the control we do have and live our lives to the fullest.

We all know that there are good things out there. People receive blessings all of the time. Why wouldn't we? We can either believe for the good, or for the bad. We have no ultimate control, but why would we want to live with bad expectations? What is the worst that could happen? A bad outcome. But what do we have to lose? Living with a negative attitude and bad expectations is a waste of good life if the outcome turns out to be a good one. And, it is a waste of good life if the outcome turns out to be a bad one, too. Bad outcomes are hard enough without having spent all of that time beforehand adding to our misery. Either way, living with positive expectations is a better use of time. Since our attitude does not control God but does influence the quality of our life experience, it is simply logical to have a positive expectation. This is where helplessness is our best friend. When we fight it, we fight God. When we accept it, we are able to do what we can, and make the best of our life right now, as well as the best of what will happen. Choice is possible when we accept our helplessness and release the future to God.

Be a fan for yourself

The Chicago Cubs have not won a World Series for 95 years! That is a long time! And yet, the Cub fans always turn out for their team, with annual attendance at home games numbering in the millions. They are enthusiastic and endlessly hopeful: "This is going to be the year we win!" None of the fans are even old enough to remember the last time the Cubs won the Series, yet here they come, year after year, with positive expectations and a great and passionate support for their team. How can this be? Are they fools? Or do they demonstrate to us what we have been talking about - it feels good to be hopeful.

Imagine having this enthusiasm and passionate support for yourself! "I am great! Today is going to be my turn to have a great day!" Why not live this way? However the day turns out, you can believe in yourself, separate from any disappointing outcomes and feel good about the fact that you had a positive attitude and did your best.

We may not be able to control big outcomes in our lives, but we can control what we pay attention to in each moment. We can refuse to allow past disappointments to discourage us, for each moment brings a new possibility. We can choose to not let external events defeat our spirits or our love - in the world, and in relationship with God. We can be our own best fan, believing for the good, and finding the good in each moment.

Challenges are a part of life

People tend to forget that to be human means having to face challenges and hardships. When our turn comes to face these challenges, it is not because we have done something wrong. They are certainly difficult to go through, but they are also an unavoidable part of being alive. Throughout all of human history, people from all walks of life, of all ages and both sexes have done the best that they have known to do, from their limited human perspective. And throughout all of human history, people have experienced tragedies, as well as joy, some of their own making, some just because it was their turn to have a tragedy or a joy. We cannot know the reasons for these things.

Because we do not like to have painful experiences or feel out of control or vulnerable, we make up explanations which blame ourselves: "I'm unlucky. I can't win. I'm cursed. I'm stupid." Sometimes we blame others for our unhappiness: "Why did you do that?! This is all your fault! If it weren't for you, I'd be happy." But these explanations are not true. They are just a way we attempt to not feel vulnerable - "Bad things don't happen to me. I cause them/ You cause them."   There are three problems with managing unhappiness this way:

1. We tear ourselves down, adding our voice to the judgments of the world, deepening the illusion that we do not have the right to exist.

2. We are living as though the illusion that we can be in control is a reality. But it is not our reality, and if we are not "in reality," we must then be "in-sane."

3. We distract ourselves from being able to discover the lesson inherent in the situation.

Challenges and hardships are just experiences to learn from. We do not have a choice about receiving this homework, only about our attitude and if we use the homework to help us grow.

Prayer by an Unknown Confederate Soldier

I asked God for strength that I might achieve,
I was made weak, that I might learn humbly to obey ...
I asked for health, that I might do great things
I was given infirmity, that I might do better things ...

I asked for riches that I might be happy,
I was given poverty, that I might be wise ...
I asked for power, that I might have the praise of men

I was given weakness, that I might feel the need of God ...
I asked for all things, that I might enjoy life,
I was given life, that I might enjoy all things ...
I got nothing I asked for - but everything I had hoped for.

Almost despite myself, my unspoken prayers were answered.
I am, among men, most richly blessed!

We can beat ourselves up, blame someone else, or decide to learn from our experiences. When bad things happen to us, it does not mean anything is wrong with us. It is just a part of the human experience. We do not have to be defeated by the hard things that are natural in life. That is like doing poorly on a pop quiz in school and thinking that now you failed the class. Never give up on believing in yourself and your dreams. You may not get everything you want, or the way you want it, but your heart will remain open to possibility if you choose to live in positive expectation.

We can only become what we believe if we have the courage to dream. When we shut down our hopes and dreams, we close God out. We are not open to the possibilities that may come our way. It takes courage to allow ourselves to tolerate feeling vulnerable and out of control. It takes courage to choose repeatedly to have a positive attitude in the face of the challenges life brings us.

Dreams belong to the world of the future. It is only natural to think about the future. As much as we may try to stay in the present, we will think and wonder and worry about what the future may bring. Even if they are neutral thoughts like "I have to go to the store" or "I have a meeting," it is impossible to be human and not look ahead. We will never have ultimate control over the future - we can only do what we can in each moment. We will never have any way of knowing what is going to happen next. We have only two options – to live in fear or to live in faith. When we accept our helplessness, we can focus on the dreams and hopes of our heart, and, prepared for anything, face the future with faith. Accepting our helplessness opens us to the power of believing in ourselves, and of believing in God for better things.

Chapter 9

~ *Claim the Real Power in Your Life* ~

Have you ever thought about, *really* thought about what an incredible brain we each have? It is capable of the most amazing abilities that defy explanation. Have you ever considered how it is that we are able to talk? How on Earth do we do that!?! We want to say something – maybe it is only a split second urge to speak, or maybe we do not even consciously realize that we want to speak – we open our mouths and *talk*. How can that be??? Unless we are giving a speech, we do not practice what we say beforehand.   Nor do we write it out. We do not develop concepts in preparation for our speaking. (Imagine how slow conversation would be if we had to do all of that!) It is automatic and effortless. How is it possible that we are capable of such a remarkable feat as the use of language?

We have other remarkable abilities, as well, but are often distracted from using them.   When we attempt to control the uncontrollable – outcomes, the future, other people – we keep ourselves busy fighting our helplessness and vulnerability. We may not have ultimate power over what is important in our lives, but we *do* have power. Our strength lies in knowing the difference between what is God's power, and what is our own.

You have inner guidance for a reason

Jan: When our son, Seth, was an infant, Al's brother came to visit us. Seth started to cry, and Ken told me to just let him so I wouldn't spoil him. This is a well-known and respected way to deal with babies, but I just didn't feel good about it. I was a new mother, though, and unsure of myself. I also felt afraid that Ken would be critical of me, so I let Seth cry. After a few minutes, I couldn't take it anymore, and picked him up to discover that his diaper was sopping wet. I felt sick inside. I vowed right then that I would always listen to myself, regardless of how much I loved or respected anyone else who was giving me different guidance. I have never regretted decisions I have made by listening to myself. I may have felt sad about the outcomes, but knew that I had done the best I could. The only times in my life I have kicked myself for the decisions I have made were the times I <u>*didn't*</u> *listen to myself.*

We have inner guidance for a reason. It shows us the path to follow that is the right one for us. There are endless possibilities in the world. Our inner guidance is the compass that enables us to find our way. Strengthening our inner guidance is similar to the process of making a compass accurate. A compass needle is magnetized over time until it always points to true North. As we listen to and follow our inner guidance, it also strengthens and becomes more accurate, ridding itself slowly of fears and illusions so that it is able to give us true direction. When we listen to our inner guidance, all of the infinite positive possibilities of the Universe are open to us. Fear does not shut us down. We become open to inspiration and creativity. Our ability to imagine and to dream is limitless.

While we do not have ultimate control over outcomes, the power that we each do have is amazing and miraculous. Look at the incredible abilities, accomplishments and discoveries we human beings have to our credit, while only using that well-known 10% of our brains. Why would we limit ourselves out of fear? We have two choices in life:

1. We can *risk* failure by trying to follow our dreams.
2. We can *guarantee* failure by not trying to follow our dreams.

When we live at peace with our vulnerability and limited control, we will have the strength and freedom to go for broke and follow our dreams. We will not be spending our energy trying to protect ourselves from feeling helpless, defeating ourselves before we even begin. That will enable us to maximize the true power we have in our lives. Accepting our right to exist, we will do our part to remain open to the infinite positive possibilities God provides us with.

Intent
<u>Intent</u>

Intent is the decision or resolve to act. If we want to walk, we do not question - our intention makes us begin to walk without even thinking about it. We have enormous confidence in our ability to walk.

Our ability to use language is the same. We open our mouths with intent to speak, and we do. We are capable of the most intricate and involved discussions, without preplanning. It is spontaneous action. It is amazing to contemplate our ability to speak! We have intent, then take a leap of unquestioning faith, a leap into the void and the unknown. We open our mouths and are able to communicate coherently! Without even thinking about it, we release control and leap without planning. And we can all do it.

On the basic physical plane, we do not question the ability of our brain to allow us to act. Most of us have had no reason to *not* trust that if we have intent and leap, there will be spontaneous fulfillment of our intent.

This remarkable ability to speak or walk is a basic part of each of us. But intent is not limited to physical actions. We all have the ability to use intent to access our potential in all areas, including finding and actualizing our ideas and dreams. Just as we can "magically" speak, we can also "magically" live in order to have the best chance to make our dreams come true. We do not have to develop something new - we already have the ability to live our intentions and access the tremendous power that is our birthright.

Steps to Power and Possibility

Most people are familiar with or have even experienced "beginners' luck." Before we get self-conscious and watch ourselves, we are able to just act freely. Because we do not know what we are doing, we can release expectations, judgment and inhibition, and leap into the unknown. In the experience of beginners' luck, we have stumbled on our power.

Al: I was studying with a classmate for a difficult exam in graduate school. We both needed a break, so he asked me if I played tennis. I told him I never had, but that I was a pretty good athlete. He said he had a couple of racquets in his car, and why didn't we take a break a play a bit at a nearby court. He offered to give me a few pointers, which I was glad to receive, and then we played. At first we just volleyed, and then he wanted to play a set. I won - 6-4. He seemed surprisingly angry that I had won, and said he wanted to play another set. I won, again - 6-4

The Steps to Power and Possibility is a process that will allow us to harness the unrestricted flow of intent and power that beginners often have when attempting something new and unusual, and that all of us continually experience.

1. <u>Focus on being in the present moment</u>. Do not think about the past or the future. Bring your mind to full concentration on just being *here, now*. Release everything else.

Al: Without any ideas about what I was supposed to be doing, I was completely focused on how to play, as I had never played or taken lessons. I certainly had no thoughts that I might win. I just hit the ball.

2. <u>Do the best you can without judgment</u>. You have the right to exist - remember, you are the child of God! You can only do what you can do, given the fact that you will always be learning more and be able to do more, later, based on the growth you make from lessons you have, today. That is good enough for God. (Remember, He did design you this way!) Let it be good enough for you.

Al: I knew I was a beginner and had no expectations of myself. I just wanted a break from my studies. When I didn't hit the ball well, I had no judgment, because I had no expectations of myself. I felt completely relaxed and enjoyed the experience of playing "at" tennis.

3. <u>Feel your intent, and *leap*</u>! Release the outcome. Remember, that is not your concern, as it is not within your power to create outcomes. Just as God gave you the ability to speak, He also gave you the ability and the *right* to have dreams and hopes. Get out of the way and let the effects of what God put inside you begin to grow freely. Allow the blessings from God to emerge.

Al: I had a surprising experience following this game. Somewhere inside, I felt like I <u>should</u> feel proud that I had played so well, but it was absolutely clear to me that it couldn't have been just me playing. Without thinking about it, I had followed this four-step process. I had gotten out on the court just wanting to hit the ball and have fun. The extra gift of winning did not feel like it had anything to do with me, and it had certainly not even occurred to me as a possibility.

Harnessing our intent is not a passive process. We will either facilitate or prevent it from happening. If we do not allow ourselves to follow those steps, if we are trying to protect ourselves from being vulnerable and out of control, we will be unable to access this power. It will not matter what potential we might have, we will never be able to access it. We cannot both watch ourselves and be "in the flow." Self-consciousness divides our attention and our intent. We are divided between the intent to do something, like talk, and the intent to protect ourselves. We are watching ourselves with the illusion that we can keep ourselves from feeling vulnerable. But it never, ever works. That divided intent makes us stumble. It makes bowlers get gutter balls and makes skaters fall. Instead of being solid and living from the inside of us, we are watching ourselves from the outside.

Sports fans know about the phenomenon of "being in the zone." Fans, teammates and coaches watch in utter amazement as occasionally a player just cannot do anything wrong! The most unlikely moves from the most impossible places result in baskets, home runs, and goals. People watching scream, hit each other, fall over in astonishment, laugh with wonder and joy that such a thing could happen. Michael Jordan, the best basketball player who ever lived, regularly played "in the zone." During a playoff game, a cameraman caught him running down the court after such a play. He looked at his team and shrugged! *He* did not understand how he could be doing what he did, either!

When we let go, something miraculous happens. God takes over. It does not feel like us, anymore. Letting go gives us access to living in our full potential. Following the Steps to Power and Possibility allows us to access that "zone" where there is no separation between our self and our actions. There is no separation between us and what we are doing.

Jan: I had an amazing tennis experience, too, almost as good as Al's. He and I were taking lessons with another couple. We each bounced a ball on our racquet for a bit, and then got to face each other across the net. It was so exciting! I watched a ball come directly to me, pulled back my arm and with joyful intent let go with a mighty "Thwack!" It was awesome! All five of us, the instructor, too, stopped to watch where the ball landed.... but it didn't. We looked up - not there, all over the court - not there. I finally looked at my racquet and found it tightly lodged in the "V" beneath the oval stringed part.

Obviously, there is never a guarantee that living as the active partner of God will always result in what we want, but it gives us the best chance we can have. And, we will always give ourselves and others lots of reasons to laugh!

We already possess everything we need to have a successful and fulfilled life. All we need to do is allow it to work by doing these Steps. We all have to practice new skills. As you practice these Steps, they will become an automatic and natural part of you, just as walking did. Our ability to walk and to talk is proof that something operates within us that we do not have to control. We only facilitate or prevent it from happening by our degree of openness. We have all had a brilliant idea or intuition that seems to come out of nowhere, when we are not even thinking about anything in particular. It just comes to us. This is all proof that something amazing and supernatural can happen. We do not need to develop some new ability - we each *already* possess it! By using the Steps to Power and Possibility, we can cultivate our openness. Soda cannot flow through a collapsed straw! Open up! Let God's blessings and your potential have a chance to flow through you!

But I'm trying!

We often tell ourselves and others that we are *trying* to do things in life. *Trying* simply is not good enough. *Trying* cheats you of being victorious! *Trying* means that you are fearful of *doing*. Doing does not always guarantee success, but it gives you a chance to succeed, and to learn from any unexpected results of your actions.

Exercise: Try to pick up a pen.....
There is no such action! You either pick it up, or you do not.

When we experience ourselves as *trying*, we are wanting something without *intent*. We are wanting without the commitment to do what we need to for it to happen. We are wanting without the courage to be vulnerable, because it is less important to have what we want than it is to keep from feeling raw and exposed in our wanting. We are wanting without the courage to release control and the outcome to God, without the decision to focus on being in the present moment and leap! We are filled with self-consciousness and watch ourselves with judgment. We have split our power between wanting something, and wanting to protect ourselves.

When we are filled with fear about taking a risk and going after what we want in life, our vulnerable, nonlogical and fearful child is in charge, not our logical adult. Our logical adult self can support us through the fear in the same way we would support any frightened child. We can be kind to the fear, breathing into our frightened feelings and releasing them from our bodies. We can remind ourselves "Once I didn't have the support to go after what I wanted in life. Once, no one realized how frightened I was, or how to help me. But I have grown up into a strong and capable adult. I want this. I want to have good things in my life. If it doesn't work, that's okay, too. I'll feel proud that I did what I could. And I won't let anyone judge me or criticize me."

Let yourself be a winner. Let yourself *do* what you want to do. Do not ever settle for *trying*. Everything will not always turn out as you hope, but at least you are letting yourself have a full life experience, and are giving God a chance, too!

Gratitude helps us remember God's promise

Think back in your life to the things that have gone right for you. Regardless of the challenges you have faced, allow yourself to name some of the blessings you enjoy, things you may be taking for granted: physical health, food, shelter, family (even if they are challenging to deal with!), work, schooling, friends, clothing... See if you can come up with 10 things that are going right for you in your life.

Gratitude allows us to know that we have already had so much in our lives, despite any challenges we have faced. Gratitude acknowledges the truth, the proof that God is operating to give us full lives. Gratitude is a bridge between the *concept* of God's blessings and the *experience* of God's blessings. Imagine that you had never eaten an apple. How could you imagine what it tastes like? But having already eaten an apple, you only need to remember the taste. We have already received blessings, and only need to remember that we deserve good things in our lives. The list you just made proves that.

Focus on your strengths

When we have a negative outlook, or focus on what is missing or what is wrong in our lives, we are really doing our adult version of throwing a tantrum. We are protesting: "This is *not* what *I* think should be happening! And I don't like it!" When we ask, "Why me? Why now? Why this?" we are having a little fight with God. We are not wanting to accept that all of us have different abilities and that being human means there is no way around having hard challenges. It is only our attitude that we can control. But this attitude means the difference between being a victim or a victor in life.

Exercise: Focus on your strengths. List five things that you can do well. They may be organizing, cleaning, accounting, art, schoolwork, communicating, cooking, sports.... open up your mind to allow yourself to recognize and appreciate the abilities you have been given.

We all have abilities we take for granted, mainly because we do not struggle with them. Look at that list you just made. If you were not able to do those five things you wrote down, you would probably wish you could do them. But most likely you minimize their importance simply because they cause you no trouble. We all have our attention caught by what is wrong. It is part of our survival instincts. (Hmmm... those bushes don't look right. Are those the eyes of a lioness peering out at me?) Noticing what is wrong can help us grow and increase in wisdom. But if we *only* notice what is wrong, we distort our awareness of reality and become out of balance. Gratitude fills in the picture of what is real, and allows us to relax and feel safe.

Think of a time you thought you could not do something, but it turned out that you did a good job. You have already had success in your life. You have a miraculous power to speak, walk, do. Trust in your past, which shows you that this is already a proven fact. If you doubt yourself, simply take a walk around the block or pick up a pen and write a letter to your mother (she will be glad to hear from you!) Prove to yourself that amazing abilities flow through you at your slightest intent.

We may doubt ourselves, but maybe that is because we go to feeling doubt instead of feeling vulnerable when we are facing something and realize that we are not in control of the outcome. There is a kind of safety in failure - we know the outcome. We won't be surprised.

Jan: I once watched myself do the strangest thing. I saw a coffee mug that I really liked, and decided to buy it. I then picked up another mug, nice, but not as pleasing to me, and started to debate which of them I preferred. I convinced myself to buy the one I <u>did not prefer</u>! It was such an odd experience that I had to explore what on Earth had happened! That's when I realized that whenever, even in the least important way, I take action in the world, I feel vulnerable. By purchasing the mug I did not like as well, I guaranteed that I would never have the experience of being <u>surprised</u> and disappointed by realizing something was wrong with the mug I really loved. I had <u>built in</u> disappointment, already, and so, in an odd way, was protecting myself. If I had accepted that it didn't have to be perfect and that it was okay for me to not be aware of everything, I would have been able to have the strength to choose what I really wanted.

Think about something in your life that you do not do well. Now, think about something in your life that you do well. Notice that they are both true. You do not need to call one a bad thing and the other a good thing. One is simply a challenge, while the other is an accomplishment. How do you feel when you pay attention to the first? How do you feel when you pay attention to the second?   When we think about something that we do well, we tend to feel more confident. Focus there! You have proven to yourself that you have strengths. Do not focus in judgment on what you struggle to do or cannot yet, or maybe ever, do. Remind your vulnerable self that it is just part of being human that we have challenges. Nothing is wrong with us. Perfection will never be possible. We can feel proud that we take on these challenges and try to grow. And, we can enjoy and feel proud of what we are able to do well. We get stronger when we accept our limitations. And, we deserve to celebrate and rejoice in our victories and abilities.

Every one of us has the ability to do something well. We also have the ability to learn, when we do not already know. Reparenting ourselves allows us to choose to live with positive expectations and the vulnerability of taking those leaps of faith in life rather than trying to control outcomes. The alternative is to live in fear, to shut down our dreams and hopes, to feel alone and abandoned, as separate from God as though He did not exist. Do not allow yourself to be defeated by fear and negative thoughts! Follow your hopes and dreams with determination so that God has a chance to operate in your life.

If one dream dies, dream another

Jan: Both Al and I lost our parents very early, so our children had no grandparents. One day, we were at the airport when a planeload of senior citizens arrived. Our son sighed longingly and said, "Look at all those grammas and grampas!" It was too much for us. Our dream of an extended family had died with our parents. Realizing how much my whole family loved my mother's best friend, Marge. I called her and asked if we could adopt her and her husband to be the grandparents for our family. Fortunately, they were both thrilled, and accepted. Marge said that not being a Gramma, yet, she didn't know the job description. She quickly arranged a visit for them to get to know themselves in their new role, and our children as their first grandchildren. By adopting the family we had always hoped for, we literally dreamed another dream and made it come true.

There are many blessings in life and many people to love. When we live with faith and hope and act with determination, allowing God to do what He does, we open ourselves to possibilities beyond our imagination. And if you do not get the outcome you had hoped for, don't allow yourself to be defeated! Keep on dreaming. There will always be another dream to take the place of the old one. Remember, we cannot know what the future will bring, so we might as well hope for great things.

Our adopted Grampa always said, "You can't kiss all the pretty girls!" We will never have everything, but we can have a lot. If we keep believing and acting for what we want, then we will not be stopped by external challenges. "This goal didn't work, but I have others" or "I'll find another way." Giving up is a way of trying to protect ourselves from disappointment. The only problem with that form of protection is that it does not work! We are still disappointed, but we are in control of the disappointment, so it does not take us by surprise. But that is living small, and we are not designed to live small lives.

Follow your wants and live in faith

We do not seem to be able to avoid thinking about the future. Some of that thinking is necessary to be responsible and take care of ourselves, our families, and our work tasks. Some, however, simply feels like a plague that worries the life out of us. If we remember that our task in our active partnership with God is to choose to live with positive expectations and to do the best we can, then we will enter God's domain, the future, living in faith, with the knowledge that we deserve good things.

We have all heard about rats that are put in mazes. They are persistent! They exist in the moment, totally focused on their goal - they want that cheese, and they do not give up! They do not judge themselves, either. They just keep on going, trying new paths. What do we superior life forms do? In the maze of life, we get discouraged. If we were rats, we would say things to ourselves like, "I always run into walls. I'll never get to the cheese. I'm stupid. I just don't deserve cheese." Hey, all of you superior life forms out there! If a rat can live in faith and positive expectation, so can we!

Dogs are another example of living in faith. They expect goodness, and are always eager to accept blessings. "You want to give me *another* dog biscuit? GREAT!" Can you imagine a dog turning down a treat? They are endlessly hopeful. They stand by the door expecting their person to come home. They are always joyful to see him. They rejoice in treats and are always ready for more. They are absolutely connected to what they want, and live in the present moment. They never say that they are not worthy: "I've been sleeping all day - I don't deserve anything." They do not interpret or think about the past: "I never got a treat as a puppy - I don't deserve one now." They live each moment without judging. And we humans just *love* them.

It may seem too difficult to be as faithful as a rat or dog. After all, we have much more complicated brains and many things to worry about. But there are so many examples of how we live in faith each day. We have faith that we will wake up tomorrow. We have faith that we will not have an accident. We have faith that we will turn on the lights and the power will come on. We have faith that the car will start. We have faith that our family will come home safely again at the end of the day. Ordering food in a restaurant is an example of entering into the future with hope and positive expectation of good things coming to us. We do not order something thinking that it will not be good. We believe for the best. We can choose to live our whole lives with that same attitude of positive expectation. What is served up to us will be great!

Care for yourself as well as you care for your car

How do you maximize the performance of your car? Did you have to learn? We did, remember? We killed our first car because we did not know that we needed to put oil and water in it! Sound foolish? That is how ignorant people can be. We now know that to keep an engine running at peak performance, we need to add that oil and water regularly, and not put things in it that would clog up the motor. We know that to run at full capacity, we need to use high quality fuel. We need to make sure that the battery is strong and charged.

People do not automatically know the proper care for things, including the care and maintenance of their dreams and hopes, and how to maximize the chances of them coming true. If we do not understand how normal it is to feel vulnerable and afraid, we will shut ourselves down and settle for a smaller life than we are capable of and that is possible for us. If we do not understand that there are things we can do to help maximize our being successful in life, we will be so afraid of disappointment and the judgment of others that we do not even try. We will give up the power we have without giving it a chance to succeed.

There is a logical maintenance program that gives your car the best chance possible to have a long, well-running life. There is just as logical a plan to do the same for ourselves. The Steps to Power and Possibility help us mobilize our energy:

1. Focus on being in the present moment.
2. Do the best you can without judgment.
3. Feel your intent, and *leap*!

These are the tools to achieve the good things we are capable of, and that God promised and wants for us.

We can harness the powers that are in each of us with our intent and acceptance of our right to exist. If we live in fear and self-conscious judgment, we are creating a distorted and inaccurate world. Who said it is not okay to be human? Who said that joy, forgiveness, peace and healing are not ours by right? Those thoughts do not come from God. It is our destiny and our birthright to be human, in all of our fallibility and lack of perfection. Perfection is not a prerequisite for deserving.

We can choose to take action so that we can have a positive attitude. Not only does positive feel better, but a negative attitude and self-judgment shut us down so we can never be fully open to opportunities that are presented to us. Gratitude helps us remember that we do deserve good things.   The proof of this is that we have already received many blessings in our lives. If God did not want us to dream for great things, he would not have put those hopes and wants inside our hearts. Live *in the zone* so that God can work through you! Stretch the muscles of your power and rejoice in being alive!

Chapter 10

~ *Living in Self-Acceptance* ~

There are times when, if only for a few minutes, we feel at peace with the world and with who we are. We all have had moments when it feels like nothing can shake our sense of well-being. Life is just fine, and so are we. We can laugh at ourselves when we say or do the wrong thing, our work cannot stress us and nothing anyone else does or says makes us upset. Perhaps we are able to recognize, even as we are in the middle of this wonderful experience, that we are being given a glimpse of how it is possible to feel. But that feeling seems to come out of nowhere, and disappear without warning. We can either accept those times as temporary gifts, or we can use them as a promise of how we are supposed to live, and learn what we can do to make it possible to cultivate that sense of self-acceptance and well-being. We do, after all, have the power to create inner well-being!

Who's running this show, anyway?

Jan: Whenever I used to have the need to interact with a male who was in a position of power, I would notice the oddest thing about myself. My voice would go up an octave, and I would act in the most peculiar manner. I would get "cute." Not the real kind of cute, but rather in a giddy, mindless way. Even noticing this behavior, I could not seem to stop it. I would try to bring my voice down to a normal tone, try to speak and act like an adult... but I could do neither. I watched myself, powerless, as though someone else were in charge of my body. I could never understand this behavior, because my father – the first male in my life – was a very passive man, totally unthreatening.

When we face difficult times, as adults, the way we react is most likely determined by lessons we learned as infants. By the time we are one to two years old, we have each formed the foundation for our personality and for the way we understand the world. No child this young is very well-equipped to make sense of what he experiences. He does not have the maturity to separate emotionally from his parents and to understand why things happen and why people act the way they do. When we are very young, we interpret the world and define our place in it based on the logic and understanding of a toddler. The way we act now when things are hard is determined by what we learned as a baby. Our responses are based on our early definitions of how the world works and how to survive in it. It is as if our logical adult disappears, and the baby runs the show.

Jan: One day, I was preparing for a meeting with a state senate subcommittee about a bill they were considering. I found myself starting to cry, and heard myself thinking, "If I don't get these daddies to do what I want, I'll die." ...... What? ..... I was stunned by the words that filled my mind and heart with panic. My logical self said, "First of all, they are not my fathers. And, secondly, I will not die, no matter what they do." But I could not stop the tears or my fear. With a chill of sudden clarity, I realized that I had been trying to link my nonlogical behavior with the wrong father. My stepfather was passive and nonthreatening. But my biological father had been physically abusive to both my mother and to me. Even though we had left him when I was two, he had been the powerful male I had been reacting to for all of these years.

All of us notice that some of our behaviors and feelings are not logical responses to situations we encounter. We will observe that the way we respond sometimes seems inappropriate, and the intensity of our responses is quite out of proportion to those situations. Fortunately, it is not too late for us to grow and change. We have the opportunity to go back to that early foundation and make some adjustments based on what our adult logic and experiences have taught us. First, we have to discover the *rightness* of our behavior, rather than judge or condemn it.

Jan: I immediately realized the origin and purpose of my nonlogical behavior with men in power. To a two-year-old, a large man's anger and abuse would have been experienced as a threat to her survival. The two-year-

old Jan was trying to protect herself from being killed. And what coping mechanisms would a two-year-old have? She couldn't say, "Dad, I know you are upset, but please don't direct it at me." But she could be cute and sweet so he wouldn't want to hurt her.

Once I realized this, I was filled with such sorrow and compassion that I had gone through such a frightening time. Even though we had left him when I was very young, I had already been taught what to expect in life, and how to best survive. Realizing this, I was able to reparent myself in order to bring myself into the present where I, a capable and strong adult, now exist. Little Jan couldn't handle a large, angry man, but I can take care of myself. As a matter of fact, a few years ago, I was stopped by a policeman, and my reaction to the event was to think, "Yea, yea, yea. Just give me a ticket and go away." I felt so proud! Our basic instinct is for survival. We cannot learn to live in self-acceptance if we never experienced acceptance, but were focused, instead, on surviving. Now we have the chance to love and support ourselves in the present, taking over where our parents left off. Only when we feel secure that our strong, logical adult is there to take care of us, can we be at peace with our vulnerability and begin to accept ourselves and our right to exist. Only then can we live as strong and logical adults.

Understand the details of your past

All people, from the very youngest to the very oldest, feel vulnerable, helpless (out of control) and separate. All people have the need to grant themselves the right to exist. It is not something anyone else can give us, no matter how much they love or approve of us. Each of us, knowing our deepest and most secret vulnerable and fallible self, must come to peace with being an imperfect and evolving being, and claim our right to exist.

This is what all people face, regardless of their background history, their family, and their upbringing. Each of us has different details of what our lives have been, but regardless of those details, we each face these basic human issues. This is a universal human task. No one escapes the need to come to peace with these conditions of being human. If we do not, our lives are profoundly distorted, and we live in the world of the nonlogical. We need to understand the details of how we came to define what the world is like and what our place in life is. When we do this, we can know exactly how to free ourselves from the past and accept who we are.   For some of us, however, those details are lost from our memories, but we still have the opportunity to reparent and comfort ourselves so we are not stuck with those nonlogical behaviors. We all can guide ourselves into living in our logical present.

<u>Why it is hard to accept ourselves: Developmental factors</u>

There are two early factors which impact our ability to accept ourselves. The first has to do with how we develop as human beings. Just because we are alive, there are human issues we must all face and come to peace with. None of us want to feel separate. We can become stuck in fusion with our parents and friends, and be too afraid to allow ourselves to feel our uniqueness. Again, fusion, the desire to be the same as, or one with someone, is not a bad thing. It is a necessary part of our development and it allows us to feel safe and that we belong.

Once our daughter and her best friend, both eight, each bought a pair of the same shoes. We took them to the library, where they saw two other friends, who had coincidentally just purchased those same shoes. The four girls could not have been more thrilled! They stood in a little circle, each of them with one foot in (as though they were playing "Hokey Pokey") admiring their wonderful footwear and just as pleased as could be with themselves and each other!

It is scary to stand alone. How many people have the courage to stand before an audience and sing? The adrenaline which surges through our bodies is not differentiating between feeling exposed and feeling endangered. Our bodies react as though any exposure is life threatening.   It is one of our instincts to want to fit in and not be exposed to the judgment or reaction of others. We all want approval and acceptance, and the automatic reaction to this need is to try to be just like the people who matter to us.

The desire for fusion is so compelling that it is often hard to separate when we need to. We will always experience different needs and feelings than those of people we care about. If we do not separate – step back emotionally to realize that we are having an experience of differentness – we will react in anger or hurt.

Jan: Al likes sports and I like dancing. One Cinco de Mayo, I asked Al if he wanted to go to a street dance downtown. Being an honest kind of guy, he said "No." I really wanted to go, so I left, angry and hurt that he wouldn't come.

Often, we do not have the support to separate just because it is hard for everyone to feel different. It takes courage to stand apart from our family or group, to follow our own way or our own conscience. It takes courage to let someone we love go, to encourage them to listen to their own hearts. In trying to avoid the pain of separation, we do not always recognize, let alone take, this courageous path. We give up the sense of self and self-acceptance, in order to keep the feeling of belonging and togetherness, not realizing that we can have them both.

Jan: I didn't get any farther than the car, when I realized what I had done wrong. I had expected him to be just like me, even though I know his feelings are different. So I went back into the house, and asked him if he would come to enjoy being with me while we danced and listened to the music. Al was great. He totally could enjoy doing that - in my fusion, I had just asked the wrong question.

Al: I had the same experience with Jan when I asked Jan to go to a basketball game with me. I finally figured out that she didn't have to watch the game with the same avid sports eyes I have, but could enjoy the experience in her own way. She enjoys being with me, watching me enjoy the game, watching sometimes, observing the crowd other times. (It is important to note here that even though I have learned to accept that Jan is a different person, dancing is dumb and basketball is good!)

What we have in common are the feelings, even though the details will differ. If we all go to buy ice cream at an ice cream parlor, we do not have to buy the same flavor to enjoy and share the experience. You may buy bubble gum ice cream while I buy coconut chocolate chip, but we are both having a human experience together. Our tastes or styles may differ, but we share the humanness of having tastes and styles.

We can give ourselves permission to be unique individuals. Our logical adult can give support for separating and having our own opinions and needs. It is never too late to develop acceptance of ourselves as distinct and separate human beings who can tolerate not living in fusion.

Why it is hard to accept ourselves: Environmental factors

The second factor which affects our ability to accept ourselves is environmental. A child is a totally vulnerable being and is deeply influenced by his family culture.   Each family has a distinct culture, primarily based on the childhoods the parents, themselves, experienced. Realizing this enables us to look back at our parents without anger or blame. They only knew what they knew. They received lessons from *their* parents, who only knew what *they* knew, because of the upbringing they experienced with *their* parents. And so it goes. The importance of looking at our childhoods is not to accuse or find fault. The goal is to allow our wise and logical adult self to clarify misunderstandings we had as children. We can now look with more experienced eyes and reinterpret what once was so bewildering and hurtful to us.

There are three possible family cultures:

The first is a culture of judgment. The message to the child in this culture is that he is not good enough. The atmosphere is one of criticism and the experience the child has is of being a failure. The child is taught that he is only here for the parent's needs, not for his own life experience. He has no innate value or worth, and no right to a separate existence. Not feeling accepted by the people he most needs, the child has no sense of self-acceptance.

Emma's father was unable to ever talk about what he felt. All he could do to show his interest in his children was to lecture them. No matter what they did, they received a lecture. If they did well, they were lectured about how to do better. If they struggled or made misjudgments, they were lectured about how wrong and stupid they were. He even used to lecture them that they ignored his lectures about how to improve. Emma grew up to be a withdrawn and depressed young woman. She was angry at her father and was unable to develop a relationship with a man of her own age, even though she wanted to, and was attractive and intelligent.

The second culture is one of neglect. The message to the child is that he is not important. The atmosphere is one of indifference, as the parents are uninterested in and disconnected from the feelings and needs of the child. The child is left feeling unworthy and that he has no value or right to exist. Having no sense of belonging or importance, the child can feel no sense of self-acceptance.

Al: Once when I made the baseball All Star team, my father wouldn't come to the game. He wouldn't take time to support me and let me know that I was important. His lack of support communicated that it made no difference if I tried to succeed or to do my best. Even though I had extraordinary athletic ability, I never felt like it was of any value, and I never pursued developing it. It was a painful thing to have felt such joy in an experience and yet see that it was so irrelevant and unimportant to my father.

In the family cultures of judgment and neglect, the children receive messages of fear. They are taught shame, self-judgment (which is an attempt to anticipate the judgment of others, and do it first to avoid being startled), and the *shoulds* of life – what others expect of them. Their acts are evaluated and judged. They internalize these messages and feel pain that they are not important and valuable just the way they are.

The third family culture is supportive. The message to the child is that he is a being of value. The parents accept his uniqueness and whatever feelings the child has. The child grows up knowing that he is important and that his parents take joy in his existence. Because he is wanted and valued, the child from a supportive family culture has a sense of self-acceptance.

Jan: When our daughter was in first grade, we went to an assembly at her school. All of the youngest children sat on the floor... except one boy, who thought lying down was infinitely more comfortable. Now, if it were up to me, I would have gone over to him and asked him to please sit up. This would have been done sweetly, but it would have been a correction, nonetheless, doing nothing to help the boy understand the world better, or feel honored in his uniqueness. Luckily, I got to observe his teacher, who came over and explained to him, "This is a 'sitting up' kind of assembly, not a 'lying down' kind of assembly." In other words, there was <u>nothing</u> wrong with what the boy felt like doing. This situation just called for something different.

In a supportive environment, a child is taught to honor his

individual feelings and differences, and to find his own way. The child is helped to understand the impact of his behaviors. He is helped to choose behavior which both honors his feelings and helps him find a way to live in the world. Through this loving guidance, the child lives in an atmosphere of acceptance, and is able to more easily accept himself.

Correcting wrong messages from the past

Our culture offers us opportunities to hear messages of self-acceptance. Joel Osteen is one messenger, reminding us that we are the children of God, and God created us to be the way we are. Mr. Rogers, for decades, was another messenger, telling children across the country that "I like you just the way you are." Those messages appeal to our hearts, which long to believe them, and to our minds, which see the logic of them. Although powerful, this appeal is not enough to change our inner programming, but there are steps we can take which will.

1. We need to forgive our parents for being the kind of parents they were. People who are happy and filled with peace can only act in ways which spread kindness and love. It is too painful for *them* not to, for their hearts are open, and they feel the pain that others feel. If people act in ways that are controlling or hurtful, it is a *guarantee* that they are not happy, themselves. Even if you cannot talk with your parent, you can know that they were also human, and most likely struggling with the same issues we are talking about in this book. They knew no better way to be a parent, and they passed on what they knew. This is the basis for forgiveness. It is, however, always helpful if we have the opportunity to understand what happened to our parents, and the issues they dealt with as human beings.

Jan: When my mother was a child, my grandmother always had to be the center of attention in the family. No one's needs could ever be more important than hers, and my mother and her sister both had to take care of her, as though she were the child. Both of them suffered from this, not ever feeling that they were allowed a childhood.

When I was an adult, I remember one day talking with my grandmother about her childhood. She described how, when she was five, she had sat by the stove and watched as her mother died. She told me about her father's remarriage, and how he spent every free moment with his new wife. When my grandmother was 11, she became the bookkeeper for her father's business. They worked six days a week, with her coming after school to do her part. On Sundays, her father would take his new wife off for the day, leaving her, the eldest, to watch the other four children. When she thought her parents might be coming home, she and the others would stand at the subway exit, often for hours, waiting to glimpse their parents returning to them.

I couldn't help but cry as I realized the lost childhood of my grandmother, and the longing she had, not only for her mother, but for the love and attention of both of her parents. Suddenly, the stories my mother had told me took on a new light. It did not make the pain my mother felt any more acceptable, but I could see the legacy of pain which had been passed down in the family. I could feel compassion for them both. There was no bad person, here, only hurting children, doing the best they could.

2. <u>We need to allow ourselves to experience and express our feelings about having received the wrong message.</u> Forgiveness relieves our hearts and brings peace between us, but it does not make the wounds go away. If someone cuts us, we can forgive them their negligence or bad intent, but we must still attend to our body's reality and take steps to care for the wound so it will heal.

Al: My father died when I was 20, and my mother, when I was 21. I was surprised at how much pain and sadness I felt. The grief that poured over me was partly that I would never have the relationships I had always longed for. I also had a deep sorrow that my childhood had been so lonely, and that I had felt so responsible for my parents. I realized no child should feel that kind of responsibility. I had learned at a very young age that it was my job to take care of them, both physically and emotionally. I had never been able to have my childhood for myself. I also recognized that unless I allowed myself to grieve the distance that had always existed between my parents and me, I would spend the rest of my life shut down, trying to avoid my sadness. I would not be able to fully open up to live in emotional closeness with anyone else, including Jan.

It takes courage and strength to deliberately open ourselves up to feel the pain, anger or fear that is our response to having heard messages of discouragement and judgment when we were children. Most of us tell ourselves "Those days are over. I'm an adult now. Why linger on unhappy memories." And we try to go on. The problem is that we cannot. If we did not attend to a wound we received, we would have to adapt our behavior and thinking in order to continue on with life. We would numb ourselves physically and emotionally so we could focus our attention on other parts of life. We would be very protective about someone coming too close to us, for fear that they might touch the wound and hurt us.

This is similar to what we do emotionally, if we do not know how to come to peace with our feelings. We distort our reality and our behavior. We fight anything that threatens to stir up those feelings. We might get angry at someone who looks at us funny or honks as they drive by. Small and unimportant events or words might trigger old feelings of hurt, and our reactions would be out of proportion to the event as we try to protect ourselves from having those old feelings get triggered. We are all "walking wounded." In order to fully heal, we need to allow ourselves to acknowledge the wounds we all bear, without judgment of ourselves or of our parents.

Al: When I think about my parents, now, I can see how unhappy they were. It was not my responsibility to take care of them, but they must have felt like abandoned children, themselves. They were always sick and must have been frightened about what was going to happen to them. They loved me, but were too consumed with their own feelings and illnesses to take care of me, and allow me to be the child in our house. I have been able to grieve for all of us.

3. <u>Reparent your wounded self</u>. Your logical adult self has the opportunity to reparent your vulnerable and wounded child. (You may want to reread <u>Loving ourselves into the present</u>, Chapter 1) You are not stuck just because your parents did not understand what they were passing on, or know how to heal themselves so that they could pass on a better message. Your wounded self does not yet realize that you have grown up to be a capable and wise adult. Your job is to make a connection with him so that you can be the parent he needs. You can be the parent who comforts him as he feels and expresses his emotions. You can affirm to him that it is very sad that he ever received those old and inaccurate messages. And you can tell him that those sad days when no one could give him any better parenting are over, and that you are here, now. You can tell him that once he thought bad things

about himself, but now, in *this* family of the two of you, his feelings matter and he has the right to exist, just as he is.

The important thing to remember in reparenting is that you cannot just read or think the words and have it work. This is a daily awareness and practice. The words must be taken deeply into ourselves if they are ever to touch our vulnerability and pain.

The miracle of reparenting is that it is never too late. You can give yourself what your parents did not realize you needed. Even the most loving parents in the world cannot know your inner reality as intimately as you do. And even the most loving parents in the world cannot take away the universal task we face to grant ourselves the right to exist. You can give yourself the correct message of loving acceptance and the right to exist, now, and you can be healed.

We perpetuate our childhood experiences

In family cultures of judgment or neglect, we have a warped experience of relationships. We learn incorrectly what a relationship is supposed to be like. We expect to be treated by people the way we were treated by our parents, because we think this is what we deserve. When someone appears in our lives who treats us in the way that we are accustomed to, we do not think to send them away. We allow them in, and accept their behavior. Even if our spouse is not someone who would believe or act like we are not good enough or not important, we often train them to mistreat us because of our expectations of negative treatment. If we do not go through the process of healing from our family culture, we will perpetuate it ourselves for our whole lives.

Monique's mother was a widow. She was lonely and so self-involved that she was unable to pay attention to anyone's feelings but her own. Every discussion found its way quickly back to the mother's experience and needs. She endlessly told stories about herself, interrupting whatever Monique was trying to say. Monique was quickly trained that her needs were not important. The only role she had with her mother was as her caretaker, not her daughter. She was trained to be quiet and to focus on the needs of others. Monique married a man who was quite similar to her mother - self-involved and wanting her to be his mother. They took the vacations that he wanted, went to social functions that he felt comfortable with, and spent their evenings together focused on his interests. She was married to him for five years before she finally received the support I n therapy to allow herself to feel like an important person, to feel that she had the right to be a separate person and have the life she wanted.

Just as our minds can be haunted by unfinished tasks, nagged to complete what is undone, we are similarly drawn into situations where we have unfinished learning. We will find ourselves in situations and relationships which mirror where we are in our emotional development. Each situation gives us the opportunity to pay attention to our unhappiness, do our "homework" from God, and choose differently, so that we can grow into the complete beings we are designed to be. Accepting ourselves as growing beings allows us to get the lesson of the experience, rather than miss the real point and defeat ourselves by living in judgment.

God, the ultimate good parent

It is so confusing to believe something and yet not be able to really take that belief deeply inside of ourselves and live it. In our confusion and ignorance, we usually turn to the same tool used most often by our culture: judgment. We feel bad about ourselves. We feel ashamed and embarrassed, inferior and inadequate.

We can remember, though, that there is always a reason for something, even if we do not understand it. Instead of judging, which gives us no help at all in learning, we can seek to discover the reasons we are blocked. We can search for what interferes with our living the way we know is possible and right. The best place to start looking is in our childhoods, to discover what we might have learned that is not really true.

If we have had damaged relationships with our parents, it is harder for God to get in, no matter how much we want Him to. Our logical adult may know and believe, but the nonlogical child is stuck in his early experience of having no right to exist. We must find a way to heal, to make room to go through the anger and pain so that we can have a clear channel to God and are able to receive His messages of love and support. He is the ultimate good parent who tells us that He created us as we are, and that we deserve to be here and receive His blessings.

The way to God

Some of us can listen to the messages from spiritual sources or read the words in the Bible and leap into belief and healing. The concepts and the support to believe and accept those messages are enough to propel some of us into freedom from our wounds. Others of us do not work this way. One way is not better or worse than the other. Who are we to know what makes us the way we are or why one way of learning does or does not work? Without judging, we can just notice ourselves and what we need in order to attain freedom and our best life. Just as children are different in what motivates them or how they learn, we are different in how we each become free to receive the blessings of God.

If inspiration from the Bible or other spiritual sources fills our minds and hearts with excitement and belief, but somehow cannot penetrate deeply enough into our souls to heal us, there is no reason to despair or to judge ourselves. Each of us must trust in our own uniqueness and our own path to healing and to God. We can remember that it takes courage to stand apart from those we care about and respect. We can know that we are all heading in the same direction, but must travel in the way that fits our own particular needs. We cannot have faith the way someone else has faith. We have not lived his life. We are on our own journey, the journey that God designed specifically for us.

We can allow ourselves to be separate and not judge or compare ourselves with others. If we are not among those who leap into faith and belief, it is just fine to creep into it!

We all can follow the path of reparenting ourselves to freedom from our old pain and self-defeating patterns. Once, when we were little and knew no other way, those patterns saved our lives. They were brilliant adaptations which allowed us to survive until we grew up. They kept our hearts intact so that we could have the chance to heal, now. When that little, vulnerable self of ours was not looking, our capable, logical adult grew up. That little self will never be alone again. Our adult self will always be here, now. That adult self can support us in healing and in remembering the truth of what God promises us.

Faith is precious and inspiring, but it does not mean that our human issues are gone. We are in a relationship with God - it is not one sided any more than a relationship we have with our own children is one sided. We are not here just to receive. We have a part to play, too. We can be God's active partner and heal ourselves at the human level so that we are more open and receptive to God.

Chapter 11

~ *Take Charge of That Mind* ~

We are all haunted by fears. We may be innocently going along in our lives, when suddenly a thought strikes us and seems to take us over. We can turn away from it, try to think of something else, but we are in battle with it. We cannot seem to make it go away. We can try to exercise our will power to get back in control of our mind, but it feels like a losing battle.

That uppity mind

The left hemisphere of our brain is the domain of control. Thoughts, problem solving, information gathering, analysis and organization are all positive applications of control. The mind uses these abilities in order to try to master our environment. The job of the mind is to insure our survival.

We all admire the cleverness of an able mind. It can be a wonderful tool. However, just as we can never leave a two year old unattended, for there is no end of trouble and danger he would get himself into, we must also attend to our mind in the same way. A two year old has no idea that he is unequipped to deal with the world without supervision. A mind will similarly not realize its limitations, that it is only a tool for gathering and processing information. It cannot be the master. Our logical adult self, who is clear thinking and centered, must harness and control the mind so it will serve us and be a positive and helpful force in our lives. When we have negative thoughts, however long we dwell on them, we can know that our vulnerable child is having feelings that we are not attending to, and that the mind, with all of its tools, is incapable of helping the vulnerable child. That job lies in the domain of the logical adult.

Why do negative thoughts have such power?

Al: Growing up with two very physically ill parents was frightening. I fully expected to die young. Every time I had physical symptoms, I felt doomed. I was unable to simply go to a doctor and take care of the problem without thinking that I was dying. I really believed that I was a physically weak person. I was scared and upset every time I felt the slightest bit unwell. I could not rid myself of my thoughts that any illness was a death sentence.

When I learned about reparenting, I was able to comfort my vulnerable child about how scary it had been to watch his parents struggle with their health. I began to remind him, every time he felt afraid, that illness is just a part of life, and that I can take care of him. I knew my body was strong, so I reminded him I would heal and be fine. I told him that being ill makes everyone feel vulnerable and out of control, but it doesn't mean that something bad is going to happen. I also needed to remember that I am a separate person from my parents. Just because they were ill and died young did not mean I would.

Negative thoughts cannot stay in our mind if there is no fear or pain in us that it can attach to. Negative thoughts are a signal, just like the cry of a baby, that the parent needs to be there and take charge. Knowing that a baby will cry, parents listen and anticipate that they will need to drop whatever they are doing and go take care of that baby. Similarly, we need to realize that our vulnerability is going to be triggered *regularly*. Rather than being shocked and surprised and go to self-judgment, we need only parent ourselves the way we would a baby. "Uh, oh. Something scared you. You're just feeling vulnerable and out of control. It's okay. I'm here to take care of you."

Jan: Once I was driving our daughter and her boyfriend home from school. At one point, I signaled to change lanes, but noticed a car there, so turned off my signal and stayed put. As the car passed us, her boyfriend said in indignation, "Jan, he flipped you off!" I replied, "Oh, I probably scared him, and he just didn't know what to do with his feelings." Her boyfriend just couldn't get over my response, and kept repeating my words to himself, laughing, the whole way home.

The other driver had feelings that were not about me. Something happened in <u>him</u>. I did not have to take it personally or judge either myself or *him. I had done the best I could do with no ill-intent to anyone, and he had his reaction. I did not have to react with anger toward myself or him. I could be separate and have my own reaction, and even was able, being separate, to feel compassion for his having been frightened.*

Sometimes a negative thought is triggered by a message we receive from someone else. Our adult logical self needs to be ready to instantly separate. We would laugh if someone said, "You made me feel hungry!" It is the same thing when someone has an emotional feeling and tries to blame us as though we were responsible. When we feel the signal of pain, anger, or tightness in our hearts, or self-judgment as the result of something someone says, we need to quickly step back and separate. "This is not about me. Those are his feelings." We are each responsible for our actions, but not for someone else's response. That response is the result of his history and how he has learned to handle his feelings.

We tend to have negative thoughts when we feel vulnerable and out of control. When we fight against our helplessness and vulnerability, we experience fear. It seems to be an automatic reaction for people to turn against themselves in judgment rather than simply feel helplessness, sadness, or disappointment. This self-judgment is a distraction from the real helplessness we must all live with. Having the illusion that if we were only better people these bad things would not happen to us distracts us from the fact that sometimes bad things just happen and we have no way to prevent them, for we are limited. The more we fight our helplessness, the stronger negative thoughts become, because we are blaming ourselves whenever we feel helpless - and yet we are destined to live in ultimate helplessness. The alternative is just to accept our limited control as an inevitable part of being human.

Susan and Bob were great parents with a remarkable daughter who was a great athlete, student and active member of their church. Their son, Adam, however, had learning disabilities, and social and emotional problems. Throughout his whole childhood, they had sought the advice of counselors and teachers, who affirmed what they were doing as parents; but no one was able to find a way to help Adam. In his late teenage years, Adam became violent, and finally left home.

One day, they received a call from the local hospital that Adam had tried to kill himself. They blamed themselves for being bad parents, who should have known how to help him. They felt guilty and responsible. They judged themselves rather than feel their overwhelming sadness and helplessness. Years later, Adam was able to tell them that there was nothing they could have done to have helped him. He knew he had to find his own way.

We can either try to control our thoughts with will power ("I am not responsible for Adam's suicide attempt."), or we can bring our logical adult to compassionately take charge and help identify what we are feeling ("You did the best you could and were still helpless. It is just sad. Adam needs to find his own way. God will take care of him.")

Anytime we have a negative thought or tightness, we are struggling with feeling vulnerable, separate or helpless. Negative thoughts alert us to our need for reparenting.

We can channel negative thoughts into forgiveness and love. If we had a child who forgot his homework, in his vulnerability at being suddenly aware of being exposed, and fear of what will happen to him, he might easily turn against himself: "I'm stupid!" Our job is to help that child identify and accept the feelings that are behind the judgment. "It's upsetting to be surprised like that. You're just feeling sad and scared about what the teacher will do. But you're not stupid. Everyone forgets things." We would also analyze what action would be appropriate: "We'll talk to the teacher tomorrow and tell her what happened. We'll take care of it together. And we'll figure out how to make sure you remember your homework next time." Then the child would most likely let go of his worry and return to being open to positive feelings. His vulnerability and need to feel in charge of his life would have been attended to, and he would feel supported in facing the future in partnership with his parents. Similarly, when we acknowledge and comfort our vulnerable and frightened feelings and take the action we can with a positive attitude, it will be easier to relax and turn the future over to our partner, God.

Is God on your team?

Some people can turn their thoughts to the promises of God and be released from the hold of negative thoughts by either remembering God or by will power. Others of us need to open ourselves to God by reparenting ourselves and healing wounds which interfere with receiving the messages from God. Reparenting gives us a second chance to be open and innocent. We are not destined to be shut down, burdened with the debilitating messages we have received from our families and the judgmental world. Positive thoughts come from an encouraging inner voice. If we did not have the benefit of hearing that voice from our parents, it is still not too late to get it from our logical adult self. Then we will be able to feel valuable and cared about, and will be able to be more open to God.

Negative thoughts are also an indication that we are feeling alone and disconnected from God, as if He did not exist at all. We are over-responsible, as if it is all up to us. Knowing that we do not have the power to guarantee our future, of course we feel scared and negative. Dwelling on negative thoughts and feeling depressed or anxious are signals that let us know we have forgotten God. Because we have a relationship with God, it is easier to look at what is our part and what is His. When we do our part, it is easier to turn the outcome over to God, because there is nothing left for us to do. We can then surrender any illusion of control, making it possible to feel relief and peace. If we forget that we are in relationship with God, we will think that it is all up to us. No wonder we experience fear, anxiety and depression!

There is an expression that basketball players use often: "Leave it all on the court." This is how they remind themselves to put all the energy and determination they can into playing their best. Teams that do not feel like they left it all on the court are usually angry about the outcome of the game. Players who lose after playing with this attitude will feel no less disappointed, but they can also feel at peace, for they know that they did all that they could. "We gave it our all, they gave it their all, and they won." These players are surrendered to the outcome. The difference in their attitudes is not based on the actions of God, but rather on the difference in their human effort.

Get out there and give it your all!

Hard times come and we are likely to react like a deer in headlights - in a total panic. We either freeze, all the power to act knocked out of us, or we leap into the domain of the future, panicking about what is going to happen next. We are flooded with feeling our vulnerability and helplessness as we recognize how very out of control we are when it really matters. We often forget, in times of adversity, that we are half of a winning team. When we feel vulnerable or scared, it is easy to get stuck in negative thoughts and forget that there are things we can do to give us the best chance possible of having the life we want.

If we had a physical wound, we would not just expect God to heal us. We would know that we need to do our part, as well. If we saw a child at the bottom of a pool, we would not just pray for him to be saved. We would do our part by jumping in to get him. We have the power to be in active partnership with God, and not just feel helpless and dependent on Him.

Al: Many people write books which never are published. It would have been easy for us to get stuck in the negative thought that this book would be one of those. We could have become discouraged and pessimistic, and have given up out of fear. By being an active part of God's team, we followed our dream and did our part: stay in the present, word by word, do the best that we can do, and keep a positive attitude. Then our part was done, and we needed to separate from the outcome. God will determine the future. It was easy to then go to faith and peace, having done everything that was ours to do.

We all have the temptation to get stuck in negative thoughts. As a child, I did not feel supported in what I wanted to do. My parents seemed disinterested in the sports programs that were so important to me. I was always so sad about that, and felt that my dreams did not matter. But now I can feel separate from them and see that my parents were lost and unhappy in their individual lives and in their marriage. They did not realize how they were affecting me. It will always be a sadness that I missed out on feeling supported in my dreams and interests, but I now know that I can encourage myself.

When I felt vulnerable about my ability to write this book I supported myself in my dream. For most of my life I would not take risks. I believed what my parents taught me by not supporting me - that my dreams would never be realized. I quit sports because no one believed in me. When my fear tried to control me with thoughts that the book will never be published, I reminded myself that all I can do is to believe in myself no matter what the odds are and do the best I can in each moment. Doing this, I could then feel my positive expectation and hope: "God, I did everything I could to make this dream come true. I just know you will take it the rest of the way, and soon I'll be appearing on Oprah to share my work!"

Perhaps you had parents who did not encourage you to be your best self. Perhaps they did not know what to do when you had your own ideas about how life should be. Perhaps they discouraged you from being a powerful human being. Perhaps it was just easier for them if you were seen but not heard, if you just went outside to play or watched television and kept quiet. But it does not have to be that way anymore. You have the opportunity, now, to be a part of the most powerful team imaginable, where you do not have to be passive and submissive ever again, hiding your strength and ideas.

It's all part of the game

The biggest problem with difficult circumstances is that like football players in a pileup, we are tangled in the situation and our feelings so much that it is impossible to call the next play. We understandably feel overwhelmed, weighted down, unable to move. But, just like the football players, if we can separate from the situation, untangle ourselves enough to see what is going on, we can know that it is not about us. It is just what is happening outside of us.

Remember the idea of receiving homework from God and question yourself, "What do I have to learn here?" Just like a student, we can move into doing the appropriate steps: keep a positive attitude, do the best we can without judgment, and release the future to God. You are not a team of one.

Just as a quarterback drops back to assess where his receivers and the defensive backs are and if the play he outlined will work, we can also drop back from a difficult situation. This is not something personal to us. Things just happen, even to good people. We all must have challenges in life, just because we are alive. Quarterbacks are not shocked when a play fails. It is a part of the game and they are wise enough to expect it. It is not pleasant to have a pass intercepted or go incomplete, but even a great quarterback can expect that to happen almost 50% of the times he releases the ball.

Stuck?

Our life follows our thoughts and feelings. If they are negative, we are stuck, somehow. People tend toward the positive and the good. We have good hearts and are generous. If we are acting in any other way, fear is guiding us, rather than compassion. If we are stuck, we need to find the healing to remedy being trapped. We need to understand why we are stuck. It is not just that we are stubborn, lazy or stupid. We do not take any pleasure in acting in self-defeating ways. We are just incredibly frightened, and are holding on for dear life, even if it is not logical to be holding on to negative thoughts. If we were not stuck, we would certainly do what is logical!

Nothing is wrong with you, and you are not doing anything wrong when you get stuck in negative thoughts. How can you know how to do something you never learned to do? You never learned any better way to survive, and your vulnerable, frightened self is overwhelmed and doing the best he can. But now it is time to get him help. You can take charge of your mind. When you understand the feelings which trigger negative thoughts, you will be able to comfort and rescue him. Our logical adult self can watch for nonlogical thoughts and feelings and reparent us into what we logically know to be true. We have the opportunity, now, to choose differently than our parents taught us to choose. We have the power, now, to take charge of our minds and go for broke to become the capable people we want to be.

We will be able to release the future to God once we are at peace with our human issues: our vulnerability, separateness, limited control and right to exist. Once we take the action that we can in the present, it will be easier to leave the future to God.

We are on a spiritual quest to be close to God, but we live in human bodies. If we are not able to leap through our doubt and fear to reach God, we still have the opportunity to heal our hearts so that we can open to receive Him.

Chapter 12

~ *Keep a Good Attitude* ~

Jan: When I was young, I really didn't like Pollyanna. I thought she was icky sweet and not realistic. "What about her angry and negative feelings!" I asked myself. "What about feeling the pain of life!" I demanded. But I have come to realize that she understood something I did not. She experienced sad and angry feelings, but she knew how to let them go. She knew that the only way to have a successful life was to live in gratitude, hope and faith, and to do the best that she could, releasing the future to God. Now, I want to be just like her! So, I have started a Pollyanna Club. I'm PollyJan, the president. My husband is PollyAl, and you can all join, too!

(Al: Look, this is a great club, but I will <u>not</u> be called "PollyAl!" You can call me "Bad Dude!")

Pain serves a purpose

We have an instinctive desire to avoid pain. Of course we do not want to experience pain. But to *expect* that we *should not* experience pain is a different thing, altogether. It is unrealistic to think that we should have a perfect life in which hard things do not happen to us. And yet we get upset or angry when they do, as if they *shouldn't* have happened. It is one thing to not like pain - who would? But it is another to fight the reality of it being a part of life. It is as though we are throwing a tantrum about how we are designed to learn.

We have all had painful experiences. We remember pain. It alerts us to pay attention. It pulls us into a special awareness, away from the normal flow of our lives. It is the signal to be careful. It often directs us to specific helpful or life preserving action. At the physical level, it helps to keep us alive. If we were to step on a nail, the sensations of pain compel us to take action. If we were numb and felt nothing, we might never even notice until an infection threatened our life. Pain does not feel good, but it is our ally.

Al: My father died abruptly, leaving me no time to express and resolve feeling we had for each other. I was stricken, for it was over and I would never have the opportunity to talk with him, again. I realized that my mother was dying, and that I had still had the chance to communicate with her. I could make sure I spent time with her, doing and saying everything that was important to me, so that when she died, I would not have the experience of emptiness and incompleteness, as I had with my father.

Pain is a survival tool. Its purpose is to help us learn. The more painful an experience is, the more we will pay attention and be committed to preventing it from recurring. This is a wonderful gift. If we were not designed this way, we would be doomed to endless repetition of painful behaviors. Pain imprints our minds so that we automatically avoid that repetition. It is a good thing to be able to have survival instincts.

Memories of pain are very accessible to us so that we have a better chance to survive. They come instantly to the forefront of our minds at the slightest trigger that reminds us of the painful event. They help us choose better alternatives. They are to use, and then release. We can congratulate ourselves for learning, and then let the memories go, knowing we have used them well.

The difficulty is that we often get stuck in the painful memories. Getting stuck is the signal that we are not at peace with our nature as an evolving being who learns through hindsight. It may also be a signal that we may not have discovered the important information contained in the experience, and so it haunts us. When we use our painful memories, and recognize how they help us, we can even have a good attitude about pain. Remembering that pain is in our service, we can look for the information and lessons it holds so we will be able to avoid getting stuck.

Our vulnerability helps us survive

There are two aspects of vulnerability. One is the lovely quality of open-heartedness and sensitivity that most of us are drawn to. Vulnerability is what allows us to love and feel compassion. When we experience joy or are able to play and enjoy ourselves, we are feeling vulnerable.   Creativity also comes from the openness and non-judgment of vulnerability.

The other aspect of vulnerability is the role that it plays in our survival. It helps us be aware of when we are endangered and need to react in a way to ensure our safety. We experience the survival aspect of vulnerability as fear.   It is important to be conscious of our vulnerability so we can analyze the danger, do what is appropriate to the situation, and soothe our fear.   If we do not take action, it is possible to get stuck in negative thoughts of being a victim, and negative feelings of anxiety and helplessness.

When we feel exposed or afraid, our bodies will release the adrenaline needed to help us have the energy to take care of ourselves. Our bodies, flooded with adrenaline, cannot tell the difference between life endangering situations and embarrassing or emotional situations. We need to be aware that at the physical level, the experience is the same. Perhaps your boss asks you to give a talk on a project you are doing, and adrenaline floods your body, as you experience your vulnerability. You are not facing a wooly mammoth, but your body does not know this. It only senses danger and gives you the energy to throw your spear or run! When we experience fear, we can remind ourselves that nothing is wrong - we are just feeling vulnerable.   We are being alerted to take care of ourselves. And, when there is nothing to do to change our external situation, we still have the opportunity to change our internal reality - to be compassionate and comforting to our feelings.

As with the experience of pain, it is easy to forget that vulnerability is in our service. It increases the positive quality of life and helps us survive. But there is another service it provides for us that is even more important. It serves as an opening to God. When we are vulnerable, we are emotionally open and able to hear guidance from God that we might miss if we were busy trying to be guarded and in control. Just as in times of creativity, we are an open channel, receptive to information and awareness we might otherwise not receive. Being aware of the bigness of everything and our small part in it leaves lots of room to connect with God. If we try to avoid the experience of vulnerability, mistaking it for something we should not feel, we will miss out on an enormous and powerful positive force of guidance and love that can flow through us. Realizing this, it will be easier to maintain a positive attitude, even if our physical adrenalized reaction is telling us that we are in danger.

Control your controlling

The desire and ability to control ourselves and our environment are also survival tools. Control is the attempt to protect ourselves. When we are driving and try to anticipate what actions other drivers may take, we are not having negative thoughts. We are having protective thoughts.

Asking ourselves "What do I need to do right now?" is helpful for our survival. It is control in the present moment. We also need to think about actions to take in the present moment to keep us safe in the future: "I need to pay my insurance so it does not expire." But often our minds take us out of the present moment and make us the central figure in a scary story: "If I don't do this, my world will collapse!" Scary stories are signals that we are leaving the appropriate arena of our control, and entering into God's domain of the future. "I'm scared that if I leave this relationship I will always be alone" is a common scary thought. We cannot know that this fearful thought is true, however, and there is nothing for us to do in this moment about such a thought, except be paralyzed with fear! Such thoughts try to protect us on an instinctive level – "Don't move!" - as an animal's vulnerability might keep him from leaving his "safe" territory.   All we can do is grab hold of our frightened self, take the *right* action in the present, knowing it is only fear speaking in scary thoughts, and trust the future to God. For all we know, we will meet a wonderful person we would not have had the opportunity to bring into our lives if we had remained in the old relationship.

Al: Many years ago, when I had just formed a barbershop quartet, we performed for a large audience in Crescent City, California. Because the group was so new, I was very concerned about the impression we would make on other singers in the show. Not only was I trying to be focused and prepared for my part - singing and being the front man who introduced the songs and interacted with the audience - I felt nervous about the performance of the others in my group, and tried to control everything backstage so that we were ready and prepared. Once on stage, I was scared that they would forget their parts or not sing well.

The mind is set up to try to control. It is able to think of many alternatives. It is able to quickly evaluate situations and determine the appropriate actions. These are wonderful and life-preserving abilities. If we do not carefully watch ourselves, however, the tool of our mind can get misguided and try to take over, thinking that if it is not in control of everything, we will not be safe. It will work overtime, even when it is not needed, seeing danger where it does not exist, and trying to control what is not in our domain to control. Although these attempts to control are trying to be of service to our survival, they are misguided. They do not leave us open to the positive aspects of vulnerability, which help us create a bigger and better life.

Al: I introduced "Blue Moon," and the bass singer began to sing the opening notes of "Barbara Ann." The other three of us panicked. I walked up to the microphone and asked the bass if he would mind singing "Blue Moon," instead. The audience started to laugh, thinking we were doing a comedy routine. Now, really nervous and embarrassed, the bass began again to sing the opening notes.... of "Barbara Ann!" The audience was in hysterics! I went to the mike, again, complimented the bass on his nice voice, but reminded him that we were singing "Blue Moon" right now. Now, I know you're thinking it couldn't *happen* again... *but it did! All the blood drained from our faces, and the audience was writhing and shrieking with laughter. Once again we tried to start. This time, while the audience continued howling, our bass began to sing the correct song... but it was all too much for our lead singer, who fell on the stage, laughing with the audience, and couldn't continue. We got a standing ovation, and have been an extremely successful comedy quartet ever since!*

If we try to control everything because we are afraid, we will miss out on some wonderful surprises in life! Sometimes the best things come to us when we feel vulnerable and open to what God brings our way.

Gratitude takes practice

We are idealistic beings. We can imagine things that cannot exist. We can actually even create some of these things, with our clever and inventive minds. But we cannot create everything we can envision. We cannot create perfection or a life without pain. So while it is useful to have the instincts which help us survive by taking control of what is happening around us, if we are not careful, we can become stuck in this control mode. Our controlling minds can get stuck in overdrive. Unattended vulnerability can cause us to live constantly flooded with fearful memories and thoughts, and with adrenaline, which will cause us to feel anxious. Over time, we can even lose the specifics of the memories and thoughts, and just live in the fear and negativity, adrenaline coursing through our body without our even knowing why.

Gratitude is an antidote to this. It helps us maintain our good attitude. It takes practice to live in gratitude. We need to practice it the same as we practice any new skill or behavior. Positive memories are not the powerful survival aids that pain is. They do not have the same urgency, and so they tend to fall into the back of our minds. We can remedy this tendency by deliberately choosing to bring positive memories into the forefront of our consciousness. We can choose to train our minds so that we create a positive way of thinking. When there is no emergency to focus on, we can develop the ability to rest in our positive memories and feelings. We can develop an attitude and habit of living in gratitude. When we focus on our blessings and positive memories, we are creating an openness of heart that will allow us to experience gratitude.

In every moment, there are so many things to be grateful for. If we really paid attention to every sensation, every feeling of each moment, we would be overcome by all of the goodness in our lives. How often we look without seeing. We race through our daily existence not living in the miracle of all that we have. We will always have challenges, but we can even be grateful for them because they allow us to grow. When we remember gratitude, negative thoughts and feelings cannot take us over.

Jan: I was picking blackberries on a beautiful summer day, standing in a creek while my dog snacked on grass nearby, sometimes coming over to lick my knee - her way to ask for a berry or two. After filling my bucket, I slipped, and a good amount of berries spilled into the creek. I responded with sharp irritation. It was such a wonderful day, and I had been feeling such lovely peace, that I shocked myself, and I realized how quickly I had gone to the negative just because I lost a few berries. But how many berries had I picked, and not thanked God for them? So I returned to picking, but this time, with each berry that I successfully picked and put in my bucket, I said, "Thank you, God." And remembered how blessed I really am.

When we have negative thoughts or a negative experience, we can use gratitude to help us free ourselves. For example, all of us have felt lonely. We can comfort ourselves, but remember that this loneliness is just the feeling of this moment. We do not know what will happen in the future, and we do not need to frighten ourselves with scary stories. When we feel vulnerable and raw in our loneliness, of course we may be sad, but we can remind ourselves that our vulnerability is also a good thing. We are open-hearted and sensitive. We will be able to receive the friendship and love that come our way. Our vulnerability opens us up to being receptive. The sadness we are feeling is just the experience of *this* moment.

Life is like reading a good mystery novel. You don't stop in the middle, at the most scary and mysterious part, afraid to go on. If we did that in life, we would be filled with anxiety and negative thinking. Just as in the book, there will be an ending - we just cannot know it yet. The future will reveal itself to us. All we need to do is pay attention to the page we are on right now. We can have the attitude that God will make the book of our life full and rewarding.

Create a Memory Album

Most of us have photo albums to hold precious glimpses of events and people important in our lives. In the same way, we can create a Memory Album to collect cherished memories and feelings about experiences and people. We can either make it in our minds, or make a real book in which we can list or journal the many blessings we have been fortunate to receive, and the positive memories of people and times in our lives. We can review our Memory Album in order to saturate ourselves with gratitude. Memories will become more accessible to us, as we make this a regular part of our daily life. The positive thoughts and feelings will become a part of us. This is similar to having a song stuck in your mind. We will have gratitude as the background against which every other feeling and event is overlaid. With this background, other feelings cannot last too long, for our gratitude will be the home base that we always return to.

Al: I feel like I have struggled my whole life with having a negative and pessimistic outlook. The experiences I had in my childhood created a foundation I could not shake, despite the wonderful experiences and loving people I have had in my adulthood. When my mind is quiet or I'm facing adversity or challenges, what immediately comes to the front of my mind is a negative or pessimistic expectation. I realized that unless I created a system in which to collect positive thoughts and expectations that I could focus on when I needed to, that my life would be dominated by negativity.

All of us have had positive moments and experiences, even if they were little ones. We can gather those memories, and note them in a journal.

Al: In this moment, the first thing that occurs to me is a memory from 6th grade, of my teacher, Dr. Valley. He had a crew cut and wore a freshly starched white shirt every day. He wore shoes with taps, and we could always hear him coming down the hall. He was really smart, a great athlete and a great teacher. I loved and admired him. I remember him standing next to my desk explaining something to me. I feel so grateful in this moment for what he gave me. In the midst of a hard childhood and a difficult school situation, he was a beacon of light. I wish I could thank him. Right now I am imagining myself doing that. He smiles in return.
Memory Album entry: My 6th grade teacher Dr. Valley.

I used to love hamburgers more than anything in the world (except Jan, of course.) I only ate them at home or at fast food franchises. Then someone told me to go to a place called Hamburger Hamlet. I remembered ordering a hamburger the first time I went there. I took a bite and thought I was in heaven!
Right now, I remember that hamburger and how it tasted. My mouth is watering as I speak! Boy, was that good. Even now it is.
Memory Album entry: First experience at Hamburger Hamlet.

Last week I was driving to the market after work. I turned right, but I wasn't watching the road very well. A pedestrian was crossing the street. I almost hit her. I felt embarrassed and upset and stopped and looked at her sheepishly. She said she was fine (thank, God). But the look in her eyes was amazing. The look in her eyes seemed to be communicating that she was forgiving me and telling me she had made a similar mistake before. I felt relieved and felt camaraderie with this stranger. It was a great feeling!
Memory Album entry: The eyes of the woman I almost hit.

I went to the store yesterday and bought some gas treatment to put in my car. I only had that one item. The checker looked exhausted. She said "Do you want a bag for that?" I was surprised to hear what came out of my mouth, "No. I'll drink it here!" We both cracked up. She looked like she hadn't smiled all day. I don't think I had, either. We laughed hard and said goodbye. As I was leaving the store, I could hear her repeating the story of our interaction to the next customer, and they were both laughing!

Memory Album entry: "No, I'll drink my gas treatment here."

I don't remember a lot of good things about my mom (she died when I was 20). I do remember this. I was around eight and had an extremely high fever. I was hallucinating, and told my mom that a piano was lying on my chest. It was a horrible sensation. I can sort of feel it now. I couldn't breathe. I kept crying to her "Get it off of me!" Amazingly, she put both of her hands on my chest, and struggled to pull the piano off of me! Then she told me that she had been successful. I fell asleep and woke up with my fever almost completely gone.

Memory Album entry: Get that piano off of my chest!

I work with many people who have a lot of physical pain (MS, arthritis, cancer, back pain.) The other day when I was driving home from work, I just started thinking –"I don't have ANY chronic pain, and I rarely think about how lucky I am." So, I'm doing that right now.

Memory Album entry: Right now, I don't have any pain in my body. How lucky!

One Christmas a few years ago, I got up and looked at the tree, and my kids, and Jan and just started weeping, thinking how fortunate I am.

Memory Album entry: Me, weeping at Christmas

I was watching the movie "All of Me" with Jan, when a scene came on that was so funny, we just about died of laughter. I remember both of us, laughing so hard we could barely breathe, tears pouring out of our eyes, glancing over at each other and sharing our pleasure.

Memory Album entry: Laughing with Jan till we cried, at "All of Me."

I could go on and on. But here is my Memory Album right now:

1. *My 6th grade teacher Dr. Valley*
2. *First experience at Hamburger Hamlet*
3. *The eyes of the woman I almost hit.*
4. *No, I'll drink my gas treatment here*
5. *Get that piano off of my chest!*
6. *Right now, I don't have any pain in my body. How lucky!*

7. Me, weeping at Christmas.

8. Laughing with Jan till we cried, at "All of Me."

My Memory Album keeps getting bigger. These memories create pictures in my mind that I can access whenever I want, and wherever I am. I start every day, for five minutes or more, "looking" through my Album, calling up my memories. I take a few moments to allow the good feelings of each one I focus on to fill me up. I feel such gratitude that I have been able to have these experiences. These are my memories! How lucky can a person get? At first it was hard to find good memories, but as I realized that they don't have to be "big" events, it got easier. Now I usually find at least one new memory to add to my Album, each day.

We can cultivate the experience of gratitude. We have all had thousands of simple moments that we each feel grateful for. We can practice calling up in our mind and body the experience of gratitude and positive feelings. We can visit gratitude daily, hourly, or however often we need to. The experience of gratitude floods our bodies with chemicals which make us feel good and help to bring us peace.

Choosing to focus on gratitude gives us the power to turn away from negative thoughts and replace them with remembering that our lives are filled with good experiences. Gratitude helps us be happy in our lives and fill ourselves with good feelings. Negative thoughts are based on the idea that life should not be so hard. Gratitude is based on the idea that we are fortunate in so many ways in our life. It opens us to all of the infinite positive possibilities that exist in life that we so easily can forget when challenges come our way.

God's domain

The experiences of pain, vulnerability and the need to control are all survival tools. They are God-given, and allow us to pay attention and take care of ourselves in each moment. They call us to awareness and action so we can do our part in the partnership with God. But after doing our part, it is crucial that we release the future to God and allow ourselves to be in the mystery, in the unknown, rather than try to control what will happen.

We can never know what is coming next or what God's intentions are in having us go through our experiences. It is so easy to get scared and project into the future. "I'm lonely and will be lonely for the rest of my life" versus "In this moment I am alone and I do not know what will happen in the future." Our job is to do what we can in the present, comfort ourselves where we are helpless, and keep a good attitude so we can be receptive to what will be available to us in the future. If we scare ourselves, we will be shut down and not able to recognize the blessings that come our way. We can release the past and forgive ourselves for what we did not know to do. We can release the future to God. All we have to do is focus on doing this moment well. And the more we turn the pages of our Memory Album, the more we will live in gratitude and peace.

Chapter 13

~ *Believe in Infinite Possibility* ~

Considering how immense the Universe is, we are amazingly tiny little creatures. Even our Earth has forces that are so powerful that they determine much of our lives. Storms come, we must take shelter. Earthquakes destroy our homes, we must rebuild. Seasons cycle, we must prepare food. There is nothing wrong with the fact that we cannot control these forces. It is simply the nature of our reality. But we are *impacted* by this reality. We are instinctively aware of how very small and vulnerable we are and are vigilantly alert to anything that threatens our survival. We are designed to notice possible danger. And we have the ability to meet the challenges of our world. We do not always overcome, for catastrophes and tragedies occur, but we can always triumph by doing what we can, living in faith and believing in the existence of infinite possibility.

<u>When things go wrong, do you freeze or bolt?</u>

As limited beings, we cannot comprehend the totality of what is occurring in our lives or in the world. We only are aware of what is happening in front of our noses. We just know the small experience of what we are feeling and seeing. That is enough to make *anyone's* adrenaline surge! And the adrenaline will trigger one of two impulses: fight or flight. When we are surprised by life, we might freeze, unable to act, or, in our panic, we may bolt into unconsidered action. Neither comes from a clear and calm place of thoughtful consideration of what is happening. Both are reactions to our fear. Because of our limited vision of the future, our typical reaction is to be overwhelmed or frightened. Filled with adrenaline, it is not natural for us to react with patience or with faith. But, trying to take control when we are not clear and calm does not allow for possibilities beyond our awareness to occur.

As young adults we were traveling in what was then Czechoslovakia. At that time, tourists needed to declare how many days they intended to stay in the country, and were required to change a certain amount of money into Czech money for each day.   We exchanged 14 days' worth, but decided to leave after nine days. When we got to the border, the guards told us that the money could not be exchanged back because we had not stayed long enough. When we protested, they told us they would mail the money to us in the United States. We did not have a lot of money for this trip as we were poor students, and we needed that money for the trip expenses.   Besides, we really did not believe them.

We didn't know what to do.   We thought of going to the American Embassy in Prague and getting them to fight for us.   We thought of just leaving so that we didn't have to deal with any conflict.   Both seemed wrong. We decided to do neither.   We returned to town and spent the night.   When we returned the next day, there were different guards, and they exchanged our money without question.   Neither of these possibilities had occurred to us.   We were grateful that in this situation we did not have to fight, get angry or take action in our defense.   All we had to do was tolerate our helplessness for a while and wait.

We fight accepting the reality of what is happening by becoming frozen in horror and disbelief, by giving up, or by taking *any* action that gives us the illusion of having some kind of power.   If we can accept that we are ultimately helpless about the outcome of situations in life, we have tremendous power available to us.   Our power lies in instantly yielding control.   What is happening is bigger than we are.   We cannot see the situation in its context.   We only see this one moment, and *our fear comes from thinking the future will be a continuation of this moment.*

We have all been in a situation where we are expecting someone to show up at a certain time, and they do not appear as we expected.   At first, we may get annoyed, and then, as time keeps passing, get angry.   If enough time goes by, most of us begin to feel afraid.   But just imagine that when they do finally show up, they are holding the present they stopped to pick up for us! Here we were, feeling vulnerable and helpless, alternating between the negative emotions of fear and anger, *never having considered* the positive possibility that they were delayed because they were doing something nice for us!

God is the endless possibility of the Universe. We are always on the lookout for the dangerous aspects of life. But there also exist infinite positive possibilities that are the domain of God. What we see is determined by our survival instincts. We notice what is wrong or different from what we want, and call that danger. God is the part of possibility that we have not considered. We react from our vulnerability and expect negative outcomes. God represents the miracle. God is everything that is not us: positive possibilities, miracles, cure, and invincibility. Our survival instincts make us focus, in our vulnerability and fear, on negative possibilities. If we comfort that fear and stay positive, we will be aligned with infinite possibility, because that is what God is. We stay open to more than we can imagine or envision.

We live in a small world

Try something: get down on your knees so that you can put your nose about two inches from the floor. How far does your vision extend from down there? Are there many possibilities that you are aware of, from that position? You know without any doubt that the world is much bigger than you can see from that position, but it is not visible. And what you probably *are* aware of are specks of dirt you had not noticed before. You notice what is wrong.

We are limited, finite physical beings. We can only see things that a finite physical being can see. And a large part of what we notice are things that are not what we want or that are dangerous to our survival.

Imagine that you are in a large, beautiful garden, surrounded by exquisite flowers and trees. Suddenly a bee starts buzzing around you. Most of us would center our attention on that one tiny aspect of the garden. Our sense of vulnerability and danger would make us focus on the one thing that could go wrong. Because we feel out of control, the bee is what catches and keeps our attention. We focus on trying to control the situation and get away from that bee. Everything else disappears from our awareness until we feel safe. And if there are enough bees in the garden, we might never be able to see anything other than the threat to our well-being. We could live in the most exquisite place possible, and yet have our eyes and attention go from one danger to the next.

God's world is big!

Life is like that garden. Only God can see it in its entirety. God knows that we cannot see the whole of life. Our ability to see clearly is made worse by the fact that our attention is drawn to things that make us feel vulnerable and out of control, that threaten our emotional or physical well-being. Because we are designed to notice what will help us survive, we are not aware of all that is around us.

We cannot expect ourselves to see what God can. But we can allow ourselves to have faith that more exists beyond our limited awareness. Remember the view from inches above the floor. Did you really believe that there was nothing more than the little you could see? Faith and logic kept you from panicking and thinking that the rest of the world had disappeared. (If anyone had suggested such a possibility, you would actually think that he was crazy! And yet we live in the fear that what we see is all that exists.) That same faith and logic can allow you to believe that there is more happening in your world than you can know.

We humans are conscious of only the tip of the iceberg of possibility. Our brain receives *billions* of bits of information every *second*! We are only aware of the tiniest fraction of them, and our awareness is primarily about our body, the environment and time. Reality is being recorded in our brains all the time. In a 16 hour day of wakefulness, our brains have received *millions* of *billions* of bits of information, but there is no way we are able to be aware of them all, or integrate them into usefulness. But all of that information is there, and even more is happening that escapes the notice of our brains! It is only logical and reasonable to think that there are also more possibilities than we could ever be aware of. It is absolutely impossible for a finite being to see the whole picture. There is no way you could ever know why something is happening or what the outcome could be.

We already know the fearful possibilities - our survival instincts help us be watchful for whatever is coming around the corner. We are equipped with fear and negativity to help us prepare. We are destined to live with being vulnerable and having limited control. If we are at peace with these truths, then we can choose, in spite of it all, to keep a positive attitude. That opens up the entire Universe for us. We would then be making room for possibilities that lie beyond our power and our comprehension, in the infinite, in God.

What we can do

There is a relationship between the present - what we can do - and the future - what lies in the infinite. We are not completely powerless when something happens, for there are steps we can take to bridge the present and the future.

1. Notice what is happening.

2. Allow yourself to feel your reaction to what is happening without judging yourself or making up a scary story about the future.

3. Breathe! Take care of your vulnerable self.

4. Remember you only know the smallest amount about what is happening.

5. Let yourself feel your limited control without feeling hopeless.

6. Choose to have a positive attitude about the outcome.

7. Take any action within your control that you can take.

8. Expect help! (It may not come in the form you immediately want, but we cannot know God's plan.)

When our son Seth was three, we vacationed in Germany. At the Frankfurt airport, the third largest in the world, at that time, we turned around for two seconds and he suddenly disappeared. He had light blond hair which usually made him stand out anywhere, but here in Germany, most of the children seemed to have that same hair color, and we could not see him anywhere. Our first reaction was to panic, but we instantly calmed ourselves down and refused to make up a horrible ending to this situation. We trusted that although it was such an enormous place (with three levels!) we would find him. We contacted security to help us search for him, and walked through the airport (trying not to scream hysterically) knowing we were doing everything we could do. We knew that the only other thing we could do was pray for God to help us. That help came in the form of a question which suddenly came to our minds, "Where would a three year old child go?" And sure enough, we found a toy store, and there he was, playing quite happily.

As frightening as situations may be, all we can do is walk through the process we outlined above. It is the only way to open ourselves to take action in the most positive way possible, and to receive guidance beyond what our minds, in their panic and fear, can think of. Of course we will feel intense emotions and the temptation to panic, but our logical adults can steer us through the steps needed to give us the greatest chance possible to maximize our power and align ourselves with the possibility of positive outcomes.

<u>What you see *isn't* what you *can* get</u>

Our reality is a reflection of what we expect. This picture of the world is created and limited by our emotions and experiences. We build models of what the world outside our body is. And then we live in the reality which we have created as if it were *the* reality.

We are only able to comprehend the tiniest bit of what exists and is happening in the Infinite. Since we are limited in our perceptions, we limit our expectations, for we cannot conceive of all that could be. If our thinking is limited, then our choices about what we pursue will be limited.

Al: When I walked onto the stage with my quartet in Crescent City, the possibility of becoming a comedy quartet <u>did not exist</u>. I had no idea that I was about to have a life changing experience. If I had clung to my limited vision and had rigidly continued to try to control the quartet and our performance, I would not have been able to shift into the new possibility that presented itself and that has brought so much joy into my life.

We can open ourselves to question and explore, rather than assume that the small view of the world that we can perceive is the totality of all existence. Remember, our vision of all that is possible is as limited as our view of the room was, when we had our noses two inches from the floor. The more we believe for positive possibility, the more we will be developing our ability to see and create positive possibility. We can enlarge our vision through faith to include the reality of infinite possibilities, even though we cannot be aware of the specifics of what they are.

Opening to possibilities

Something happens when we live knowing that there is so much more than we can see. This allows us to live with questions, rather than false certainty, and to be open to discovery. We can live in the knowledge that there is infinite possibility, remembering that only by staying open will we ever be able to see differently. If we are open, our brains seem to work in a different process. Pieces of information are put together in ways that cannot be arranged by logical thought.

Einstein reported that inspiration, not logical reasoning, gave him his greatest ideas. He was on a quest to "know God's thoughts," for to him "the rest are details." Einstein contemplated the Universe, realizing, without knowing the specifics, that he faced the unlimited and infinite possibilities that are God.

We have all had little experiences of ideas or solutions just coming to us - perhaps nothing on the scale that Einstein experienced, but in the same category.

Jan: One Christmas we were having a lot of trouble getting our tree to stand up straight. We always get a tree and stick it in a bucket of stones. For some reason, this year, we couldn't figure out why it wasn't working. We finally took a break to clear our minds. I kept walking by that tree, as I did other tasks, peering at it sidelong, trying to open my mind to allow the answer to come. And it did. I suddenly realized what we were doing wrong, and we were able to set it up easily.

"Remembering" is another example of how we all open ourselves up to receive. There is no active process that we can engage in to remember something. Instead, we open our minds so that we are in the passive and receptive state which allows information to come forward to be retrieved.

By opening ourselves, in vulnerability and humility, factors of existence get put together in ways that would not have happened had we tried to stay in control and think in our logical, left-brained way. This is *living in the question.* By living in this openness and receptivity, we make room for amazing things to happen.

Most of us live in varying degrees of fear. We are guided by our awareness of negative possibility. We shut ourselves down, making our world small, in an attempt to protect ourselves. While we can succeed in making our world small, we will never be successful in protecting ourselves. Life happens, anyway. The alternative is to be guided by the dreams and hopes that lie in our hearts. If we live in openness to possibilities, we will be able to receive information we could not have conceived of with our minds. Having the positive expectation and determination to follow our dreams and hopes will enable us to change our old patterns and choices, and our lives will change.

Reality is neither set nor unchangeable. We tend to either have the illusion that we can control things, or the illusion that we are powerless to impact our environment and our lives. If we can conceive of and imagine greater things, we have the ability to make choices which open up possibilities for ourselves. If we do not believe that we have the power to impact and help create our reality, we will hold back, defeated and passive, and guarantee that we have limited lives. When we allow ourselves to wonder, to live in openness, we become channels for God to work through. Whether God works through ideas and solutions about external things, or hopes and dreams within our hearts, it is still the working of God. When we conceive of and dream about greater things, we will be able to take our real power to be in active partnership with God and make possible lives of victory.

<u>Our language shapes our reality</u>

We cannot separate ourselves from our emotions. Every aspect of every process of our body is under the influence of emotion. Chemicals accompany every emotion and serve to reinforce our memories of experiences. This is a survival tool. The moment we experience an emotion, a corresponding chemical is released into our bloodstream. Our bodies get used to certain chemicals. Negative words and thoughts create destructive chemicals which flood our bodies and weaken us. If we change how we react, the chemicals that are released will change, as well. Negative words and thoughts reflect our attempt to protect ourselves from surprise or pain. They come from our desire to survive and guard against danger, but they are describing our limited vision. When we are surprised, we usually say things like:

"That can't happen."   "I don't believe it!"
"No way!"   "That's impossible!"

Or in response to a person, we may say:

"I don't believe you."   "You're lying."
"You can't be serious."   "What are you talking about?"

These responses reflect our reaction when the illusion of certainty and control is ripped away from us by an unexpected or inexplicable event or action. If we are to stay open to possibilities, we can train ourselves to stay with just feeling surprised, using appropriate language that helps us avoid going into negative reaction:

"Wow! That's a surprise!"   "That's a shock."
"I never expected that!"   "How did that happen!?"
"What do you mean?"   "I don't understand."

Anything can happen to anyone at any time, because we are all vulnerable and have limited control. We do not have to be able to anticipate it or understand it. That is beyond our ability. We can remind ourselves of this without it being a scary statement. While it reflects our lack of control, it also reflects infinite positive possibilities. With so much possible that we cannot even begin to imagine, why would we waste our energy being focused on and talking about negative possibilities?

Our power lies in being able to change ourselves. "Negative" emotions like fear and pain help us to be able to recognize the limitations we put on ourselves. They are the calls to action from our souls. As we guide our vulnerable child self, we can also watch for negativity. Rather than getting stuck in it, we can remind ourselves that we are just feeling vulnerable. We can instantly switch to a logical truth that is more neutral, like "I don't know" or "I don't understand." We can remind ourselves that our hopes can direct our actions into the unknown realm of positive possibility, leaving us open to outcomes and results we cannot even begin to imagine. We can begin to use words that comfort us, like "I will be okay." Whatever outcome occurs, we have the control over our attitude and our choice to live in faith.

Our words can soothe the old negative emotions, therefore changing the chemicals which flood our bodies. Neutral or more hopeful and positive emotions will literally bring a new chemical reality inside us which allows us to transform ourselves from being frightened and limited to being open and positive. This new attitude then opens up the entire realm of the Infinite – what is not ours to know in this moment, but which is out there, nonetheless: God's domain.

Chapter 14

~ *Moving Through Grief* ~

Jan: When my mother died, I thought I would die, too. I could not imagine life on this planet without her. I would ask myself and others, in despair, "How can you live if part of your heart has been ripped out of you?" I would notice other mothers and daughters, and wonder why she had been the one to die. And why so young? Being a psychologist, I understood the need to make room for the feelings of grief, and so I did. For three years. And nothing changed inside me. I was just as grief-stricken as the day she had died. I was stuck.

Accepting vulnerability and our limited control in life

Why do we get stuck in painful experiences? What keeps us from being able to comfort ourselves and move on? Why can't we let go of feelings that no one wants to have? Is there something wrong with us? Are we weak, wanting to wallow in self-pity, not wanting to get well? Do we get something out of being a "victim" in life? These reactions would be so self-defeating.

None of us *want* to suffer. All behavior, regardless of how illogical it appears, is our attempt to avoid something which seems as though it would be worse. What we call illogical, is really nonlogical. It belongs to the world of the emotions, not to the world of reason. Nonlogical behavior is the signal that there is a secret battle going on inside of us that we probably cannot even identify, let alone win. It is a secret battle against our vulnerability and our lack of control. Especially when something painful happens, we fight against feeling vulnerable and helpless. But because there is no way we will ever be invincible or in absolute control of outcomes, this is a battle that takes a tremendous toll on our well-being. This is a battle that we are doomed to lose.

Jan: I clearly remember the exact moment, three years after my Mom's death, when I was hit by a bolt of lightning, of enlightenment, from God. I was in my room, when I felt the electricity strike my body with a staggering blow, stopping me dead in my tracks. "I might never be happy again," I realized in terror. Maybe if I were 98 ½ years old and about to die, that might have been okay, but I had too much life to live, and I didn't want to live it in this kind of grief.

I suddenly knew that I had been asking myself the wrong questions. A part of my heart had <u>not</u> been ripped out of my body! I adored my Mom, but she was <u>separate</u> from me. We each walk this Earth having our own life experience, growing into as complete of a being as we can before we go home to God. She, although most beloved, was as irrelevant to my wholeness as anything else that is not me: my ring, my home, my shoe. I <u>love</u> her far more than those other external things, but God sent me here to grow as <u>His</u> child, not to hold onto her.

We are a "and they lived happily ever after" culture. We want to believe what we are taught in our fairy tales and movies. We want to think that if we could just figure out the right things to do then we would be able to control our future and not have to suffer with difficult situations or painful feelings. We would rather blame ourselves than accept our human fate. We would rather suffer from painful experiences than release them and feel our helplessness.

When we remember that we are here to learn and grow, then every experience is a learning experience. We can use our "misfortune" to become wiser and more complete. We need to remember to separate from the experience. It is happening, but it is external to us. It is homework for our souls. Even events that are deeply disappointing and painful are merely homework during our school days here on Earth in our human bodies. We need to and are able to learn from them.

Jan: I realized that my despairing questions were really my fight with God and reality. They were my disguised statements that "This <u>should not</u> be happening!" I had not wanted to feel my vulnerability and helplessness, so I *fought, not with anger, but with sadness. I was battling God, and I was losing, badly.*

It is not negative thinking to remember that we will all experience pain and loss in our lives. It is simply the truth of the human journey. If we are in denial of this, then our suffering will be worse, for we will be shocked when it is our turn to go through difficult human experiences. That shock will make it more difficult to let go and heal. Being shocked signals that we are not living in acceptance of what it means to be human.

Jan: As I stood there in my room, I could feel something changing deep within me. I was no less sad, but it was as though I had changed the channel on the television to a different station. I knew the grief would always be playing on that old station - how could I ever not be sad to have lost my Mom - but it was not my focus, anymore. I realized that a large part of my grief had been caused by my not being able to accept that such a loss was a part of the human journey. Though my words of grief sounded meek and sorrowful, they were really fighting words. I had taken a stand that "I should not have to feel these feelings. This experience is too great of a loss and should not have happened to me." But fortunately, something in me had opened to accept the reality that I was helpless to have it be any different, and that this was just my turn to experience my vulnerability and my loss.

If we have a realistic picture of human life, we will not be shocked when we feel vulnerable and out of control over things which matter to us. We will feel grief and disappointment when sad things happen, but we will remember that we are only experiencing the human journey. Things can be *painful* without being *wrong*. We can experience pain, but know that these things happen to other good people, as well. People die, are injured, get divorced... why would painful things not happen in our lives, too?

We do not have to like what happens to us, but it does not have to stop us from continuing to have a great life.

Jan: One thing that helped me let go of my Mom's death was telling myself "I don't have to ever like it, but I need to accept it." That allowed me to stop my "protest" of God's decision without feeling that I had to give up a part of myself, my sadness, to do so.

We still have power

If we have a realistic picture of human life, we will know how to stay centered when painful things occur. Accepting our vulnerability actually encourages our being empowered. We tend to have the illusion that we are in control: "If I want something to happen, it will." If, instead, we know that problems arise in every area of life, we will be prepared to step up into action, rather than be in denial or avoidance.

Most people get married with high hopes that they will be together forever. Of course we want this outcome, and have positive expectations that it will be true for us. No one gets married thinking "I'll do this for a while." Our marriage vows reflect this hope, promising to stay together through all that life sends our way. Yet the reality in our world is that too many marriages end in divorce.

If we accept that bad things can happen to us, too, we will be more likely to take action, rather than be passive and hope that by magic nothing will go wrong in our lives – we will be the lucky ones who "make" it. Marriage vows or attitudes could be "I'm going to do everything I can to stay in this marriage and keep our love strong. I will not leave without learning what I have contributed to the difficulties we are experiencing, and doing my very best to do it differently." This attitude would encourage us to pay attention sooner when problems arise, for they would not be as threatening. Rather than be horrified, or thinking that something is wrong with us or with our marriage because those problems exist, we would just roll up our shirt sleeves and get to work! We would also keep a sharper lookout for problems and tackle them when they are small, rather than going into denial and letting them build to the point that they seem overwhelming. If the marriage were to end in divorce, due to difficulties that were insurmountable, it would still be painful, but we would not be shocked or ashamed. It would be easier to let go of the marriage because we could feel proud that we did our best.

All things pass

Nothing lasts forever. When we accept feelings, we will experience them intensely, and in time they will pass. Most of us have no difficulty accepting positive experiences and feelings. We relish them and wish they could last forever. But they do not. They pass. Most of us fight accepting negative events and feelings. We do not want to have to go through them, and so we fight experiencing them. That fighting tends to make us stuck in them. If we recognize this and learn to accept *all* feelings and experiences as a natural part of the human journey, we will not get stuck, ever. If good feelings pass, so will bad ones. If we are open to the natural flow of the human journey, we will be carried from one experience to the next and not even the worst of experiences will get stuck in our bodies.

Some people hold onto pain because it keeps them from feeling vulnerable and helpless. Sometimes the pain is all that they have left of someone they have lost. It keeps them feeling connected with their loved one, even if it is a negative connection. They are not being masochistic or unwilling to heal - they simply do not want to totally release the person they have lost. They are also not wanting to face the loss of their dreams and hopes for the future. They are fighting the reality of their vulnerability and their helplessness, and pay a high price for maintaining this connection. They are so stuck in their grief that they might never have happiness again.

When we accept our vulnerability and limited control, we can choose to dwell on the gifts we have received in life, not on the grief, which is unavoidable on the human journey.

Jan: One night, Al and I were sitting on the couch, each of us crying about our mothers, who were both dead. I was crying because I loved mine so much and had lost her. He was crying because his mother had never been able to give him the love that he wanted, and he had lost her. I looked over at him and suddenly felt so grateful for my tears. How lucky I was to be grieving such an incredible mother! My grief was over having had and having lost. How sad that his grief was over not having had. I could rejoice in my great fortune and feel blessed that I was the one who got to be her daughter. I did not have the power to avoid the loss that all people must face, but I had the power to appreciate the blessings I had been fortunate to receive.

As we accept everything that life brings us, we will be in harmony with God's plan. We will not waste our lives fighting what is unavoidable to us all. We will be able to appreciate the many blessings we have, and learn to take the power we *can* have as we pass through difficult times.

Names people call us

No one likes to feel helpless. When hard things happen, people want to comfort each other and be supportive. It is hard to watch someone hurting. Everyone feels better when people finally recover from painful experiences. It is a relief. Sometimes, though, no matter what we do, we cannot seem to let go of grieving feelings, or help someone else through their grieving. We feel helpless. And this is when we tend to fall back on that old familiar tool that keeps us from having the unpleasant feeling of helplessness - we turn to judgment. We call ourselves or the other person names. We either feel worthless and ineffective, or say that the other person is wallowing in his feelings and doesn't want to get better.

One common accusation is "victim." Not understanding why someone would be stuck in a feeling, we say the person is "just being a victim," as though this is something he is enjoying. No one enjoys suffering. It is simply the best alternative he could come up with to handle a situation. He is stuck in feelings and the other alternatives seem like they would feel worse, or, he cannot even find another alternative.

True victims have gone through a traumatic experience and had no power to prevent it. They were truly vulnerable, and were assaulted. A child who has been abused is a true victim. An adult who has been robbed at gunpoint is a true victim. People who *feel* like a victim in a situation have been living with the illusion that bad things cannot happen to them. They may not have a sense of their right to exist, and so do not recognize that they have the power to change situations. They may not be able to see and understand their part in having created an unhappy situation. They might not realize that they have the power of choice and do not need to passively, like frightened children, accept whatever happens to them, or what another person says or does. They most likely have avoided dealing with problems, and so are shocked when something so negative occurs that even they cannot ignore it.

Both types of victims can get stuck in not knowing how to come to peace with their vulnerability. They are in secret battle that they should not have to feel vulnerable or helpless. These things should not happen in their lives. When we accept that we have limited control over what happens to us and that we are all vulnerable, even when we are not consciously aware of it, then it will be possible to comfort and reparent ourselves through these hard feelings into peace.

"Self-pity" is another name that is used when we do not understand why someone is stuck in his sadness. Here is a simple test to determine whether or not we are deserving of sympathy for our feelings. When we are sad, if we were to see our situation in a movie, would we feel bad for our "character?" If the answer is "yes," then we are not feeling *sorry* for ourselves; we are just feeling *sorrow*. Every feeling of sadness always deserves empathy and comforting.

"You don't want to get well" is another accusation made when someone is stuck in sad feelings. It might be more useful to ask "What would you have to feel if you <u>accepted</u> this situation?" Most likely, the response would be "sad" or "helpless." When we identify the true feelings, it is easier to come to peace with them. "These things happen. Nothing is wrong. We are just having understandable human reactions to them."

All of these accusations we make come from feeling our lack of control in helping ourselves or someone we care about recover from their trauma and go on with life. We mean well, but feel frustrated and helpless when our efforts do not work. Not understanding what is going on, all we can think is that something is wrong with that person – they are being willfully stubborn and masochistic.

People who are stuck in feelings do not know what to do with their vulnerability and helplessness. They do not want to feel powerless. (This is understandable – no one does!) They are in battle with the reality that all of us must accept these conditions as part of our destiny. They are fighting acceptance with thoughts like "Why did this happen to me? This should not have happened to me. What did I do to deserve this? It's not fair." This fighting keeps them from being able to accept that it is their turn to go through a difficult part of the human journey. Until they come to peace with this reality, they will not be able to accept comforting or complete their grieving.

We can help other people identify this struggle, and we can comfort ourselves and others who fight the feelings of vulnerability and helplessness. We can comfort and reparent ourselves through the grieving process, affirming that:

1. No one wants these things to happen.
2. These things have happened to people since time began. It is just a part of the human journey

3. Nothing is wrong with us, even if we can see through hindsight that we could have avoided the problem.
4. We can see if there is anything to learn from the experience, and then fortify ourselves to use this "homework" to become more wise and compassionate.
5. Without judgment of ourselves, we can release the future to God, for we do not know why we were given this "homework."

We do not have answers to the question of why we are given painful experiences in our lives. This is outside of our human capacity to understand. Our power lies in how we choose to conceptualize the existence of these experiences, and how we choose to act when they occur. We cannot change the fact that we are vulnerable and have limited control. We can, however, choose to look at difficult times as opportunities to grow and to affirm our connection with God. We can accept the "homework" we are given and commit ourselves to growing in wisdom and coming more to peace with what it means to be human. We have all the tools we need to be able to support ourselves in feeling the grief and then letting go. Times of pain provide the greatest opportunities for us to become more than we are. When we learn to accept and use these opportunities, we live in triumph.

Chapter 15

~ *Ignorance Is Not Bliss* ~

It is an enormous challenge to understand human nature. So much of our behavior and emotions seem nonlogical and bewildering. We are not a stupid species, and yet so much of what we do makes no sense, causes us grief, and keeps us from having the life we want to have. To even attempt to understand ourselves, we have to be like detectives. When we act in a self-defeating way, we must know the right questions to ask ourselves in order to look for clues about our behavior. The alternative is to judge ourselves and think that something is wrong with us or that we just do not want to be happy.... and we know that is not true. People unconsciously choose to live in a way that *seems* as though it will be less painful than the alternatives. So even behavior which limits our lives and causes us unhappiness, *seems* to be less painful than the other options available. We are doing the best we know how to do.

<u>Oh, no! I'm just like my father!</u>

Steven wanted to explore the reasons behind how easily he would get frustrated and impatient with his wife. He gave the example of being in a restaurant. If she took more than a few seconds to order, he would become irritable and critical of her. His logical adult self knew that this was probably unreasonable, but he couldn't stop thinking about the waiter needing to attend to his other duties,, and that he and his wife were holding him up. He didn't want to be like his father, who was very impatient and critical, and he felt really bad about his behavior.

Often, our emotional responses to situations simply do not make sense. If we are to truly understand ourselves instead of just trying to beat ourselves into submission by judging what we do, we must ask ourselves where our behavior comes from. The best place to start is with our childhood: what did we learn from our experience in our families that shaped how we protect ourselves in the world now? Because we are all vulnerable and helpless as children, we all are wounded in some way. In addition to our animal reaction against our vulnerability, we have also had life experiences which teach us that it is dangerous to be vulnerable.

Steven talked about how it was hard having such an impatient and angry father. As a child, he never knew what would trigger his father to get angry and criticize him. But he also noticed his own behavior, which distressed him. When Steven was waiting for his wife to order, he was, without realizing it, reliving the sense of vulnerability and lack of control he had experienced as a child. He had learned to protect his vulnerability by moving quickly in his life, trying to accomplish a lot, giving no one the opportunity to criticize him. That feeling of not being carefully in control in the restaurant brought back the sense of danger he had when he lived with his father. Even though it was nonlogical, he reacted as if his father was about to criticize him for taking up the waiter's time. He tried to control his wife because he felt vulnerable to being attacked. He was stuck in the past without even realizing it. When he felt exposed and not in control, his fear took over, and he behaved toward his wife as his father had behaved toward him. This realization also helped Steven understand what his father might have been feeling. After all, his father had a father, who had a father.... and they had never learned how to deal with their vulnerability, either. Steven could feel compassion for his father when he was able to step back and see the situation from a different perspective.

As children, we did not have the power to defend or protect ourselves in our relationships with our parents. No child has the ability to separate from his parents and understand that the words or behaviors of the parents are due to the struggles of the parent, not the behavior of the child. Children learn to cope with their feelings as their parents did. Because children are too young to separate from their parents, the parents become the models of how to live in the world.

Jan: I remember one time when my mother did something that hurt my feelings. Within five minutes, I found myself doing the same thing to Al! The two situations had happened so close together, that I was able to catch *myself. I was amazed. Because I had not separated from my mother and talked about my hurt with her, I internalized the hurt and had <u>become</u> her, going on to treat Al the same way she had treated me! (Al: Good. Now next time, try to figure this one out about five minutes earlier, and then your wonderful husband doesn't have to get attacked due to the sins of your mother!)*

When we understand the causes of our behavior, we can separate the present from what happened to us in our past. We can comfort and reparent our nonlogical self into the reality our logical adult knows to be true. The vulnerable child part of us will no longer need to react as if he has no power or ability to take care of himself. Our logical adult self will be able to choose behavior which is more in keeping with who we want to be.

<u>Separating gives us power</u>

It is not the act of another person that makes us stuck in old behavior patterns. It is our inability to separate and choose another way to respond to what they did which keeps us trapped. Unable to separate, our experience is the same as it was when we were defenseless children. We are left feeling vulnerable and out of control, unable to mobilize the choices and powers we do have over our own actions. The inability to separate leaves us stuck in nonlogical behaviors, feeling victimized.

This does not only happen to children.

Beth brought her husband to therapy, after 20 years of marriage. Our discussion made him feel willing to work on the issues in their marriage. As soon as he committed to this work, Beth burst into tears and said that she didn't know if she could ever forgive him for all the years he wouldn't talk with her. She expressed fear that she just had too much hurt and resentment stuck inside her and would never be able to recover from it. For 20 years, Beth had been unwilling to separate from her husband and insist that if they were to continue in their marriage, they would have to learn to communicate differently. She had victimized herself by not being willing to go for broke. She had chosen to sacrifice her own need for closeness in order to avoid the risk of divorce. She had given up her power, leaving herself victim to whatever he, in his unconsciousness, did. The result was that she had built barriers of hurt and bitterness between them, and divorce was a greater possibility now than ever.

As adults, we need to forgive ourselves for what we did not know to do earlier in our lives, as either children or as adults. Few of us grew up being supported in feeling that we were important and that our feelings matter. Few of us were supported in separating and speaking our own truth. How then can we automatically be different in adulthood? All of us need reparenting in order to be able to give this permission to ourselves. Without this permission, we are stuck in the past, repeating our powerless and self-defeating coping styles.

When Beth could forgive <u>herself</u> for not having known to be stronger in her relationship with her husband, she could also forgive him for what he did not know to do. Both of them, out of their love for each other and their commitment to make their marriage work, had compromised themselves too far. But it was not too late for them to choose differently. Once they could separate from each other to understand their own fears, they could see the situation differently.

They realized that both of them were innocent. Neither had wanted to hurt the other. They were each just stuck in old survival patterns, feeling vulnerable, out of control, and unable to let go of each other. Separating allowed each of them to bring their logical adult self to the relationship. Suddenly, it was not so difficult to communicate in ways they both felt good about. They were able to speak up for what they each needed, and hear each other's needs with compassion instead of feeling threatened.

We will no longer feel like an angry victim when we realize that we now have an adult self who can speak up for what we feel and want. We can separate from the other person and make our own choices. We now have the ability to take care of ourselves. Forgiveness is possible, for when we separate we are able to recognize that we are not a victim, and that we helped to create the difficult situation. We can also see that the other person is struggling, too. With understanding and compassion for ourselves, we can learn to transcend our old survival patterns.

Many people confuse *responsibility* and *blame*. If we do not live in the world of judgment, blame is irrelevant and a waste of time. Taking responsibility for our part of a problem gives us power. When we can identify what we can do differently in a situation, we are no longer a victim.

Victims can't forgive

Forgiveness is not possible if we continue to feel unsafe and vulnerable. We get stuck in bitterness and resentment when we feel powerless. We are unable to let go of a "wrong" done to us because our inner experience has not changed. We feel exactly the same as we did when that "wrong" occurred. As long as we still feel that unprotected vulnerability, we will have no way to move beyond the past.

There are two steps to being able to find our power and move ahead in our lives. The first is simply to take the time to release and express our anger and pain. In situations that have occurred when we were adults, most of us have done this, to some degree. In situations that happened when we were children, it is more likely that we just endured and went on. Instead of expressing their pain, children tend to shift their self-image to fit in with how they feel they are being perceived by their parents. "Mommy is mad at me. I am a bad boy." Understanding this, our logical adult self can reparent our vulnerable child self by allowing him to go through his sadness and anger.

The second step is to go back to the event and examine it from the position of separateness. From this position, we do not experience it in the same way. Something happened *to* us that was painful, but it was not *about* us. The other person is accountable, but not to blame. People who have peace and love in their hearts and know how to handle their feelings do not behave in ways that are hurtful to others. The worse their actions are, the more they are lost and suffering.

Jan: Andi's daughter was killed, and her murderer had not yet been found. Andi was stuck in her anger and grief, and could find no comfort. She was haunted by knowing that her daughter lay dead, yet the murderer could go on with his life, unaffected. I told her that even if he did not realize it, he was suffering. How could he ever feel the peace in his heart that comes from being proud of who he is? How could he ever feel the joy of having love and compassion for others? Even if he felt clever and thought he got away with something, she and I knew he was unable to feel the kind of happiness we know is possible. A devout Christian, Andi was able to feel compassion for someone as lost as the murderer, and from there, was able to forgive him and find peace.

For situations which occurred when we were children, we can take that same step of examining the event from a position of separateness, with the eyes and understanding of the big adult self we have grown up to be. Once we were defenseless children with no way of protecting ourselves. If we do not separate and reparent ourselves, the frightened child in us will still feel vulnerable that this type of situation can happen again. We get stuck in victim feelings, behaviors and attitudes because we are not connected to the power of our logical adult. We cannot see our situations in life through the eyes of that logical adult. Our vision is tinted by our past, and everything and everyone threaten to be a painful repetition of that past.

Jan: My father, Leon, was physically abusive of both my mother and me. Even though we left him when I was two years old, I looked at the world through Leon-colored glasses. I remember walking around my house, peering at Al through the corner of my eye, telling myself, "He's not my father" over and over, trying to get the message into my very cells. I needed to help my two year old self know that those scary days were over. I was no longer that defenseless toddler, but a strong and capable adult who could take care of myself, now.

When we can separate from the situation and the struggle of the other person, it no longer is about us. We no longer have to define ourselves in their terms. We can feel that we now have choices, unlike when we were powerless children who were stuck in the situation. Separating allows us to have a different way of seeing what happened to us. We can see the whole picture, including how the other person simply did not know what to do, either. When we have a distorted view, it is hard to heal or forgive. If we can see accurately, we will be able to move through our feelings more easily.

Al: In the early years of our marriage, Jan and I fought like most other couples. I would always be hurt by her words of anger, and would withdraw into myself. Once she revealed that when she got angry, she was really feeling scared. The anger was a mobilization to try to protect herself. Suddenly I was able to see her as a separate person with something happening in her that had nothing to do with me, and that she didn't know how to handle. Instead of the fight being something happening to me, it became something that was happening to us. I was hurt, she was scared. It wasn't me against her. Both of us were just struggling with our vulnerability in different ways. Understanding what was going on helped me not take what she said personally. I didn't need to forgive her for hurting me, for I now knew her anger wasn't even about me.

Forgiveness comes easily if we feel safe. Without feeling the power of choice and separateness, we still feel like vulnerable children. From the position of non-separateness (fusion) we feel vulnerable to having the past repeat itself and being victimized again. From a position of separateness, we can see that what the other person did had nothing to do with us. It was done *to* us but was not *about* us. We can feel our choice and power to act now. From this position of safety and with the ability to speak up for ourselves, we can afford to see the other person in his vulnerability, with compassion and with forgiveness.

<u>Laying abuse to rest</u>

In addition to the normal experiences we all have, some of us have been subjected to serious emotional or physical abuse. As horrifying and tragic as this is, the reparenting process can help all of us attain freedom from our pasts and bring ourselves into the present where our logical adult understands that we did nothing wrong, and that we survived that awful time. We need to separate what does not belong to us and remember that we were innocent and did nothing to deserve abuse. What the abuser did affected you, but was not about you.

Exercise:

1. If you have experienced mental, physical or sexual abuse, imagine yourself at the age it first occurred. Comfort that hurt child. Tell yourself "No one deserves to be treated the way you were. There is nothing you could have done which would have justified that kind of treatment." Take a deep breath and try to take those words deeply into your heart. Take as long as you need to do this. It is not a simple or quick step.

2. Imagine holding your vulnerable self close to your heart. Allow yourself to visualize the face of your abuser. Stretch out your arm and put your hand up as if to say "STOP" to him. Look at his face and feel your feelings towards him. Are you angry, hurt, sad? Whatever they are, your feelings will probably be saying that you do not like what he did, and that it is not okay with you to be treated that way. Those feelings can help you separate from any illusion that whatever happened was your fault. Something wrong was done to you, not by you.

3. Remind yourself that you survived that awful time. It is over, and can never happen again, because you have become a strong adult who can take care of you now in a way no one knew to do when the abuse happened.

The important thing in reparenting is to correct the misinformation that got into our hearts and minds. That misinformation was our attempt to make sense of something that was beyond our ability to understand. That misinformation was our way of trying to survive. We do not need to go to anger or blame, although we might need to go through those feelings to get free. Ultimately separating will be enough, and we can remember, as we comfort ourselves, that no one who is at peace in his heart or with himself could ever treat another human being abusively, as if that human being did not matter.

Beware the false expert / You are the real expert

Jan: The first time I saw him, Michael was already crying as he walked down the hall to my office. He curled up on the couch in a fetal position and sobbed as though his heart would break. He choked out that the psychiatrist he had been working with had told him that he was hopeless, that he could never expect to be any better, but should just go home and take his antidepressants for the rest of his life. Within 20 minutes of our being together, Michael was laughing with joy and amazement. He knew he had begun his journey of healing and hope.

If we believe that someone in our world has authority - whether he is a parent, teacher, spouse, doctor, pastor, employer, psychiatrist, or psychologist - we tend to listen with submission to their words. They have power with us. They especially have power if their words are negative, for we all fear judgment and cringe in the face of it, feeling exposed and diminished. If their words are logical and have even the slightest grain of truth to them, we tend to accept their message and their attitude toward us without question. In the face of their logic, we take the complementary position of feeling wrong or stupid. In the face of their judgment, like frightened children, we may snap ourselves into "good" and logical behavior. Judgment triggers our fears that we are worthless, and so we shrivel inside and allow that authority person to diminish us. Neither their logic nor their judgment help us empower ourselves to look for what blocks us from having access to our own logic and wisdom.

Jan: The "expert" who (in his "all-knowing" certainty) told Michael that he was hopeless, was not talking about Michael! He was revealing <u>himself</u> - <u>his</u> ignorance, <u>his</u> hopelessness (for he did not know what to do), and <u>his</u> helplessness. Because Michael was in a very vulnerable state, he took in the psychiatrist's words about him as if they were the truth.

Especially during a time of crisis, if we still struggle with our right to exist, and are not firmly grounded in separateness, we will think that an "expert's" words are about us. In the face of their judgment and "expertness," it may not occur to us that their words reflect more about them than they do about us. We forget, in the vulnerability that we feel when we hear negative messages about ourselves, that even people in "power" are human, and struggle with the same issues we do.

How often do "experts" lay judgment on us in the name of "helping" us? How often do their "logical" assessments make us despair and feel like fools? How many times have you heard an expert "help" someone by making them seem stupid to have not followed logic in their choice of behaviors? These "experts" are not helping us to develop our own strength, and they are not being honest. "Experts" who make negative statements about someone are not revealing their own feelings of vulnerability and helplessness. They are acting as if they do not struggle like the rest of us do. But such perfected beings *do not exist*! And in pretending that they are above struggle, (by omission, if nothing else), they are doing all of us a terrible disservice. In the name of "helping," they are perpetuating a myth that it is possible to be perfect, *but it is not*! "Experts" who do not openly struggle with and share their human journey are dangerous to those who come to them. However "logical" they may be, if they do not live and speak with the humility of knowing their own humanness, they contribute to the illusion that something is wrong with us. They do not support us in claiming our *own* strength. They shame us into leaning on *their* strength.

Jan: Diane came to me after leaving another therapist in town, who for years had been extremely supportive of her. But one day, Diane got angry at this therapist for something she had said. The therapist responded to her by saying, "After all I've done for you, how can you be angry at me!!!" (Translation: It's okay with me if you are powerful in the world, but you had better not try to be powerful with me.)

"Experts" will use their words and position to throw judgment back onto the other person. Diane's therapist was not willing to be vulnerable and address her own feelings. She probably felt surprised, hurt, and threatened facing Diane's anger. Instead of talking about her own reactions, person to person, she assumed a position of power and tried to make Diane feel guilty and ungrateful.

Al and Jan: Many times we sit in silence in our office, facing someone who is struggling and in pain, opening our hearts and minds to ask for guidance from God, for we do not always know what to do or say. What we do know is that all of us grope our way along this human journey.

No one is so expert that he can know another person's experience or answers. But we can explore together, share our knowledge and information, and hope that somehow, out of that mix will come something helpful and clear. Clarity *does not* come from the "expert." That is the height of arrogance. We are each the **real** expert in our own lives. We just have not received the support to be able to accept this and to strengthen our ability to listen and understand our own inner guidance.

Jan: I once said something particularly brilliant to a client named Doug. He sat, stunned, looking at me in complete wonder and amazement. When he was finally able to regain his speech (ah, yes... my wisdom is awesome!) he said to me "I knew that! I just didn't know that I knew it until you said it!" I was thrilled! He absolutely pinpointed the perfection of two people accompanying each other on this journey of self-discovery. We help each other remember.

We help each other along the path. We do not create the path for the other person. Each of us is supremely capable of knowing all he needs to know in order to find his own way. The role of a *true* "expert" is to be a companion who trusts and believes in the developing truth of the other person.

Al and Jan: One of the first things we do when we meet new clients is watch for where they create a false image of us as the "experts," doctors who know it all. Our culture does not support our right to exist or our belief in ourselves. It has fostered the idea that ignorance means that we are "less than." From the first session, we let our clients know that we struggle as much in our areas of ignorance as they do in theirs. That nothing is wrong with this, or with us, or with them. We let our clients know that we will explore together, but that they are the experts in their own lives. If we let people idealize us into "perfected beings" we do them the ultimate disservice. They would be coming to us for help, but we would be perpetuating the same harmful message they come to us to get free from. By allowing them to project their power onto us, we would be undermining their strength, and the development of and trust in their own wisdom.

If an authority figure or "expert" in any field cannot speak with compassion about the rightness of how you have learned to survive, if they cannot speak with humility of their own journey so you do not feel alone, if they do not focus with kindness and empathy on supporting and empowering you to grow and learn, then their words are *not* in your service. Their words are spoken to use your humanness to support *their* goal of protecting themselves so they do not feel *their* vulnerability and helplessness. You walk away in shame; they walk away having used your shame to make themselves feel "superior." God did not give you life to be food for another's fear or insecure ego. God did not intend us to feel shame or to have our souls shrivel because of the words of another. *No one* has the right to judge or shame us. *Ever.*

God gave you all of the tools you need to be a strong and capable person. Do not let anyone speak words to you which diminish this truth. Remember with pride that if you are sometimes ignorant, it is the design of the Most High God that you are here to learn. Remember with pride that if you have unexpected outcomes to your actions, which you see with the tool of hindsight, it is the design of the Most High God that this is the way you learn. Remember with pride that if you are vulnerable and have a heart of compassion that feels deep emotions, this is the design of the Most High God that enables you to deeply connect and love others, and receive guidance for your life. If the negative words of any "expert" or authority make you feel shame, embarrassment or guilt, you are not receiving a message that honors the design of God. Turn and walk away, and remember who the <u>real</u> experts are: you and God!

<u>We are innocent</u>

Our hearts are innocent and blameless. We have always done the best we could within the limits of our awareness and knowledge. We may not know what to do when we feel threatened or frightened, hurt or sad, but we are acting out of fear and ignorance. We can revisit events from our past to find the power and choice we now have. We can transcend our ignorance and the pain that resulted from it by learning how to listen to the guidance of our logical adult self. We can remember that the human journey each person is taking is not about us, but is between them and God. We do not need to let bitterness overcome us if we separate and take care of ourselves. Then we will be able to feel compassion for us all, and if forgiveness is necessary, it will flow effortlessly from our compassion.

Chapter 16

~ *Triumph Over Adversity* ~

Although we may try our best in life, not everything turns out as we hope it will. Sometimes things happen that are so disappointing that we have trouble getting over our feelings. Sometimes we do not know how to come to peace with an outcome that haunts us with how sad or how unfair it seems. We can agonize over what happened, search our souls for what we could have done differently, and rage at fate or at someone we may think "cheated" in some way. But that just leaves us exhausted, grieving and angry, for we are helpless to change what has occurred.

We will, of course, wonder why misfortune has happened to us. (What could Mr. Lucky have been thinking?!) The answer is, as usual, that we do not and cannot know. It is impossible for us to see or understand all the variables at work in any situation. Too much is occurring for us to ever be able to comprehend it all. We may never know the cause or purpose of any situation. As much as we long to know, we are not designed to have that kind of knowledge. We can only experience life at the human level and release what is beyond our control to the forces beyond our control.

Keep an eye on yourself!

While we do not have power over the grand forces of the Universe, we have enormous power over ourselves. Our job is to watch ourselves, to reparent what is nonlogical and wounded in us, and to help ourselves grow and develop into the people we want to be. It is hard to keep an eye on our every word, tone of voice, and action, watching to see that we are centered in our hearts and living true to ourselves and with compassion for others. It is as exhausting a job as working and running a household at the same time as we are raising an active toddler!

Our job is not to raise someone else's toddler, though, regardless of how poorly behaved we think he is. Not only do we not have the time and energy for this task, but we cannot know what is going on in other people or why they behave the way they do. That is theirs to figure out. Our task is to separate from them and live in a way that we are proud of being who we are.

Al: When my son was very young, I took him to a gymnastics class. All the other children got onto the mat, except for my son, who wasn't sure that he wanted to participate. I immediately felt pressure from the other parents, who were all watching me, and from the instructor to get him to participate. I knew that wasn't the right thing to do, that I needed to wait for him to go through his feelings and find his own way. But I found myself starting to feel self-conscious. I had to keep reminding myself that I was doing what felt right to me. I kept telling myself that even if other people were critical of me, I had to not take it personally, and not pressure my son just to avoid my discomfort.

When something happens to us, our task is to watch ourselves so we can continue to guide our development into being the person we want to be. The first step is to separate from the uncomfortable or disappointing situation and from anyone else who is involved. We may never understand why this situation occurred, but it is not about or because of us, so we need to not take it personally. We will never be able to make someone act in any way - their behavior is their responsibility. And, we will never know what forces or lessons came together to create any particular outcome. All we can do is separate: step back and disentangle ourselves and our feelings from the situation so that we can choose how we are going to react. Separating allows us to choose to be our best self.

Reactive or proactive?

Just as we would need to keep our eyes on a toddler to make sure he stays out of mischief and does not hurt himself, we also need to constantly watch out for our own well-being. Regardless of the face we present to others, we are each sensitive and vulnerable. We are deeply affected by the words and behavior of others. Hurtful words, sharp tones or critical looks can pierce our hearts. They assault us. It is extremely hard to not respond to such painful attacks with angry words, tones and looks of our own. Such a response is an understandable animal "fight" reaction. The "flight" reaction would make us feel helpless and defeated, and we would withdraw from the conflict, feeling incapable of facing the assaulter. Another reaction is one of fusion - we shift our self-image to correspond with the words of the person who is criticizing us. We become the incompetent or valueless person they say we are.

We do not have to allow the actions of the other person, or the details of the situation, no matter how painful they are, to set the tone for how we choose to be. Instead of being *reactive*, we can be *proactive*, separating and determining how *we* want to behave. We can watch our emotional response and determine from it the lessons we have yet to learn so that we can feel proud of our behavior. Each moment gives us information about what we need to do to be the person we want to be. We are not here to watch others - we are accountable for ourselves and our own growth and integrity. We do not need to base our feelings or behaviors on the feelings or behaviors of others.

Al: My brother-in-law asked several of his friends and me to help him move. I noticed that while I labored away, everyone else seemed to be taking lots of breaks to play around with each other and have cold drinks. My first reaction was to feel like I was being taken advantage of, and feel resentful and impatient with them for not being as focused as I was. Instead, I decided on the amount of time I wanted to spend helping out. As soon as I did this, I felt separate from whatever anyone else wanted to do. I happily finished working for the time I had chosen to help, said goodbye to everyone, and left. I had no bad feelings left over, and no longer felt taken advantage of, because I did what I felt good doing. My actions were no longer connected to theirs. My emotional well-being was no longer dependent on their behavior.

Having choice gives us power

One of the hardest experiences for a human is to feel helpless, or trapped. We like to have choices (consider the popularity of buffet restaurants!) especially when it comes to our well-being. We tend to not like someone else having power over us. We may not have control over external conditions, but the good news is that we *always* have the choice of our attitude and of how we use an experience. We can remember that every situation provides us with a mirror to our inner selves. Our reactions reflect back to us the emotions we are struggling with. Unless we respond with peace and compassion, we have something to learn from *every* experience.

> *Sandy hated her job. The corporate culture of her workplace was disrespectful of the employees. Supervisors in the company took credit for the creative work of the lowest echelon of workers, who worked long and hard with no recognition or reward. There was an atmosphere of fear, coming from the top, down, as the company president would proclaim frequently that fear makes employees more productive. Sandy wanted to quit, but had not been able to find another job. She felt trapped and miserable.*
>
> *In therapy, she found a way to change her thinking about the job, taking her out of her role of victim. She looked for the nonlogical reactions from her vulnerable child, and came up with a list of goals for her to focus on while she was doing her work. They included challenges like separating from the behavior of the corporate officers so she could see their behavior as having nothing to do with her, but rather as their fearful reaction to the work environment. They felt insecure and did not act in compassion. She also determined to make sure it was her logical adult self who interacted with her supervisors, rather than feel like a bad little girl who was helpless and worthless. Instead of feeling used and mistreated, she focused on how she was using the situation to grow. She congratulated herself on being paid by the corporation to do her work on herself! No one else knew this, but she did!*

We have the choice over our responses - no one can make us feel something. We can choose to feel powerful in *any* situation, regardless of how difficult it may be. We can *use* painful or unjust outcomes as homework from God, choosing to work with our feelings so that regardless of what happens, we can feel proud of ourselves and take steps to become our best selves. This gives us true freedom - not the kind of freedom that comes from having everything go our way, but the kind that says, "No matter what happens to me, nothing can take away my gratitude for what I do have and my pride in the kind of person I am. I am going to use every situation I am in to help me grow." With this attitude, we can never be trapped.

We also have the power to choose how we react to people, regardless of what they have done. When people do hurtful things, it is totally normal to feel shocked, assaulted, hurt, and unseen. As painful as these experiences are, we can separate from them, and ask ourselves if they have acted with compassion. If our answer is "no," than we can remember that their behavior has *nothing* to do with us, *even* if there is some truth in what they say. We have the power to speak with compassion in *any* situation. It is our job to take hold of our upset child and separate so we can live in compassion. Not that this is easy! But if we are unable to do so, it is not anyone else's fault. When we respond to someone, *we* have the power to speak with compassion. If people do hurtful things, they are suffering enough - do we really want to add to their wounds by counterattacking?

Some people find themselves in situations that are very hard. They may be in bodies that are racked with pain. Their marriages may have become bitter and hurtful. They may be working in terrible jobs. Some men have had to live through captivity or other hardships during a war. All of these painful situations are challenging, because, ultimately, we are helpless to change reality. What we can do is look for how to take care of ourselves, in the midst of a difficult reality. We can commit to keeping a positive attitude and feeling grateful for what we have had in our lives. We can pull out our Memory Album! (Remember Chapter 12?) We can do the Steps to Inner Peace (Chapter 6) of acknowledging and having compassion for our feelings, doing what we can with a positive expectation, and releasing the outcome to God.

Am I holding my breath till I turn blue, or am I just feeling disappointed?

There is nothing wrong with feeling our emotions. We are designed to have them, and feeling them is as natural as breathing. But sometimes we get stuck in a feeling and do not know how to free ourselves, even though we may truly want to. It is not stubbornness, masochism or wanting attention - it is ignorance that keeps us from being able to let go. Our initial emotional response to a situation is completely understandable, but after a while, everyone, including us, may notice that we are unable to release it and move on to other feelings and experiences.

There is a difference between hopes and wants, and expectations. Hopes and wants are inevitable as we face life. They come up automatically from our hearts, as do dreams. They give us directional guidance, telling us which of all of the possibilities of life is the right path for us to follow. Expectations are about control, not direction. Having an expectation is the attempt to avoid feeling vulnerable. An expectation is a demand, whether it is done in hope, anger or sadness.

When we feel unable to recover from a sad or disappointed feeling, we are stuck in a demand. "This should have been different! This is not right/fair/nice!" Expectations about reality are a fight against God. Our job is to do what we can to attain our hopes and wants, and then release the outcome. This gives us the best chance possible for success in affecting our own lives, and guarantees that we will have success in feeling proud of ourselves. This is very different than having an expectation that doing the best we can *will* result in worldly success.

Jodie really wanted the promotion that was coming up in her department. She knew she was a hard worker and was well regarded by her supervisor, and so she had high hopes that the new position would be hers. When the position was given to someone else who was new to the firm, Jodie was hurt and devastated. She felt a combination of anger at her supervisor and a sense of being worthless. Weeks went by, and she could not shake those feelings, dragging herself into work each day, hardly speaking to anyone. She was finally sent to therapy by her employer, who did not want to terminate her from her job, but who also knew that her behavior could not continue. Jodie was able to come to an understanding of her feelings. Beyond disappointment, she had feelings stirred up from her childhood. She had always been a "good girl" who was rewarded by her parents for conforming to their ideas of who she should be. She carried on this approach to life in her work environment, and was therefore not only disappointed, but angry when being a "good girl" did not result in reward. She had a secret demand that she receive her reward for her "good" behavior. That was the secret agreement she had with her parents that let her feel in control: "If I try hard, I will get what I want." Jodie was fighting against not only her feelings of disappointment, but the feeling of being helpless. Hard work did not guarantee the results she wanted.

Jodie was able to reparent herself by acknowledging and comforting her feelings of disappointment and helplessness. She was able to remind herself that she really never had control over anyone's response or actions. When she was young, it was too hard to feel vulnerable and disappointed, but now she is grown, and __can__ tolerate those feelings. Her expectation had changed her hope into a demand. Once she was able to reparent her disappointed self, the feelings melted away, and she returned to work at peace with the reality that she has only limited control. She was able to feel proud of herself for what a good employee she is, without needing approval from anyone else, in the form of a promotion.

God's dreams for us are bigger than we are capable of imagining. Instead of seeing this possibility, we get stuck in disappointment over not attaining our goal. And, His goal for us in any situation may be quite different than what we are hoping for or expecting. While we hope for the fulfillment of worldly accomplishments, the true purpose of any situation might be the growth of our soul. Whenever we experience disappointment or frustration in the accomplishment of our intent, remember: we are being called into school for homework.

Jan: I remember my family sitting around, one night, very discouraged by having our plans to go to Disneyland fall apart. We all felt disappointed, somewhat adrift and confused about what to do, next. I remember sitting there, looking at the others, and suddenly realizing "This isn't about getting to Disneyland, at all! This is about all of us needing to learn to be more determined, more communicative, and more patient." Having the desire to go gave us a goal to reach for while providing an opportunity for our human lessons to be revealed to us. Our real job was to work on our own growth, as evolving beings. And maybe, if we were lucky, and did a good job with our "homework," we'd get to have a vacation, as well.

Inner success

As much as we may try hard to be our best self, we have no control over anything external to ourselves. We can guarantee that we are successful in feeling proud of ourselves, but we cannot guarantee that we will get what we want in the outcome of life events. When we keep an eye on our sensitive and vulnerable heart, we will keep from being reactive. This enables us to mobilize our energy to act in ways we are proud of. Analyzing situations to see if there is any lesson for us to learn enables us to possibly do better next time we face a similar situation. But that is all. The rest is beyond our control and beyond our understanding. Even when an outcome is disappointing or unjust, we do not have to be angry at ourselves, other people, or at God. We can simply allow ourselves to not understand, and to keep faith with ourselves, and with God. Regardless of what happens *to* us, we have the power to guarantee that we are using every situation for growth of our soul. Then, we can never be defeated!

Chapter 17

~ *Fight the Good Fight* ~

Poppy is a very brave woman. Doctors can do nothing to help her with the constant pain she suffers from. On a good day, she may have an hour or two without agonizing pain before she must take the medications which numb her enough to make life bearable, but also numb her mind, keeping her from the life she once enjoyed. Despite this, Poppy is able to find joy in her life.

Sometimes life brings us such hard challenges that it is almost impossible to keep up our spirits and continue. Such adversity can be an acute and immediate emergency, or a chronic situation that seems to last forever. Either way, the intensity of the difficulty tempts us all to lose heart and to lose faith. In adversity, we feel our vulnerability and helplessness so absolutely that we can easily feel completely overwhelmed and hopeless.

Fighting or acceptance

What makes the difference between people who despair and feel defeated when facing adversity, and those who are able to mobilize their strength and their best selves? What can we all learn from those who are able to steadily maintain their positive attitude while facing struggles that would bring most of us to our knees?

We have all heard the expression "Fight the good fight." But what, exactly, does that mean? How do we know when to struggle against the challenges we face and when to yield and flow with what is happening? So many times we wind up bashing our heads against the wall of reality, leaving the wall untouched, but our heads quite bloody.

What makes the difference between fighting the *good* fight, and fighting the *bad* fight?

There are two reasons why people become defeated by adversity. Some fight the bad fight. They fight the reality of their vulnerability and helplessness. They fight what they are absolutely powerless to change. There is no possibility for them to be victorious. Other people who become defeated get worn down by the constancy if the struggle to survive and to keep up their spirits. They end up feeling too alone in the struggle. They lose heart and lose faith, feeling like there is no one but themselves to depend on. They tend to think that they must be in control of everything, and this is simply not possible. Trying to do the impossible, they are doomed to feel despair and hopelessness.

People who do well in adversity are not fighting the *existence* of the crisis. They like a crisis no more than the rest of us, but they are in acceptance of having to face it. They are not arguing with God in the hopes of making it go away. They accept what is happening. They do not fight what they can do nothing about. They are at peace with their feelings of vulnerability and helplessness. Because they are free from the impossible fight against what is real, they are able to mobilize all of their energy to fight the good fight - to do what they can, what is in the realm of their control.

Poppy has found a way to find meaning and joy in her moment to moment existence, whether she is in a period of respite from her pain, or whether she is confined to her bed, unable to move from either pain or medication. She does not fight the reality of her condition. She fights the good fight of finding ways to have a good life, despite it.

Accepting our human destiny

Jan: My favorite type of book has always been historical fiction. I have pored over biographies of people living in different times, as well as stories of people who didn't themselves exist, but who represent the nameless unremembered multitude who did. I read about their hopes, their dreams, their discoveries, their successes, and their defeats with a great hunger to learn about them, and with deep empathy for their human struggles. Since time began, in every country of the world, in every social class and profession, both men and women have experienced not only the joys of being alive, but great sorrow and tragedy as well. Sometimes the sorrow came as a universal and nonspecific tragedy, as a plague, for example, striking everyone in its path. Sometimes the sorrow was the result of a person's ignorance, his not being able to foresee the results of his choices. I rejoiced and grieved with them all. I identified with them, and shared their triumphs and despair.

After many, many years, I discovered why this type of literature held such a powerful appeal for me. I realized that through learning about what it has meant to be human throughout the ages, I was affirming that <u>nothing is wrong with me.</u> When I create problems because I am ignorant, nothing is wrong with me. When bad things happen to me, nothing is wrong with me. When I struggle or am defeated in a goal, nothing is wrong with me. It is just <u>my</u> turn to experience the painful aspects of our human destiny. It is not a statement or a judgment about <u>me</u>. I am innocent. In all my human imperfection, I am traveling the path all of my ancestors have traveled before me. This is just what it means to be alive.

When we remember that to be alive means that we are born into the conditions of vulnerability and limited control, we will not blame ourselves when something happens that makes us aware of this. We will not think that we have done anything wrong, but will remember that, for reasons we cannot understand, it is our turn to face adversity, which is as much a part of being human as is joy.

Jan: I remember standing next to Al, as we were being married. I had the feeling of being in a procession of brides and grooms, billions of us, stretching from the earliest time of humanity, and going forward, endlessly into the future. all of us with our love, our hopes, our fears, our dreams. I remember thinking that it was my turn to be feeling and doing this. I remember the sense of being deeply connected to everyone who had ever stood next to someone they loved, repeating a ritual that would remain as long as there is love.

Accepting our human destiny means understanding that *all* experiences we have throughout our lifetime, whether they are celebrations or struggles, are natural and human. Vulnerability opens us to accept that we deserve the joys of life. Some people are afraid to allow themselves to feel happy, for they fear that the happiness will end. All things come to an end in the temporal world. But while we are here, we can embrace the joys of life and be grateful for them. We can embrace the times of adversity and know that they, too, can keep us connected with God, as we grow into the people we are designed to be. Each experience, joyful or challenging, gives us the opportunity to fully embrace our humanness and celebrate the human journey of becoming our best selves.

Our right to exist gives us power

Although in adversity we are deeply aware of how vulnerable and limited we are in controlling what matters so much to us, we can also have the power of feeling that this is our turn to have our life here on Earth. We can remember that we have the right to our feelings and our wants, and that we deserve good things. We do not have to take the presence of a difficult challenge as the proof that we are not valuable or worthy. Hardships are simply a part of being alive, and we all must take our turn to face them. If we try to face them without feeling our right to exist, we will be defeated. We will be overwhelmed by hopelessness and despair.

Al: A friend I hadn't heard from in a while called me to visit. When I asked how he was doing, he told me about the challenging time he was having with his teenage son, and that he was struggling financially. I told him that I was sorry he was having such a hard time, but he corrected me immediately. "This is my life, and I don't feel sorry about the things that are going on right now, just because they're difficult. It's just what's happening right now."

We can remember that nothing is *wrong* - it is only *difficult*. This frees us to take charge of our lives. Acceptance of our human destiny frees us to mobilize the power that we do have. In accepting our ultimate helplessness, we are free to recognize where we can make choices. We may be the victims of external events beyond our control, but no one has the power to determine our attitude and how we take action in our lives. No one can bring us to our emotional knees, regardless of what they may do to our body.

Take the steps to take your power in adversity

All of us need to follow the Steps for Inner Peace (Chapter 6) all of the time. We need to constantly be keeping an eye on our vulnerable self and accepting guidance from our logical adult. If we don't, that vulnerable self will be the one running the show when we feel threatened, and no child is equipped to be able to handle adult challenges.

When we face adversity, the stakes are higher. In difficult times, the process of doing the Steps is not any different, but we *really* need to be committed to doing them. Adversity necessitates our drawing on our strength, training and knowledge. We must focus and be deliberate in our practice of the Steps, or we will fall prey to the temptation to despair. We must commit to the process and attempt to live it with each breath. *Then* we will be able to feel our power.

Poppy is an inspiration to all who know her. She is aware of the temptation to be angry at her body for being in such pain, so she works hard to separate her sense of self from her disability in order to be able to accept what is going on. She tries to stay in her feelings of compassion for herself and how hard it is to be disabled and in such debilitating pain. Staying in compassion allows her to remain centered in her true feelings of sorrow, rather than go to anger or self-pity. She tries to be aware in each moment of the power she <u>*does*</u> *have. Whether it is choosing to turn her head, blink her eyes, pat her dog or drink some soup, she recognizes each moment all the little ways in which she determines the course of her life. Her rejoicing in such simple freedom causes the responses of others to range from weeping to deep respect and admiration. She is living proof that even in the most horrible adversity, it is possible to focus on what is right in our lives, not what is wrong.*

When it is clear that our vulnerability and helplessness are unavoidable, we can choose to accept them absolutely and not fight what is beyond our control. Then we are free to really get to work and do what we can without dividing our energy by fighting against our human destiny.

Build your inner strength

Al: Inner strength is like a muscle - the more we practice and flex it, the more familiar we become with how it works, the stronger we feel. Even though we don't like them, we all recognize that we must face trials in life. How can we mobilize ourselves to face these trials?

Self-defense classes are one example of a way to prepare. No one really expects to ever have to fight another person, but look how many people take those classes. Jan took one, once. Not one series of classes, but one class. The first thing the instructor taught the class was to bend their knees, make fists, and make a fierce bellowing sound. When Jan heard the sound she made, she felt such enormous power that she quit the class. She had gotten what she had come for. (Yeah, a new way to wake me up in the morning.)

I do a similar thing to connect with my inner power. I know that feeling vulnerable is inevitable. I remember practicing fire drills in grade school. The risk of fire wasn't eliminated, but I knew what to do should one occur. So when I'm approaching something that feels scary that I know I have to do, I try to walk myself through the danger I am anticipating, just as I used to walk through fire drills as a child. I watch myself walking through discomfort, so I know that I can do it. I redefine what I am calling my "fear" as "energy," and can feel myself go from feeling vulnerable to feeling empowered. I am taking steps to find my inner peace, and to maximize my power. There are two positive outcomes for me in doing my "fire drills." First, I feel like it builds up inner strength to face the danger. Secondly, having done my preparations, it makes it easier for me to then ask for God's help so that I'm not facing challenges alone.

The Steps to Inner Peace address an internal need for self-acceptance. When we are facing adversity, or either an external or inner/emotional crisis, we can additionally take the Steps to Power and Possibility, which maximize our ability to face the unknown with the power we do have and accomplish our goals, as best as possible.

Al: When my son was born, I was thrilled! My first child! As I watched Jan bond with him, I first felt so incredibly happy. Then it hit me. I was completely overcome with grief about what I had <u>not</u> felt with my own mom when I was a little boy.

1. <u>Acknowledge your feelings without judgment</u>. Anyone facing a difficult challenge in life will feel shaken. We will experience, shock, grief, fear, and anger - understandable human reactions. There is nothing wrong with having these feelings. They are the body's instant response to danger or assault. There is no shame for anyone, woman or man, who experiences these emotions. It is absolutely necessary when facing adversity to acknowledge these feelings so we

are not using energy to hold them off. This allows us to fully mobilize all of our inner resources to go on to the next step.

Al: I felt ashamed at all of my pain. Why wasn't I overjoyed for Jan, our son and myself? I was, but I also felt huge waves of sorrow for my experience as a child. Every child should have received what Jan and I were giving our son.

2. <u>Feel compassion for yourself</u>. Take the time to be as loving and sympathetic to yourself as you would be to a young and vulnerable child. You deserve all the compassion and kindness you can give yourself. It is not easy to be going through adversity. We need love and support. Remind yourself of how completely understandable it is to have the feelings you are experiencing. Remind yourself that you have grown up into a capable and intelligent adult, and that it is this competent adult who will be facing all of these challenges. You may not know what to do all of the time, but you can commit to always being lovingly present with yourself.

Al: Although I felt compassion for my childhood grief, I got stuck in the past and I suffered. I didn't know what to do, and the pain from my memories wasn't going away.

3. <u>Focus on being in the present moment</u>. It is especially crucial during times of adversity to stay focused in each moment, rather than look back with regret to the past, or with longing to the future. Both of those tendencies divide our attention and focus, and diminish our ability to take appropriate action, now. All you can do is be right here, right now. There is no other time to live.

Al: Finally, I realized I had to do something to release the past, because I couldn't concentrate and do my life in the present. I was embarrassed - here I was, a counselor, and I needed help! I had to look at the judgment I had for myself that I was supposed to be strong and overcome my problems alone. My logical adult had to comfort my "child" and remind him that everyone needs help in their life, and I could feel proud of my willingness to seek it.

4. <u>Choose a course of action and keep a positive attitude</u>. This is definitely the time to mobilize our ability and permission to consider choices. Even if it is easy for you to explore options, this is a good time to build a team of people who care about you, so you do not have to go through this alone. They can help brainstorm possibilities you might not come up with on your own. Let your guidance from within direct you to the choice which seems to be the best for you in this moment. Believe for the best. The choice does not need to be perfect.

Al: I thought of all the years I had silently suffered with my childhood pain. This time, I was determined to face and overcome it. I decided to go into counseling.

5. <u>Do the best you can without judgment</u>. You may feel vulnerable in the moment, but take positive action, anyway! Hindsight will help you evaluate your choice. Use it as a gift, not as something to beat yourself with. Hindsight will help you refine your future actions. You can only know what you know, and it is a guarantee that you will know more, later. When later comes, you can analyze and learn so your subsequent choices can be even better. But later is not a time to judge yourself, either. Remember, it is your destiny to learn by hindsight. It is <u>not</u> a mistake that you are designed that way.

Al: I wanted to feel free to enjoy our new child and my family. I didn't want to be stuck in grief, anymore. Most importantly, I wanted to feel at peace with being an imperfect being.

6. <u>Feel your intent</u>. Focus on *your* goals, not on the situation. You have gathered up your vulnerable self so that you can feel centered and clear. You have brought your attention to what is possible to do in this moment. Now is the time to bravely and boldly feel your determination to be the best you can be and to actualize your goals. Those goals might be internal ones, about how to be the person you wish to be given the difficult situation you are in, or external ones, focused on how to impact the world as much as possible.

Al: Feeling very vulnerable and nervous about facing my long stored up grief, I made the call to a counselor. I had to have faith that with both of us

working together, I could find healing. More than that, I had to have faith that
God would be there for me and keep me going in the right direction.

    7. <u>Release control and *leap*</u>! This is the step where we engage our active partnership with God, and leap into hope, faith and relationship with Him. Like a child leaping trustingly into the outstretched arms of his parents, we must release control and act. Having done everything we can think of to do, there is nothing more available to us than to trust in the infinite positive possibilities that are in God's domain.

    When we love and support ourselves, sympathizing with how difficult it is to have a human life, when we remember that everything we experience is a part of what it means to be human, when we choose to live with hope and belief in ourselves, we are able to feel the peace of having done everything we can do. We can feel proud of ourselves that we are choosing to be as brave and as alive as we possibly can. We can be proud that we refuse to despair or fight our reality, but rather rise to meet it with determination and faith. And, as the result of all of this human effort, we are led to God, because God is all that is left when we have done our part. When we leap into His arms, we can feel the freedom of having left nothing behind.

Chapter 18

~ *Living with Uncertainty* ~

Our language plays tricks on us. For example, have you ever tried to "grow" a plant? It is impossible. We do not have the power to do it. A seed has its own natural ability to become a plant. We can provide a nurturing and protected environment to give that seed the best chance possible to grow and flourish. We can plant it in the right location, give the soil the nutrients that will nourish its growth, and water it, but we do not "grow" it. We do not get impatient and crack open a seed because we want to hurry the growth, or peel back the petals of a bud to hasten its blooming. If we were to take these actions, we would destroy what we are eager to nurture.

Like all life, we also have our own natural timing for unfolding and growth. The best thing we can do to maximize our ability to become our best self is to provide a nurturing environment, just as we would for a plant. We need to find the right location for ourselves, where we are surrounded by supportive and understanding people. We need to give ourselves the nutrients we need which will nourish our becoming as strong and developed as possible - compassion, reparenting, support to keep a positive attitude, acceptance of our limited control and vulnerability, and permission to separate so we can exist as our own distinct and individual selves. And lastly, as with "growing" plants, we need to cultivate patience. Everything happens in its own timing, and we are not in control of that. Anything we do to try to manipulate the timing will only harm the outcome.

Hurry up! I'm feeling vulnerable, here!

Our natural response to feeling vulnerable is to try to control the situation so that we can stop whatever is stirring up our feelings. If a mosquito dive-bombs us, we swat at it without the need to stop and think - "Hmmm. That's annoying. I wonder what should I do about it?" If we grab a hot pan, we will release it immediately without pausing to reflect on the situation and problem-solve - "My, but this hurts. I wonder what the best solution would be to stop this unpleasant sensation."

At the physical level, these automatic responses are most often absolutely appropriate and life furthering. But even with physical pain, our life preserving instincts must sometimes be guided by our logical adult self. If we are in need of an operation to repair a heart valve, immediate pain avoidance does not serve us well. We need to fortify ourselves to walk through a painful operation because the result will truly be life preserving, as opposed to the temporary relief of immediate pain avoidance.

At the emotional level, our automatic responses to avoid pain must be carefully monitored by our logical adult self. At the emotional level, we very often must walk through a painful situation in order to prevent ourselves from stunting our growth and diminishing our lives. This means that we need to have a strong and supportive relationship with our vulnerability. While our instincts cause us to leap into action in order to prevent ourselves from feeling vulnerable and out of control, we need to embrace our vulnerability as the unavoidable companion to growth. This is not an easy thing to do.

Jan: When I first learned the tools we are talking about in this book, I sensed the enormous and wondrous freedom that could be mine. I felt myself longing to be free. I wanted more than anything to grow and to rid myself of the illusions and fears which burdened my soul and kept me from becoming whole and liberated. I progressed for years, calling on God to "burn me free," grateful for the self I was becoming.

Then, a challenge came up for me which was excruciating, and which I had not anticipated. Suddenly, God had turned up the fire. I was way out of my comfort zone. This new issue took me by surprise and left me feeling extremely out of control. The approach and tools I had used for years which challenged me and allowed me to grow were of absolutely no help or comfort! I remember stopping suddenly and thinking, "Maybe I don't really want to be free, after all." While I laughed at myself for this thought, I was also more than a bit serious. It was very hard to deliberately walk into such a painful issue, especially since I had no clue how it would get resolved.

What is interesting to me now, looking back, is that I don't even remember what the challenge was, at all! What I do remember is how hard and shocking it felt to be so out of control. It is not necessarily the difficulties of life, themselves, which are so awful. Things come up, and they pass. What we are really fighting against is the reality of feeling vulnerable and out of control.

If we are to become our best selves and have the best life possible, we must learn to tolerate our vulnerable and helpless feelings. We can even befriend them, realizing that their presence signals the fact that we are having an opportunity to grow.

Jan: When I am facing a really hard challenge that I know is giving me the perfect opportunity to grow, this is how I think about it: "I'm so theoretically happy. Experientially, I'm miserable. But I'm theoretically happy."

We can *know* that we are going through important and unavoidable growing experiences, but it is still hard to go through them. And, as it is not in our power to rush time, we must learn to be at peace with the way reality unfolds and with the vulnerability we experience from not knowing what will happen next. When we do what we can, we are then left, again, with the choice to turn the rest over to God, for it is beyond our control.

Living with uncertainty

The average person lives 75 years. If we were to define a "moment" to last as long as one eye blink, we would have two moments each second. *(Do you like the image of us standing in front of our clock, researching how many eye blinks there are per second?)* There would be four billion, 730 million, 400 thousand moments in an average lifetime. *(Al: I like math!)* Of all those moments, we are only aware of one at a time, and even then, we are only guessing about what is really going on in each moment, for we only see what is in front of our nose.

We had a small backyard wedding. We worked very hard to plan a simple, but nice wedding, focusing on all the details which would create the feeling we wanted. We decorated on a budget, prepared a nice buffet, and treated ourselves by hiring a little band to provide dance music.

Everything was going perfectly - the yard looked beautiful, the food was bountiful and inviting - until the band came. Our first clue that something was wrong was that they were not dressed in formal attire, as they were supposed to be, but were, instead, in very odd clothing. Next we noticed that they had no instruments. (Hmmm. Subtle, but even we realized how odd that was!) But the worst was that they started doing some ritual in which they chanted things repeatedly, then sat transfixed in different poses of prayer or yoga. It seems that between the time we had hired them and the day of our wedding, they had joined some kind of cult!

As limited as we may be, the greatest power we have is in living each moment (blink!) as fully present as possible. We will never be able to anticipate what will come next. If, however, we focus on being right here, right now, when things occur, we will have a better chance to be clear minded. This increases our ability to be aware of our environment and of our inner state, and to be able to make the best choices possible for our actions.

With all of our planning and efforts, there was no way either of us ever would have thought to come up with a plan about what to do should our band happen to join a cult! (Do you think this should be added to "To Do" or "How to Make Your Wedding Memorable" lists in wedding preparation books?)

We can only live and act in this one moment. Sometimes that means planning and taking action now for the future. Mostly, though, it means simply attending to where we are now. If we plan on walking up steps, we can know that they are coming up, but we must center our awareness on where we are right now. If we try to walk up them before we reach them, we will fall. Our bodies will be out of balance from trying to take an action before its time. If we are strong and solid in this moment, and the next, and the next, chances are our lives will be a series of those good moments. There is no guarantee, but we will be doing our best.

P.S. The police made our band leave, and some musician friends of ours stepped up and provided us with great music!

Accepting the moment

Jan: When our daughter was eight days old, my mother became very ill and came to live with us. Our son was getting ready for kindergarten, Al and I were both working, plus Al was still in graduate school. It was a very intense time, filled with the joys of our young children, the deeply satisfying and demanding nature of our work, Al's school schedule, and facing the imminent death of my mother, who was very close to all of us. We were up several times a night with our new baby, and a couple of other times a night caring for my Mom. (We were so exhausted that one night when our daughter was crying, Al got up, prepared a bottle, and took it into my Mom!) We received a lot of comments about how hard it must be for our family, but we spent no energy feeling either proud or sorry for ourselves, or thinking ahead about what would happen next. For survival reasons, we needed to just be in each moment and do our best. We all worked hard to stay present in the moment with each other.

Whenever we come to peace with reality, we are doing ourselves an enormous favor. Life is hard enough without fighting the impossible. Engaging in the Steps to Inner Peace assists us in being able to be at peace with the vulnerability that accompanies living in uncertainty.

Humility gives us a way to be at peace with the truth that we know so little of what is going on. All the moments of our lives that speed by, all of the bits of information that our brain is processing - yikes! It is impossible for us to be aware of them all. If we accept this, with humility, we can more easily focus on making the best choices we can, and keeping positive expectations. There are so many possibilities out there; we might as well focus on the positive ones and watch for ways to leap into action, should one appear!

Our minds have such a desire to control that sometimes we would rather predict a negative outcome than feel vulnerable. Both optimism and pessimism are ways of trying to create the feeling of being in control, so we do not have to feel the vulnerability of living in uncertainty. Neither of them is based in logic or reality. Both create an illusion that narrows our world, and narrows our awareness of possibilities, because we are shut down. We cannot see the truth of reality, because we are locked into our coping mechanism. An optimist cannot respond to *problems* well, because he is in denial of trouble being a part of reality. A pessimist cannot respond to *possibilities* well, because he is locked into a defensive and protective stance, ready for problems.

Jan: My favorite position on a football team is the defensive back. I like him. Before the snap, he shifts his weight quickly, back and forth, from one leg to the other, ready to move quickly in any direction, following the receiver's moves. He has no idea where he is going to go until the snap. He has no idea what the offensive team is going to do, so he tries to be as relaxed and ready as he can be. He doesn't stand rigidly. He doesn't rush headlong following a predetermined plan. He watches, and waits, dancing. (Now I think that shows some class!) He is ready for whatever happens, and is light on his feet so he can take off in any direction. (In fairness to Al, he begged me not to use this example. But it's how I see football. Don't think poorly of him!)

(Al: I'd like to say a short prayer: "God, please forgive her. She knows not of what she speaketh!")

God doesn't tend to share His plan with us... does He with you? Actually, is life uncertain, or is it that *we* just don't know the plan? A very young child has not yet learned that when a toy is covered up and he does not see it, it has not disappeared. It still exists - it is just out of sight. We are like that child. When we do not see the plan, we think it does not exist, rather than thinking that we are limited in our awareness. Adolescents struggle with being in a hurry. They want to be grown-up, but they cannot be. They simply have not lived long enough to have gotten the experience of an adult, so they cannot see all that an adult can. We will never live long enough to see all that God can.

Live like you are opening birthday presents!

The excitement of looking for gifts to bring joy to people we love, sitting around together by a birthday cake - these can be very happy moments. With all of those presents in front of us, there is no reason to be impatient. Take your time and enjoy each moment. We do not know what is inside those beautifully wrapped packages, but chances are we will be happy. Even if we get presents that are not quite what we would ever think to own, we know that the person giving them to us had the desire and intent to please us and make us happy.

Al: When I was 12, I asked my parents for baseball cards for my birthday. I didn't care how many I got, but they were all I wanted. My father gave me an electric razor. No baseball cards. I was stunned and hurt. Looking back now, able to separate from my father and see with adult eyes, I understand his intent. He gave me the razor to help usher me into feeling like a man. It was a symbolic gift. He wanted me to know that he accepted me as a man. I didn't understand at all, at age 12, but I do, now.

We can think of life like it is a wrapped up birthday present. We do not know what the moment will contain, but we can trust that God has something important for us in each moment. We may not like it at the time, but everything that comes our way lets us have the opportunity to grow.

Is there a happy ending?

Jan: For much of my life, when I read a book, I could not tolerate the suspense of not knowing the ending to a story. The tension was too much for me to stand, and it took away all the pleasure from my reading. As soon as I got attached to a character, I had to go to the end of the book and make sure that nothing bad happened to that character. Even knowing the ending, I had to race through the reading to know all that occurred. I couldn't bear the not knowing, feeling vulnerable because of my emotional involvement with the characters. I would stay up late, put off doing chores, anything to get through each book and feel relieved that everything turned out okay.
Now, more at peace with living in uncertainty, I can read my books in a leisurely way. I am able to put them down and stay in the mystery of what will happen next. I do not have that horrible tension wondering if everyone will be okay. I don't even peek at the end, anymore!
(Al: I wish she'd read more books and watch less football games!)

We each are living as the central character of a great book. We can look back at our lives and see the patterns woven in our past. We can see events that affected us and caused us to develop in the ways we have. We can see how our choices and our ignorance have affected us, leading us to this present moment. We can see the blessings we have received, and how unexpected events have influenced us. And just as in reading any book, the ending is there. We just have not gotten to it yet. Our future will come, the book will conclude. We cannot know about it, however. Our job is to be in this moment and live deeply engaged in this chapter of our life. The rest will unfold over time, as we go from word to sentence to paragraph to page of our autobiography.

We might as well relax and enjoy the story, for it is going to happen whether or not we do. As we attend to each aspect of NOW, we maximize our positive possibilities, for we are centered and alert. We cannot know the storyline. We cannot know what God has in store for us. But we can luxuriate in the life we are fortunate to have received. We can look forward to the next chapter while we enjoy this one, living with determination and a positive attitude, trusting that it will all turn out just fine.

Chapter 19

~ *Trials Make Us Grow* ~

We do not always understand why disappointing things happen or challenges come our way. We do not think of them as gifts. But they are. Every time we have a difficult experience, we have an opportunity to learn something and to take a step toward becoming the person we have the potential to be. And that is a gift.

We are comfort addicts

Comfort is blissful. It is seductive. How could we *not* want it? We are very familiar with it. We are conceived into a state of well-being. We were one with our mothers, fused and floating in warmth and ease. This is how we begin life. It is the foundation of our existence, and like home, it has a powerful pull on us to return.

As we grow, we add dimensions to ourselves. Each of us starts with being a baby. With learning, time, knowledge, and experiences, we become toddlers, children, teenagers, young and then older adults. None of these states of being are lost. Each succeeding one builds on the selves who have come before. And at the heart of us all is a little baby, whose foundation for what life is, was the experience of fusion and comfort.

Nothing is wrong with either fusion or comfort. They are both wonderful places of rest and closeness with those we love. They are both havens from the struggles of being out in the world, of needing to experience our separateness and hold onto ourselves. We each face an experience of this relief when we climb into bed at night and can let go of being big and strong. We can let go of the need for the constant watchfulness over our vulnerable selves. It is like the deep relief we have at the end of the day when we finally get the children to sleep and can just focus on taking care of ourselves.

The only time fusion or comfort might cause us difficulties is if we try to cling to them, to hold onto being in that state. Holding on diminishes the richness and possibilities of life.

Al: I resist leaving the comfort of home. Jan has planned many vacations that sound like they will be fun, but when it comes time to commit to going, I am reluctant. I don't want to leave my home. I don't want to get on the airplane. I don't want to leave my dogs. I don't want to leave my work. I don't want to leave my town. These are all my comforts. They are familiar and safe.

The bliss of comfort and fusion is seductive. Of course we do not want to leave that bliss. Only the fact that our lives would be diminished makes us need to be able to leave the refuge of fusion and comfort and go out into the world to face the challenges of life. Comfort and fusion are like recess at school - they are places to rest, to renew our energy, to remember how sweet it is to feel love and connectedness with the people who matter most to us.

It is the most natural desire in the world to love comfort and fusion and to want to feel it. If we view these states as the dessert of life, after we eat all the vegetables that will help us stay strong and grow, there will be no problem. As much as we might want to fill up on brownies and ice cream, we will not have the health we want, if we do so. Just as people can easily become addicted to sugar, alcohol, drugs, television, sex, work, shopping and just about anything else, we can live addicted to comfort and fusion, wanting to always be "high" on it. If we remember that they are the rewards for doing our work as a human being, they will take their appropriate place, and cause us no trouble.

Comfort is what scares coaches of athletic teams the most. They are always cautioning their players: "Don't become complacent. Don't get comfortable. Just because we were champions last year doesn't mean we will be this year." Coaches know the pull of settling into ease.

Married couples often become complacent. They settle into a comfortable routine which does not stir up conflict between them. It is as though they sink into bottomless easy chairs, farther and farther away from each other, lethargy keeping them from mobilizing because it is oh, so easy. And soon, the relationship is in a crisis. It feels dead, stale, empty.

Successful marriages, athletic teams, and businesses all have in common an aliveness and zest for challenge and growth. They resist the urge to disappear into comfort and the past. Just because we have had success in life does not mean that there will not be other challenges. Those challenges keep us sharp and alert, ready to mobilize our strength and take on the world.

Trials are trials only if we're clinging to comfort

Jan: How many of us stay in the same job because we are used to it and it is comfortable? I was working for a YMCA as a program director when I realized that I needed to go to graduate school. People would talk with me about their problems, but only knew how to be sympathetic. I knew there was more that could be done to help them, and I couldn't stand not knowing what it was. But I was scared to try to be a psychologist. I was very successful and comfortable in my job, and the thought of leaving it for the unknown felt very frightening. I was also so aware of my own struggles, and thought "How could I have the arrogance to try to help someone else if I'm not perfect, myself?"

So, I did the logical thing... I waited. I waited and waited. But although time passed, I wasn't any more perfect. I realized that my whole life might go by, without my ever achieving perfection. I might die and never get to go to school! I realized that the true issue behind my thinking that I needed to be perfect before I could be a psychologist was that I thought perfection would be a shield for me. It would protect me, so I wouldn't have to feel vulnerable or stupid. (Or, rather, reveal how stupid I really felt!)

Realizing the futility of this wait, I took deep breaths, braced myself, and (in terror) started school. I made it through the first night of class by wrapping my arms and legs around the desk so thoroughly that I wouldn't be able to just bolt out of the room, for I would trip and make a fool of myself. (Evidently, I felt making a fool of myself physically was worse than exposing myself intellectually and emotionally to be the fool I truly was.) And, I decided that if it took me 10 times as long to complete school as everyone else, then I would just take 10 times longer, for I passionately wanted to become a psychologist.

We have the opportunity to use our time here on Earth to grow into the fullness of our potential, to become the best selves we possibly can before we return home to God. It is our human destiny to learn. Learning will not occur if we cling to comfort and fusion. Whenever we enter the world, we are aware of our vulnerability and of the existence of uncertainty. As much as we might try to control our world with little tricks like following the same routines, staying in the same jobs, going to the same places, eating the same foods, we are only creating illusions of security, not real security.

Like any animal, we fight feeling vulnerable by trying to control our world. The only difficulty with this is that it is not possible. All we succeed in doing is to create illusions or distortions. We are not living in the truth of life, but in a distorted creation that is not real. The truth of life as a human is that we live in the unknown, which means that we all must learn to be at peace with uncertainty and discomfort. Remember the concept of homework from God? We are always being stretched to learn and grow beyond where we are. Nothing is wrong - it's just homework.

Al: When my mother was dying, she moved out West because she wanted me to take care of her. The rest of her support system was on the East coast - I was the only one here. I felt like I had spent my whole childhood taking care of her, and this just felt like too much. But, there she was, and although I had reason to feel resistant, I stepped up to help. But I didn't really embrace and fully accept the trial. I internalized my feelings about it and got sick frequently. Although I did an excellent job taking care of her, and she died feeling very grateful to have had me there, I suffered through it.

Thirteen years later, Jan's mother came to live with us when she was dying. I wanted her to be in our home, and happily took care of her. As my own mother had, Bette expressed gratitude to me for my love and care. Both Bette and my mother appreciated all that I did for them in their last months. No one watching would have known, but my experiences were very different. I felt sadness with both deaths. But where I resisted the experience with my mother, I embraced the time with Bette. Both situations were trials. The difference was my attitude, and how that affected my experience.

Trials are only trials if we are fighting them. If we resist accepting the reality of their existence, we are once again fighting with God. "I don't like the way You designed the Universe! I like my way better!" If we do not cling like addicts to comfort, then a trial would not be a trial - it would just be the next thing that we are facing. It would be our next homework assignment. And, if we can accept that learning is not only a part of life, but the purpose of life, then we will not have to make our lives harder by resisting and fighting the presence of a trial. We can bend our heads in humility and acceptance, and feel proud of ourselves that we get the opportunity to become more than we were. (Remember being theoretically happy?)

The mirror of consciousness

In a play or movie, a character discovers himself as people and situations whirl around him. It is as though he is watching his development in a mirror of consciousness, and telling us about what happens to him, internally, as events unfold, externally.

That is how we can each use the experiences in our life. We each have a mirror of consciousness - though not all of us realize it and know to look into it! (It really is difficult to remember to look at ourselves... after all, our eyes *were* designed to look outward. When something happens, it is easy to be mesmerized by the event or by what someone else has done or said, rather than to pay attention to what gets stirred up in us.)

We can go through our lives watching ourselves in our mirror of consciousness. We can watch for our reactions in order to discover what they reveal to us about ourselves. If we experience a trial, we can watch to see where we have the potential to grow and become our best selves, as a result of that trial. None of us faces everything with peace and equanimity. All of us are works in progress. We all have areas where we can grow and become more clear, more compassionate, and less angry or judgmental. There is nothing wrong or shameful about this. Remember, this is how we are designed.

Danger sharpens us

Recess, vacations, comfort, and fusion are all wonderful, but it is danger which challenges us and causes us to take the steps that help us grow into our best selves. During trials, our minds work harder. We are stretched beyond our limitations to become more than we were before. We all know the expression "Necessity is the mother of invention." During difficult times, we have the opportunity to reinvent ourselves - the new improved version!

Trials strip away our comfort zone and leave us more raw and vulnerable. It is during extreme trials that the best of us is revealed. A tragedy or catastrophe occurring anywhere in the world always brings out acts of generosity and courage, as people everywhere respond with their best selves to help each other. Fortunately, most of us do not suffer such devastating catastrophes. But in our own trials, we have the same opportunity to respond with generosity and courage. We can accept our vulnerability and limited control, and choose to act with faith and positive expectations, reaching to fulfill our potential. And at the end of all of our efforts, where we cease to have knowledge or control, that is where we can find God.

Chapter 20

~ *Giving Helps Us Live a Centered Life* ~

Since our destiny is to live as a human being, the most empowered we can be is when we yield to that destiny and live in acceptance of it. Our birth as human beings gives us the opportunity to learn and to grow into wholeness and completeness. This is not a reward or a punishment - it is simply our reality. Rather than fight to have a different destiny – say, to be a mythical creature like a "perfect person," or to be a saint - we can fully embrace the tasks and the strengths that we have been given.

Selfish or centered?

If we know that our primary task in life is to work toward living in acceptance of ourselves and our destiny, we will recognize that every experience in life is "homework," which allows us to practice these tasks. Before we are accountable to our employer for our work, our family for our relationship, we are accountable to God for our soul. As dear as our family is, as important as our work might be, we are here on Earth to grow into our best selves. Of course, this might *include* family and work, but even if we did not have family or work, we would still have our life journey to make - we are the center of our own life. Responsibilities for family and work can be included in our life choices, but they are not the center of our existence.

Being the center of our own life and of our own existence is often confused with *selfishness*, which means concentrating on our own advantage or well-being with no regard for others. *Centered* living means that there is a core *me* living in or as *my* body, which exists separate from anyone and anything else. It is the source of my aliveness, and all of my thoughts and feelings. Whatever I do comes from this centered me, and serves my purposes, even if other people happily and coincidentally benefit, also. If we were to give one million dollars anonymously to a charity, are we being selfish? One answer is "no" because our action does have regard for the well-being of others, and so does not fit into the definition of selfishness. But another answer is "yes" because we would feel good doing this, even if no one else knew.

Everything we do comes out of our "self." There is no action possible that is not "self - ish" - just as someone from England is "Engl – ish." That is not good or bad. We have a self. It is where we live. We have no choice in the matter. If we took selfishness to its logical extreme, a truly selfish person, who wanted his own well-being, could not help but be concerned with the well-being of others. If others suffered, his heart would hurt, and as he wants to prevent feeling pain himself, he would need them to be okay, as well. True selfishness would entail concern for all people. We will talk of this kind of extreme selfishness as *centeredness*. *Centered* living would include the well-being of all involved, because it would be too painful to have something for ourselves at the expense of another. Their pain would cause us pain.

Selfishness is seen as an extremely negative quality, and people often confuse it with centeredness. People are afraid that if they speak up for themselves, they will be seen as selfish. The label "selfish" is often put on people who say what they want by people who are afraid to do so. In other words, "You're selfish because you're speaking up for yourself and I can't." Or "You're selfish because you're not doing what *I* want you to do." Speaking up for ourselves, however, gives us the best chance possible to have a deep and positive connection with others, for it reveals who we truly are. If everyone spoke their inner truth, with compassion for others, we would be able to achieve intimate and respectful relationships where everyone's needs were considered.

Our culture tends to look at "selfish" people as being too self-involved, greedy, narcissistic... the names go on and on. They appear to have no concern or compassion for anyone but themselves. But, looked at in the context of our human destiny as beings who are here to learn and grow, what would cause a person to be that way? If people truly have good hearts, then how could they do hurtful behaviors which range from thoughtless to cruel? What happened to them?

"Selfish" people are frightened people

The story of Ebenezer Scrooge is a portrait of a man consumed with fear. His life is cold and empty, with money his only companion. He lives in self-imposed aloneness, for only in his restricted world can he feel safe and in control. He has narrowed his vision to be able to see only his own needs. Opening his heart to others would make him aware of his vulnerability, which he protects himself from feeling.

Selfishness is a way of avoiding the human condition. It is a way of living that is based on fear. It fights the reality that we are vulnerable and without ultimate control. It operates under the illusion that we can shore up our defenses and insulate ourselves against feeling vulnerable and helpless. It seeks to establish control where it is not possible to do so. It is an attempt to find safety. It is an attempt to make oneself feel invulnerable. As this is not possible, given the truth of our existence, selfishness is doomed for failure.

Similar to "selfish" people, those who are narcissistic also live in fear. Narcissism is a signal that people are stuck in fusion. They cannot overcome their anxiety about separating, and cannot move beyond the infant end of the fusion-individuation continuum. They have not developed the internal support to know that they will survive. Like a two year old who is stuck on saying "No!" to everyone else, they are consumed with the need to control. When a two year old is with another child, his major communication is "Mine!" and his major activity is grabbing every toy within reach. A narcissist, although an adult, has not developed the inner sense of safety which would allow him to feel vulnerable. He is not connected with God, which would enable him to be at peace with his helplessness. He cannot share his "toys." Totally focused on his own well-being, he fights his vulnerability and helplessness by using all of his energy to maintain a sense of control.

Selfish people are frightened people. They try to control the external world, hoping that will ease their anxiety and make them safe. They may feel better for the moment, but it is illusory, for there is no way to avoid the human condition of vulnerability. Soon they will have to do or get more. Selfishness is the pathway to gluttony - more is necessary to quench the fear. The temporary relief of "getting" cannot last, so they need to keep getting - more, bigger, better. But nothing can work to make a person not feel vulnerable and helpless, because our human destiny includes these conditions. It is our task to come to peace with this reality. We cannot change our true nature and destiny. We can only choose how we deal with being human.

With support and encouragement, Scrooge made different choices for his life. Once aware of the price he was paying for his illusion of safety, he opened his heart and was filled with the joy of being human and alive.

Centered people live in peace

Centered people accept their right to exist, and are at peace with the human condition of being vulnerable and having limited control. They are able to find the peace of living in each moment with compassion for themselves and others. They know they must constantly be ready to love themselves out of the past, into the present, healing old hurts and correcting old misunderstandings. They know their power lies in making the best choices they can. They do not need to judge themselves, for they accept their limitations. And, lastly, they know that in the end, they must release the outcome to God, for it is not theirs to control.

Giving helps us live a centered life

It is a moment to moment challenge to stay centered. This way of living is nothing our culture or family has known to support us in doing, but it is something we can guide ourselves to do.

When we are living a centered life, we cannot help but respond empathetically to those around us. There is a sympathetic connection between hearts when they are vulnerable. It is as if those often spoken of "heartstrings" actually exist and are physically tugged on when life touches life, when we are not armored and protected, but are living connected to our own vulnerability.

Have you ever passed a hurt animal by the side of the road, seen someone with a physical challenge bravely struggle to walk or do a task, or watched a touching movie about someone having a sad challenge, and felt your heart ache in response? Our heart response is the basis of generosity. The pain of another person travels along our heartstrings and echoes in our own hearts. Knowing and feeling compassion for our own pain, our bodies empathetically feel the pain of others.

Jan: I had a break in between sessions at work, and so drove home, looking forward to using the time to write on this book - this chapter, as a matter of fact. Driving down a busy street where there was no place to pull over and stop, I saw a man standing up from his wheelchair, struggling. Swept along by the traffic, I felt awful for him, but told myself, as I pulled off onto the street leading to my home, that he was probably fine. I'm sure he was smart enough to not be on that street unless he knew he could manage it.

But the image of him was haunting. I remembered, years ago, walking up our very steep hill from the park to our home, staggering under the weight of our young daughter, who had collapsed like a dead weight into sleep on our way home, exhausted from playing. I remembered praying that some Good Samaritan would stop to offer me a ride home... but none did.

Almost home, I couldn't stand it anymore. I returned to the busy street, parked as close as I could to him, and ran over to see if I could be of assistance. He was sitting, now, calmly spreading mayonnaise on his chicken sandwich. He was very friendly, and in no need of help, at all, happily picnicking by the side of the road. I returned to my car, relieved. The need to give doesn't always need to result in actual giving. The real gift, this time, was my peace of mind. And I sincerely appreciated it!

Staying connected to our own vulnerability gives rise to the desire, even more, the *need* to give. And giving helps us stay connected to our own vulnerability so we can live a more centered life. It is a wonderful, self-perpetuating cycle.

Giving pulls us out of self-involvement and fear. Rather than fighting our vulnerability and lack of control by trying to acquire success or possessions, we release our well-being to God, and live in an attitude of faith. Selfishness gives the illusion of comfort - but just for a moment. It cannot last, because control is something we cannot attain. Selfishness, in seeking to control, does not acknowledge the existence of God. A selfish person lives in fear that his well-being is totally dependent on his own actions. Selfishness pulls us away from the opportunity to be at peace with our human destiny and to be connected with God. It is an attempt to find safety by insulating ourselves against feeling vulnerable. It not only cannot work, but there is an enormous price - this insulation prevents our feeling a connection with God, for the *vehicle* of that connection is our vulnerability. To be connected with God we must find a way to be at peace with the discomfort of being vulnerable. Giving is one way of doing that. Giving transforms the discomfort of vulnerability into the joy of human connection. When we open our vulnerable hearts to feel our compassion, we cannot help but give. We have opened ourselves to being filled with love.

Coincidence, or is giving a self-perpetuating cycle?

Al: Neighborhood sports are activities that fill non-athletic kids with shame and anxiety. It is a sickening feeling to watch other kids get picked to be on teams, and be the "leftovers" that no one wants. As a child, I couldn't stand seeing the faces on those kids. The best athlete in my neighborhood, I was always asked to be a team captain, and those were the kids I picked to be on my team.

Something amazing would happen, then, something that all the kids soon noticed. My team always won. My players were so enthusiastic and happy that we seemed to have a spirit that pumped us all up and made us play better. Soon, the other team captains were picking these kids, too. A simple act of giving that began with picking the "bad" players changed the whole feeling of sports in my neighborhood. The goal of playing well and winning as a team *became more important than who were the best players, and all the kids felt included and valuable. And for me, I could go outside and not have to feel the pain of someone's suffering.*

The need to give can come about in different ways. Some people, so connected to their pain about not having received, cannot tolerate seeing pain in others. Another's pain reverberates in their open and vulnerable hearts. Other people have had so much love and support given to them that the pain of another person is an irresistible call to action. They are compelled to pass on what they have received, for not doing so creates too much pain in them.

Jan: Al's childhood was one of loneliness. No one saw or knew to address his feelings of unimportance. I had a different childhood situation. My mother was always present to love me, even when times were very hard for our family. I never felt abandoned, but knew I could always count on her help and creativity in facing my challenges in life. When I saw people hurting, I wanted to give to them the way I had been given to by my mother.

Giving is a gift to the giver. It soothes and comforts pain in the giver's heart. It is a necessary release for empathy, because we *know* the pain of another, having been there, ourselves, and it is intolerable to watch that pain without taking action.

We were driven into psychology by our hearts. We knew that we <u>had</u> to learn how to help people get free from the pain they were trapped in. We got our degrees, and set up a counseling practice together.

Over the years, we found we could not turn people away when they had no money to pay us, or lost their jobs and their insurance while they were working with us. We opened our practice and our hearts to them, and found that 1/4 to 1/3 of our practice was devoted to people whom we saw for free. This has never changed, and yet, we have so much for ourselves. We are actively sought after, very busy, and continue to love our work. It feels as if we get to talk to the best people in the world about the most important topics in the world... and money falls from Heaven! All this joy, and we get <u>paid</u>, too?

Who is to say who benefits most in giving? Giving creates a love flow which sweeps all of us up so that it is impossible to tell the difference between "giver" and "recipient." In opening ourselves to give and receive, we overflow with love, and we all become both givers and recipients.

<u>Compassion connects us with all of life</u>

When we live in compassion for ourselves and for our vulnerability, a peace fills us. (At a chemical level, the chemicals released in our bodies when we feel peace, forgiveness and compassion certainly feel better than what is released when we are feeling angry and bitter.) Centered in our vulnerability, we are connected to everyone else, for we all share the same human conditions. That state of openness and sensitivity makes us intuitively connected with others. We cannot help but feel compassion. And, who can explain why a mother dog would adopt a litter of kittens? Why would a pod of dolphins risk their own safety to save a swimmer from sharks? Yet these things happen. At a deep level, life responds to life, and in compassion, even the boundaries of species are crossed. Intuition and the sensitive heart are not limited by logic or differences.

Al: Has this ever happened to you? My daughter and I were driving on an outing. As we were getting off the freeway, the car ran out of gas about a block from a gas station. I told my daughter to steer the car while I got behind it to push. Within 30 seconds, three people had stopped their cars and were helping me push the car to the gas station. Why?

Knowing vulnerability and distress – even if minor – we respond from our best selves when we see someone in need. Every time there is a tragedy, people all around the world rally to help each other, driving across the country, flying to a far off place, raising and sending money to help others rebuild their lives. We all feel deep inside of us the truth that it could be us struggling to survive. The people who are most connected to their vulnerability tend to be the ones who respond with the most compassion and generosity. This feeling of kinship is one of the many benefits of being connected with our vulnerability. We feel our oneness with each other – we are less alone. Although we resist – no one wants to feel pain – it is the experience of that pain which opens our hearts to others.

Giving keeps us connected to God

Incredible things can happen when we live in peace with our vulnerability, not trying to control what is not ours to control. Feeling more open in our hearts, we are also more open to each other. Connected to others, we are moved to act on the deep compassion we feel. Giving is the inevitable outcome of this connection.

We are also more open to all of the unlimited positive possibilities that are beyond our conscious awareness. Because we are not focusing on the impossible – control and perfection – we are open to the possible, sometimes without even realizing it. Many of us have "picked up" on information that we cannot categorize or explain. We "tune in" to others at a deep level that is beyond logic or normal consciousness. We "know" things without being able to explain how we can know them. We are tapping into the realm of the ultimate giver, God. This is the realm where unconditional love resides. When we live in that place of love, everything we do is an act of giving. Giving completes the cycle which keeps us connected to God.

Chapter 21

~ *Bridging Heaven and Earth* ~

Just as children learn and grow, we do, too. We have limitless potential. This is a miraculous trait of our species. Just think of it! There is no end to who we can become! Can you think back a few years ago and find something that you did not know, that you now do? Have you learned anything that has made your life better, or made you feel more at peace with yourself? That can continue to happen as long as you live.

One of the best parts of growing older is that we always have the opportunity to grow, if we know how to *use* our life experience. And just as miraculous is the truth that no matter what happened to us in our past, no matter how tragic or traumatic, we have the ability to love ourselves out of the past into the present. We are not crippled and stuck, the victim of forces that are bigger than we are. That wounded, vulnerable, nonlogical self has been waiting, all of these years, for our logical adult self to find him. It is never too late to heal and go on to create the life we want to have. *That* is a miracle!

We deserve to be happy

At this time in human history, we are realizing a new kind of awareness. We are like scouts making inroads into our unconscious selves, discovering and naming the feelings, survival patterns, assumptions and old wounds which drive our lives. Today we have permission to take our feelings seriously. We have been given the idea that we deserve to be happy. When we are not, we are more likely to pay attention and to know that something is wrong, although we often mistake that "something" as being something wrong with *us*. Now, however, having read this book (!) we can remember that when we are unhappy, we are only being called out of "recess" to learn. Nothing is wrong. It is just time to get to work and fulfill our purpose in being alive!

Most of us have wondered, at some point in our life, why we are here. Since time began, people have sought to find meaning and purpose in life. It is impossible to understand the human journey. Why do some of us endure such hardship while others of us seem to have a life of ease? Why does tragedy exist, in the first place? Are we being punished? None of us will ever know. All we can know is that here we are!

Answers to the question "What is life all about, anyway?" are as varied as people are. Some of us seek solace in doing good works. Others seek to avoid the feelings of vulnerability and uncertainty by seeking to gain control over things or other people. Some people find satisfaction in acquiring more or better than others have. Some long for union with God, seeing life on Earth as exile. Some see life as nothing but the physical experience we have in our bodies, and feel no connection to anything bigger than themselves.

Regardless of how we answer the question of meaning, all of us find ourselves with a decision to make. How are we going to *use* this time on Earth? Our decision will profoundly and absolutely determine the quality of our life. In order to have an answer to this question that supports our having a good life, we must believe that we deserve to be alive and we deserve to be happy.

<u>The key to having your best life, is to be your best self</u>

Al: I always admired Jan's mother, Bette. She spent her whole life dedicated to being her best self. Whatever she did, she did wholeheartedly, without self-consciousness. She had no sense of rhythm, but never hesitated to get up and dance. She was tone deaf, but sang joyously and exuberantly. She smiled big and laughed big, loved big, made mistakes and apologized big. She did not cheat herself out of anything in her life. She lived big.

While we can never see or understand the big picture, we can decide that since we are here having our human experience, we are going to have a good attitude, trust in the existence of positive possibilities, and *go for broke*! We are here, why not throw ourselves into life with enthusiasm! Why waste precious time being afraid or depressed? Why let the judgment of other frightened and self-conscious people stop us from having a big life?

When we live the goal of having a centered life, we have the best opportunity to live big. When we accept our vulnerability, we are at our best. Our hearts are open to experience the joy of being alive and to celebrate our growth as we become more whole. Vulnerability allows us to feel kinship and connection with others, knowing that they, too, share this human journey. It leaves us free to experiment, to try things, knowing that we have the right to look at unexpected outcomes with hindsight, not judgment.

We all have the opportunity to choose our attitude and dedicate our lives to what gives us meaning and satisfaction. We can commit ourselves to a life we can feel proud of. It is easier to have our best life when we are our best selves.

Our hope for you

What we have shared with you in these pages are the thoughts, beliefs and tools which are transforming our lives. They are more than theories - they are helping us to heal and learn and grow into people we are happy to be. We offer them to you with love, and with the hope that they will give you the ability to find the same help and peace we are finding.

What words can we now leave you with that will fill your hearts and souls with hope, with joy, and with both faith and belief in the possibilities of this human journey? Here are our wishes for your best self, our words of blessing to you:

May you have peace in your heart. May you accept your human destiny as vulnerable beings with limited control. May this acceptance vanquish judgment and allow love and compassion to be your companions on every aspect of your journey. May you give yourself the right to exist, knowing you deserve to be happy and to receive God's blessings. May you find peace in your separateness, knowing it allows you to grow to your fullest potential. May you feel in harmony with life and savor every moment.

May you have freedom. May you love yourself out of your past into this glorious present where you have a turn to walk the Earth and be alive. May you experience comfort and healing so that your fears and your wounds are laid to rest. May you be able to grow beyond your nonlogical survival patterns, knowing that the wise, logical, capable adult you have become will always be there to protect and take care of you.

May you feel proud of yourself. May you have a life which stretches you to live at your highest potential. May you meet every challenge with faith and strength, determined to learn, determined to free yourself from illusions and fear.

May you have power inside you. May you have pride in the strength you were designed to have. May you know that whatever challenge comes your way, you have the strength to use it to grow, to become wiser, stronger and more free. May you use every feeling of pain or anger, of fear or sadness as an opening to the opportunity to become more than you were before.

May you live in gratitude. May you rejoice in the blessings of each moment, knowing that as a child of God, you deserve every one. May you remember, in difficult times, that even challenges are blessings which allow you to grow into your greatest potential.

May you live a life of service. May you have the joy of giving, of sharing, of loving those around you, for when you do so, you will be doing God's work. You will have the blessing of feeling a connection with every human being who has ever lived.

May you live with joy and enthusiasm. May you have a life committed to rejoicing in every moment, whether of struggle or of ease, as a moment given to you to celebrate life and God. May you dedicate every breath, every act to God.

Bridging Heaven and Earth

We are living our human experience, but are spiritual beings. We must have balance to be complete. If we were intended to just be spiritual, we would have taken form as angels or saints. If we were meant to just be of this Earth, we would have been born a less self-aware and less complex animal. To have a life which fulfills our greatest potential, we must attend to the challenges and lessons of our human journey. To develop in our souls, we must learn how to find peace and faith.

At the end of each moment, as you take your power to be your best self, may you find joy in the richness of Life. May you find yourself at peace and in harmony with the Mystery. May you find yourself friends with Mr. Lucky. May you find yourself safe and loved in the arms of God.

In love and in kinship,
Your brother and sister,

Al and Jan